THE ROMANTIC SUBJECT IN AUTOBIOGRAPHY

The Romantic Subject
in Autobiography

Rousseau and Goethe

EUGENE L. STELZIG

UNIVERSITY PRESS OF VIRGINIA
CHARLOTTESVILLE AND LONDON

The University Press of Virginia
© 2000 by the Rector and Visitors of the University of Virginia

Printed in the United States of America

First published in 2000

⊗ The paper used in this publication meets the minimum requirements of the American National Standard for Information Sciences — Permanence of Paper for Printed Library Materials, ANSI Z39.48-1984.

LIBRARY OF CONGRESS CATALOGING-IN-PUBLICATION DATA
Stelzig, Eugene L.
  The romantic subject in autobiography: Rousseau and Goethe/Eugene L. Stelzig.
  p. cm.
  Includes bibliographical references and index.
  ISBN 0-8139-1975-4 (alk. paper)
  1. Rousseau, Jean-Jacques, 1712–1778 — Criticism and interpretation.   2. Goethe, Johann Wolfgang von, 1749–1832 — Criticism and interpretation.   3. Autobiography.   4. Self in literature.   5. Romanticism.   I. Title.

PQ2043.S74 2000
848'.509 — dc21   00-36665

TO THE MEMORY OF MY PARENTS

Susanna Füreder (1900–1970)

and Josef Stelzig (1895–1980)

CONTENTS

ACKNOWLEDGMENTS

Goethe once stated that we understand the strategy of life only after the campaign is over. Perhaps the same is also true of writing a book. When I started on this one a decade ago, my original scheme was to have Wordsworth as a coequal member of my team of Romantic autobiographers. But by the time the Rousseau and Goethe sections took shape, including a study of *The Prelude* would have made the book too unwieldy.

I want to thank a number of people who helped me in one way or another as I worked on this project. James Olney in his 1983 NEH Seminar on the Forms of Autobiography gave a new impetus to my interest in the (then-rapidly) emerging field of autobiography studies. Although his recent book *Memory and Narrative* (1998), with its chapter on "Jean-Jacques Rousseau and the Crisis of Narrative Memory," appeared too late for me to make use of, his work and encouragement over the years have been a stimulus and an inspiration. So have those of John Eakin, whom I must also thank for reading and commenting on the Rousseau chapters. Jane K. Brown, Cyrus Hamlin, and Paul Hernadi sharpened my understanding of Goethe in their 1990 NEH Institute on *Faust*. I am grateful also to Jane Brown and to my Geneseo colleague Ken Asher for reading and commenting on different sections of the Goethe portion of the book. John Barbour of Saint Olaf College offered timely words of encouragement. My home institution, SUNY Geneseo, supported me with a sabbatical leave and a Spencer J. Roemer (Geneseo Foundation) summer fellowship. I must acknowledge as well the many Geneseo students who in various autobiography courses I have taught, including two senior seminars on Romantic autobiography, have challenged my understanding of Rousseau and Goethe with their honest and probing responses. I have also benefited from the intense discussions with the participants in my 1992 NEH seminar for secondary teachers on Rousseau and Wordsworth. I must also thank my editors at the University Press of Virginia, Cathie Brettschneider and Ellen Satrom, for their support of this project. My greatest debt, however, is to my wife, Elsje van Munster, who has given unflagging support to all my academic ventures.

I am grateful to the editors of the journals in which earlier versions of the following chapters originally appeared: the introduction, in *Neohelicon* 18, no. 2 (1991): 249–71, and chapter 4, in *a/b: Auto/Biography Studies,* 10, no. 2 (1995): 39–51.

THE ROMANTIC SUBJECT IN AUTOBIOGRAPHY

Introduction

Modern Autobiography and Romantic Subjectivity

Although it has its sources in the Renaissance and is already much in evidence in leading texts like Montaigne's *Essays* and Shakespeare's *Hamlet,* the emergence of modern subjectivity, and of a full-fledged literature of the subject, is one of the significant developments of the later eighteenth century. As Jerome Hamilton Buckley has emphasized, the following century "was certainly the first period to speak self-consciously of the self as a major source of literary material, and the first, beginning with the Romantics, to write a great deal subjectively" (3).[1] Clearly, the growing literary preoccupation with the singular self is one of the leading indicators of the transition from the culture of Enlightenment to that of Romanticism. The rise during the second half of the eighteenth century of a type of writing that Georges Gusdorf has suggestively called "the literature of the self" ("L'autobiographie initiatique" 978) helps to account for the new prominence and popularity of certain closely allied literary forms such as the autobiography, the fictional memoir, the epistolary and first-person novel, the *journal intime,* and even the travelogue.[2] Just as eighteenth-century fiction writers used autobiographical devices (the letter,

I

the diary, the first-person narrative), so autobiographers made use of the resources of fiction to emphasize and highlight the subjective and the personal. Patricia Meyer Spacks has noted the "close connections" between eighteenth-century English autobiographies and novels as forms of imaginative literature, because "imagination . . . both helps to create developed subjective identity and testifies to that identity in the same way that memory does" (311, 19). What Spacks calls "the conversion of life into story" (18) begins to take on a much more subjective coloring in the eighteenth century even in a very traditional but newly revitalized and popular genre like biography, which, as Donald Stauffer sums it up, became not only "a work of the creative artist," but also increasingly "subjective in its emphasis" with its centering on "the individual . . . for his own sake" in the latter part of the century (11, 457, 166).

Even Edward Gibbon, the leading historian of the age, could succumb to and indulge in the subjective penchant in his autobiography (1788–93). The ironic detachment of Gibbon's self-presentation in his posthumously published *Memoirs of My Life* has become justly famous, but what the reader perhaps recalls most vividly are the two points of the narrative at which he slips into a mode of lyrical reminiscence as he recalls the occasions of the conception and the completion of his ambitious historical project: "It was at Rome on the fifteenth of October 1764, as I sat musing amidst the ruins of the Capitol while the barefooted fryars were singing Vespers in the temple of Jupiter, that the idea of writing the decline and fall of the City first started to my mind" (136). If this is a rudimentary Wordsworthian "spot of time," with its powerful mixture of circumstantial fact, personal emotion, and latent sense of sublimity, Gibbon's recording of the moment of completion registers the same admixture in a yet more affecting manner:

> It was on the day or rather the night of the 27th of June 1787, between the hours of eleven and twelve that I wrote the last page in a summer house in my garden. After laying down my pen, I took several turns in a *berceau* or covered walk of Acacias which commands a prospect of the country the lake and the mountains. The air was temperate, the sky was serene; the silver orb of the moon was reflected from the waters, and all Nature was silent. I will not dissemble the first emotions of joy on the recovery of my freedom and perhaps the establishment of my fame. But my pride was soon hum-

bled, and a sober melancholy was spread over my mind by the idea that I had taken my everlasting leave of an old and agreable [*sic*] companion, and that, whatsoever might be the future date of my history, the life of the historian must be short and precarious. (180)

This is the high point of Gibbon's life, in the recording of which his public identity and his innermost aspirations are fused in a secular and highly individualized confession.

How did this secular sense of the modern self as an individual identity come about? I take as paradigmatic as well as representative of a larger historical consensus the recent account of that self's emergence by the philosopher Charles Taylor, who locates it in a very long developmental perspective in the Western phenomenon of "Inwardness," the title of part 2 of his epic *Sources of the Self*. According to Taylor, "it was Augustine who introduced the inwardness of radical reflexivity and bequeathed it to the Western tradition of thought," and in turn "the modern epistemological tradition from Descartes . . . has made this standpoint fundamental" (131). Augustine, of course, "makes the step to inwardness . . . because it is a step towards God," who "is to be found in the intimacy of self-presence" (132, 134). But in the early modern period, beginning with the Cartesian *cogito*, which helps to found modern individualism and which is prepared for by the Bishop of Hippo, the self-presence of inwardness is increasingly secularized ("the Cartesian proof is no longer a search for an encounter with God within," 157). From Locke, whose "radically subjectivist view of the person" makes personal identity not a substance but a function of the continuity of consciousness and who provides the psychological foundation for the Enlightenment view of the self, to Montaigne, who "inaugurates a new kind of reflection which is intensely individual" with his assertion that "each of us has to discover his or her own form" (and who in his stress on individual difference diverges from the Cartesian "science of the subject in its general essence"), the early modern period adumbrates a new sense of a secular and individual self that "by the turn of the eighteenth century" is "recognizably . . . in process of constitution" (172, 181, 182, 185). The instrumental "inward turn" initiated by Augustine makes his *Confessions* "the first great work in a genre that includes Rousseau's work of the same title, Goethe's *Poetry and Truth*, Wordsworth's *Prelude*" (178), secularized versions all of the first great Western autobiography.

If Gibbon's account of his peak experience represents his own approach to the secularized epiphanic modes of Romantic autobiography, the three foremost self-chroniclers of the new genre, whose autobiographies constitute its classic moment with their distinctive self-conceptions and their very different accounts of the problematic relationship of the self to the world, are the ones cited by Taylor as following in the footsteps of Augustine's turn inward: Jean-Jacques Rousseau (1712–78), Johann Wolfgang von Goethe (1749–1832), and William Wordsworth (1770–1850). Each of them accomplished the definitive self-inscription of a highly developed individuality in a genre revitalized and transformed to allow for the full display of that individuality. Each wrote with a different purpose in mind, which in terms of the rhetoric of their confessional self-presentation can be respectively epitomized as *self-justification* (Rousseau), *self-completion* (Goethe), and *self-authorization* (Wordsworth). If these three are the first truly modern writers of French, German, and English literature respectively, an essential part of their modernity is the self-reflexive and subjective character of their writings. They create their best works from within themselves, out of the widely varying and rich resources of their own experience. In so doing, they exemplify the thesis of Friedrich Schlegel, that pioneering theorist of literary modernity who concluded in his *Dialogue on Poetry* (written at the end of the eighteenth century) that "the modern poet must create all . . . things from within himself . . . like a new creation out of nothing," and who also presciently pointed to the autobiographical tendency of so much fiction since the eighteenth century: "What is best in the best of novels is nothing but a more or less veiled confession of the author, the profit of his experience, the quintessence of his originality" (81, 103).

The quintessence of the originality of Rousseau, Goethe, and Wordsworth as autobiographers was to give distinctive imaginative forms to their lives in *The Confessions* (written 1766–70), *Poetry and Truth* (written 1811–31), and *The Prelude* (written 1799–1805 and revised for the remainder of Wordsworth's life). Between them, they wrote the classic works of Romantic autobiography—Rousseau's, indeed, is legendary as the first and still most influential, notorious even before its posthumous publication (part 1 appeared in 1782, part 2 in 1789); Goethe's has been preeminent in German literature since its first appearance (though it has been slow to gain international critical recognition); Wordsworth's, finally, because of its delayed publication (1850) and its even more delayed critical recognition, has had to wait until the twentieth century to achieve its rightful place as a poem, and has not until recently assumed its proper place in the history and theory of autobiography.

Each of these autobiographers enacts different modes and strategies of subjectivity. Goethe, on the surface, at least, the most objective in his outlook, stresses in the famous assertion of his preface the crucial role of historical circumstance in forming the selves we come to be, to the point that each individual "would have been quite a different person if born ten years before or after, as far his own cultural development and his effects on others are concerned" (*Poetry and Truth* 17). The impersonal moment of history itself governs the possible forms of our subjectivity and determines the horizon of our aspirations and achievements. However, despite his persistent penchant to look to the world around him in telling the story of his life, Goethe nevertheless has to acknowledge the overall subjective character of his writings. In book 7 of *Poetry and Truth* he reviews the state of contemporary German literature as he had come to know it as a very young man in the 1760s, only to conclude that it did not provide him with essential impulses for his own poetry: "If I wanted true source material, feeling, or reflection for my poems, I had to delve into my own bosom" (214). Indeed, the young Goethe's prolific writing of poetry fits the Romantic formula of composition—*the spontaneous overflow of powerful feelings*—immortalized by Wordsworth. Goethe goes on to acknowledge in a well-known passage that this subjective tendency has defined his career as a writer in its entirety, and that actually all of his works are but "fragments of one great confession" (214)—a seriatim self-reflection that his autobiography itself is intended to fill out and finalize.

Far from disguising or downplaying itself, like Goethe's, Rousseau's subjectivity is so transparent and rhetorically insistent as to stand as a kind of exclamation point of his entire being. In the draft introduction to his *Confessions* he voiced a sentiment that we hear a few years later in Gibbon's preface to his *Memoirs* (2), and one with which Goethe and Wordsworth would have agreed, namely, that the best biographer is none other than the autobiographer: "No one can write the life of a man except that man himself. His manner of interiority, his true life is known only by himself" (*Oeuvres* 1:1149). With the notorious *braggadocio* of his self-proclaimed "sincerity," Rousseau goes on to claim that whereas other self-biographers have always disguised who they were and what they did, he will present nothing less than "the most secret history of my soul" (1155). This ringing prologue to the later Rousseau's sensational confessional career has its attenuated epilogue in the lyrical self-portraiture of *The Reveries of the Solitary Walker,* ostensibly written (unlike the *Confessions*) only for himself, as a kind of barometer of his soul and in order to double his existence by bringing his past back to life (*Oeuvres* 1:1000–1001).

Finally, to complete this Romantic triptych, another solitary walker, Wordsworth, ends up both championing and divinizing his own subjective self-awareness in blank verse on the threshold of his poetic maturity, not as an achieved magnum opus or definitive self-sounding, but as a poetic rite of passage and proleptic act of literary self-empowerment. His aim was to write an epic poem commensurate with his artistic talent and ambitions. However, in his search for a suitably elevated and serious subject, he ended up, without quite setting out to do so, writing his autobiography at a remarkably early age. At the end of the first book of *The Prelude,* in which he has been casting about for a topic for a major work only to find himself returning to his childhood and "those recollected hours that have the charm / Of visionary things" (659–60), he takes this return and concentration upon himself and his past—"the story of my life" (667)—as his proper focus. It is, *faute de mieux,* "a theme / Single and of determined bounds" (668–69), and thus he will "chuse it rather at this time, than work / Of ampler or more varied argument" (670–71).[3] With this apologetic note, Wordsworth commits himself to the single theme, the expansive song of his own self.

It has not escaped critical notice that the emergence of modern autobiography in the later eighteenth and early nineteenth centuries is coeval with the rise of Romanticism. Roy Pascal, who considers this "the classical age" of modern autobiography (36), notes in passing that the growth of the genre "to full stature in this period . . . accompanies the break-through that is called Romanticism, though it transcends any of the narrower definitions of this term" (51). Several years earlier, Gusdorf observed that "with the exaltation of genius the romantic period reinvented the taste for autobiography" ("Conditions et limites" 111), and in a later essay concluded that the "primacy of autobiography . . . considered as a privileged means of understanding culture, is a contribution of romanticism" ("L'autobiographie initiatique" 977). Jacques Voisine has pointed to the deliberate blurring of the line between author and protagonist as a distinctive feature of Romanticism ("Confession religieuse" 355), and Georges May has linked the related phenomena of the development of modern individualism and "the beginnings of romanticism" (in connection with the "posthumous works of Rousseau"), as decisive for the emergence of literary autobiography (24, 20). Rousseau, of course, is not only the father of modern autobiography but also gives a powerful impulse to the subsequent rise of Romanticism, of which he is seen as a fateful harbinger. As the author of the first book on French autobiography points out, Rousseau "did not invent the genre: but he realized in a single stroke nearly all of its possibilities." Although Philippe Lejeune does not connect Rousseau's achievement with the rise of Romanticism, his correlation of the birth of modern autobiography in the middle of the eighteenth century with a "transformation of the notion of the *person*"—that is, the discovery of the historicity of the self and of the "desire to return to the sources" ("L'autobiographie" 65–66, 64)—clearly points to some of the favorite concepts of the Romantics and their early sources in thinkers like Rousseau and Johann Gottfried Herder, who were so concerned with the primitive or "folk" origins of language and culture, and whose ideas influenced the young Goethe and Wordsworth.

I use the term Romantic autobiography, then, to denote a type of life-writing the most prominent instances of which are *The Confessions, Poetry and Truth,* and *The Prelude.* As a generic label, the term is, of course, problematical. Autobiography, a neologism of the late eighteenth century that appears to have surfaced first in Germany and then in England, has received considerable and growing critical attention in the last three decades without, however, any clear consensus as to what exactly it means or what kinds of writings do and do not qualify as autobiography.[4] Voisine epitomizes it as an unstable chemical compound that defies definition (356–57); James Olney concludes "that there is no way to bring autobiography to heel as a literary genre" and points to "one of the paradoxes of the subject: everyone knows what autobiography is, but no two observers . . . are in agreement" (4, 7). Yet he sees this not as a failure, but as an index of the irrepressible vitality of the genre. Other critics, most notable among them Paul de Man, deny the assumption that autobiography is in fact a genre—de Man famously asserts that "attempts at generic definition seem to founder in questions that are both pointless and unanswerable" ("Autobiography" 68). One of these unanswerables is the generic boundary line between autobiography and fiction and the richly complex and mutually determining relationship, since at least the eighteenth century, between the kinds of narrative modes employed by autobiographers and novelists. One of the most penetrating students of the genre, while concluding that ultimately there may be no "essential difference between the novel and the autobiography" (May 194), nevertheless posits the useful model of a spectrum, with the hypothetical extremes of pure autobiography and pure fiction and various shadings of different combinations of autobiography and fiction in between (188–94). Still other critics, impatient with such dilemmas, summarily dismiss them, like Paul Jay at the beginning of his book, as "finally pointless" (16).

Granted such difficulties of definition and classification, I nevertheless find Romantic autobiography helpful as a working term for a type of confessional narrative of the self in the later eighteenth and the early nineteenth centuries that, as a retrospective account and interpretation of how the writer's identity and personality were formed, artfully merges reality and imagination, the historiographic and the poetic poles of narrative—or what Goethe calls the "poetry" and the "truth" of a life. Because of their concern with the achievement of identity, Romantic autobiographers are most in their element when dealing with the period of childhood and youth. It need hardly be emphasized that this developmental focus closely aligns Romantic autobiography with the new genre of the *Bildungsroman*. However, while Romantic autobiography and the *Bildungsroman* share a common interest and indeed intersect and overlap at many points, as is readily apparent in *The Confessions, The Prelude,* and *Poetry and Truth,* it is still possible to distinguish the two. In the *Bildungsroman* the poetic or imaginative dimension preponderates or is in full ascendancy—as it is, for instance, in Novalis's *Heinrich von Ofterdingen*—over the biographical and historical. This is also readily apparent if we place Goethe's *Wilhelm Meister's Apprenticeship* next to *Poetry and Truth,* or Rousseau's *Julie, or the New Héloïse* next to his *Confessions.*

To date, no substantive study of Romantic autobiography has appeared, and no one has examined Rousseau, Goethe, and Wordsworth as the foremost instances of it, though Roy Pascal's brief commentary on *The Confessions, Poetry and Truth,* and *The Prelude* as instances of "the classical age of autobiography" (39–49) may stand as a modest beginning.[5] The periodizing procedure, to be sure, has not been absent from autobiography studies, as witnessed by a number of books—on, for instance, seventeenth-century, eighteenth-century, and Victorian autobiography— and the three figures who are the focus of my discussion have of course had been individually scrutinized as autobiographical writers. Several recent books devote sections to two out of three, but again not in the context of Romantic autobiography.[6] Ironically, the only book-length investigation of autobiography in the period in which Rousseau, Goethe, and Wordsworth were writing takes so narrowly prescriptive a view of the genre that it consistently castigates these writers by identifying as a flaw the most striking achievement or innovation of Romantic autobiography. According to Heidi I. Stull, for leading autobiographers during this period, "personal experience, subjected to artistic demands, is turned into a literary creation and, though basically and fundamentally of an autobiographical nature, loses its claim to the conventional autobiography, for the author has—in the interest of *artistic* considerations—changed or modified the true nature of events and experiences" (38). The (undefined) ideal of "the conventional autobiography" serves as Stull's touchstone for a naively referential view that she uses to castigate Romantic autobiographers (specifically, Rousseau, Goethe, Wordsworth, and Thomas De Quincey), for blatantly violating "the established norms of the traditional autobiography" (98, 165). The very energy of her repeated charge, however—as if "the true nature of events and experiences" were readily available to the self-chronicler's retrospective gaze, and not a problematic matter or challenge of self-interpretation—points unerringly to what is new and central in Rousseau's, Goethe's, and Wordsworth's autobiographical self-presentations.

How can we begin to account for the rise of autobiography as a major literary form in the later eighteenth century? Taylor's persuasive and synoptic charting of the emergence of the modern self along the axes of philosophy and religion (199) provides a conceptual framework for modern autobiography as a genre, a cultural and literary phenomenon that came about in the eighteenth but that was not really theorized until the second half of the twentieth century. While there clearly is no single or simple answer to explain the emergence of modern autobiography as a major genre, one important factor behind this new literature of the subject is the modern sense of individuality which had been powerfully in the making since the Renaissance. Two important studies of eighteenth-century German autobiography, by Klaus Detlef Müller and Günter Niggl, correlate the impressive achievements of the genre toward the end of the century with its increasingly individualizing character and its attachment to the idea of individuality, which come to the fore as autobiography's true subject (Niggl 38, 97; Müller 124, 339). Generalizing to the level of European culture, the historian Karl Joachim Weintraub posits the notion of individuality as "a specifically modern form of self-conception" coming "fully into its own at the time of Goethe," that is, "only at the end of the eighteenth century" (xiv–xv). It was only at that time, in the wake of Rousseau's *Confessions*, with their ringing insistence on the uniqueness of his self, that the interest in autobiography by both readers and writers took a quantum leap. In Germany, the philosopher Herder, friend and intellectual mentor of the young Goethe, championed the concept of individuality and declared the reading of "confessions" to be the most useful means of revealing the particular and the specific in history, and of displaying "those small traits, through which . . . the single individual gives himself away." For Herder, autobiography is the surest index and disclosure of individuality: "*As someone is, so he acts:* as he thinks, so he writes; most of all, if he writes about *himself.*" The teacher in Herder also saw a pedagogic value in reading the autobiographies of notable individuals and in 1790 called for the publication of an anthology of "confessions about themselves" to serve as productive models and exemplars of achievement for others, a call that was to be met by two separate collections in the following two decades: Johann Georg Müller's *Confessions of Notable Men* (6 vols., 1791–1810), and David Christoph Seybold's *Self-Biographies of Famous Men* (2 vols., 1796, 1799).[7]

To this we might add that the rise of individualism in the eighteenth century was aided by both secular and religious currents. On the one hand, the influential tradition of British empirical psychology from Locke to David Hartley, which makes personal identity a function of our particular experiences, memories, and associations; and on the other hand, the Protestant examination of the conscience, which gave an impetus to religious autobiography and, by extension, to a psychological scrutiny of the self. Thus Taylor points to the religious provenance of modern autobiography not only in Augustine's founding text but also in "the Protestant culture of introspection," which "from Bunyan to Pepys to Boswell, and arguably even Rousseau . . . becomes secularized as a form of confessional autobiography" (184). Indeed, as a popular but essentially nonliterary form of a forward-thrusting artisan class, eighteenth-century Pietist autobiographies in Germany and Wesleyan and Methodist autobiographies in England (a very rich vein that runs literally into thousands of manuscripts in archives), did their part to stimulate the development of literary autobiography as a secular scripture of the self. As Gusdorf has shown in his summary of what he calls "the Pietist international" ("L'autobiographie initiatique" 979–93), the seeds of a new and popular religious movement that called for intensive introspection and minute self-analysis were to yield a rich literary harvest.

Voisine arrives at the skeptical conclusion that because of its ubiquitous and uncertain character, autobiographical literature between 1760 and 1820 cannot be defined in terms of a distinctive style or technique ("Confession religieuse" 352). He bases this negative view on his review of the broad spectrum of genres across which the autobiographical impulse is discernible, but a more limited focus on what I take to be the constitutive moment of Romantic autobiography yields a more positive result. Admittedly, Rousseau, Goethe, and Wordsworth share no identifiable style of writing—indeed, each of them registers a variety of styles, which can range with different combinations and emphases from the lyric, the idyllic, and the epic to the ironic, the picaresque, and the satiric. Nevertheless, if we are to speak meaningfully of Romantic autobiography, then it must be possible to characterize its leading texts in terms of similar assumptions and features operative in them. One such similarity is that, in the context of a secularized view of the world in which God has largely dropped out of the picture, Rousseau, Goethe, and Wordsworth write a sort of theodicy of their selves. What Carl J. Hammer has concluded of the first two as autobiographers is also true of the third; they are concerned with "the inner life, the inner light" (105). Goethe is aware of a "daemonic" and fateful force at work within himself; Rousseau also attends to his inner voice, most notably so in the famous illumination on the road to Vincennes; and Wordsworth in the "spots of time" records a series of epiphanic moments that uncannily reveal the psychic stresses of his inner world and the life of his imagination.

Romantic writers differ fundamentally from our late-twentieth-century postmodern and dispersive sensibility in their root assumption that there is a core self, no matter how mysterious or elusive, and their most telling experiences are intimately bound up with and often indeed are experiences *of* it. Unlike some influential twentieth-century autobiographical works, which according to Paul Jay have abandoned the Wordsworthian belief in "the wholeness and the coherence of the self" and "whose subjects are represented in fragmented discursive forms" (36–37), Romantic autobiographies show a subtle and pervasive attentiveness to the inner rhythms and larger shapes of their subjects' lives. As William C. Spengemann has written of *The Prelude*, "The need to locate the fixed personal center that lends pattern and value to unstable reality, and the necessity of approaching that center through one's own moving experiences . . . stipulate autobiography as the prime instrument of Romantic knowledge" (77). Moreover, the three major Romantic autobiographers also give us three differing portraits of the artist in rendering their lives, and thus make their contribution to the Romantic legend of genius, in which the creative, the sensitive, the morbid, and even the pathological are never that far apart—a psychological truth that is as dramatically played up by Rousseau as it is discreetly downplayed by Goethe.

As the classic and constitutive exemplars of Romantic autobiography, Rousseau, Goethe, and Wordsworth also share the optimistic and in fact utopian presumption that their lives can be narratized, that they can be translated not only into a sequence of words but into a coherent and unified narrative. Contrary to the pervasive pessimism of our own century, with its decentered discursive forms and its multiply fragmented and perspectivally proliferating reflexivities, and despite momentary hesitations when they seem to strain against the limits of language and self-understanding, their most confident assumption is that they can render the plenitude of their experience in and through language, and that they can be at home with themselves, if anywhere, in their texts. In order to do so, however, and to impose order and coherence on their recollections and feelings, they call upon the shaping powers and resources of the imagination: Rousseau in a characteristically neurotic and defensive manner, Wordsworth in a high religious-sublime mode, and Goethe in a playful and poetically expansive fashion that makes autobiography very much an instrumentality of creative writing. In their retrospective life-narratives and self-accounts, imagination comes to the help of memory, or—to use a favorite word of Rousseau's—*supplements* it. Their pasts are stylized, poeticized, even fantasized. So in the *autos* of Romantic self-writing, poetry facilitates telling the truth of the *bios*. In a departure from strict biographical truth that Stull finds reprehensible, life takes on the coloring of fiction, as in Rousseau's account of his stay at Charmettes with Mme Françoise-Louise de Warens, or in Goethe's account of his love affair with Friederike Brion, or in Wordsworth's tale of Vaudracour and Julia (a very distant fictional echo of his French love affair).

Another feature that these autobiographers share is that they do not subscribe to any orthodox or conventional religious confession while nevertheless manifesting an openness to spiritual impulses and supra-rational dimensions and experiences. They are willing to fashion for themselves an undogmatic spirituality based on the awareness of their own mental powers and on the feelings of their hearts. Their religious impulses typically find expression in a quasi-pantheistic perception of nature, which in the case of Goethe and Wordsworth has a common philosophical source in Spinoza. Theirs is a vague religiosity both secularized and individualized, which transfers—in the well-known Romantic redistribution—to the mind and nature the powers traditionally reserved to the deity. Thus Romantic autobiography has not only its spiritual, but also its hieratic side, for these writers see themselves, in different ways and in differing degrees, as soothsayers and sages.

Their view of themselves as sages, as writers who not only have something to say about themselves but something to teach their readers, points to the moralizing and didactic nature of Romantic autobiography, which may be a secularized version of religious autobiography's need (by way of presenting an exemplary pattern of sin and conversion), to enlighten and to edify. Goethe's objectivizing tendency—to repeatedly locate and fix his subjective self within a panoramic historical framework—and his penchant for general reflections and moral aperçus arising from his experience attest to the didactic cast of *Poetry and Truth*. Rousseau in his original introduction insists on the value of his *Confessions* as a piece of comparative psychology by making the extraordinary claim that they are "a piece of comparison for the study of the human heart, and . . . the only one in existence" (*Oeuvres* 1:1154). Even more so than Goethe's and Rousseau's, Wordsworth's autobiography is nothing if not didactic, for its stated focus and sublime subject is the growth of the higher, that is, of the imaginative type of mind into the fullness of its powers.

To be sure, this desire to instruct by discovering a representative value in one's experience is evident in other eighteenth-century autobiographers, including Franklin and Gibbon, and—though it can put off the reader, especially if the moralizing is too bald and prudential, as is sometimes the case with Franklin—may simply point to the fact that during the period in question autobiography has not fully constituted itself as a separate and distinct genre. These autobiographers feel in need of some larger warrant or higher purpose than merely the telling of the stories of their lives, which in and of themselves would not be worthy of such literary treatment. Thus Goethe's self-biography has to be a *completion* of something already in the public domain (his other writings); Rousseau's is conceived not only as a pioneering psychological casebook, but also as his public defense of the slanderous image of him promulgated by his enemies; and Wordsworth's is, as we have seen, presented under the disarming guise of being a transition to an indisputably major and certainly more public work to come.

For Romantic autobiographers, with their imaginative investment in nature and the organic—"Fair seed-time had my soul" (305), wrote Wordsworth in the opening book of *The Prelude;* Goethe initially intended to model his autobiography on the metamorphosis of plants; and Rousseau made the devotional cult of nature a European fashion—and their emphasis on *Bildung* (education, growth, development, process), being *is* becoming. Hence also their special interest in the formative stages of their budding lives, which they render with particular power and varying degrees of vividness of detail and intensity of feeling—Wordsworth the most lyrically, because he is closest to it in time, and Goethe the most ironically, because he is the furthest removed from it. Even their eddying and uneven styles, with shifts and swerves from the nostalgic to the sublime to the pathetic to the prosaic to the ironic, seem to suggest in retrospect the irregular patterns of individual development, a mysterious compound of inborn capacities and external circumstances, of fate and accident, freedom and necessity. Their organic view of nature and the self, and their genetic perception and dynamic ideal of the free and harmonious unfolding of our faculties, also makes acculturation and the relationship of the individual to society a core problem, from Rousseau's crass and polemical polarization of the two, to Wordsworth's difficulties in moving from the love of nature to the love of man, to the later Goethe's diplomatic accommodation of the outer world, not as the stifling antagonist of our wishes and desires—

which it had been in *The Sufferings of Young Werther,* that confessional romance of his Storm-and-Stress youth—but as the necessary instrumentality of our self-realization and *Bildung.*

Let me at this juncture attempt a provisional characterization of the new or transformed genre in which the subjectivity of the modern self that achieved prominent literary representation in the later eighteenth and early nineteenth centuries found its definitive expression in Rousseau, Goethe, and Wordsworth. As the retrospective self-account of a highly individualized identity posited on a dynamic developmental sense, Romantic autobiography inscribes the specific forms and modes of the writer's subjectivity in a narrative interpretation and stylized reprise of the past that merges memory and imagination, thought and feeling, inner and outer, into a higher unity of the written self.

ROUSSEAU, GOETHE, AND MODERN AUTOBIOGRAPHY

Because the critical impact of Wordsworth's *Prelude* was delayed until nearly a century after its posthumous publication (1850), the most important English autobiography of the first half of the nineteenth century played no significant historical role, unlike Rousseau's and Goethe's influential life narratives, in the development of modern autobiography. A contributing factor here too is that unlike Goethe and Rousseau, who were authors of European renown when they wrote their autobiographies in their later years, the young author of *The Prelude* was largely unknown, except to a small if discerning coterie who had admired his *Lyrical Ballads.* For some reason, the foremost English Romantic writer has never effectively crossed the English Channel, and unlike his notorious younger contemporary, Byron, did not establish a European reputation even after he became a poet of national stature in the country of his birth. And when Wordsworth did achieve high canonical stature in the Victorian era, his reputation was based on his shorter poems, which were praised by the most influential critic of the age, Matthew Arnold, as his best and most representative work. Then too the critical preconception that autobiography is a prose genre, a position unreflectingly assumed even by some contemporary theorists (for example, Lejeune), has kept Wordsworth's epic blank verse *Prelude* from significantly influencing the development of modern autobiography.

The opposite is true of Rousseau and Goethe; indeed, it is hardly an exaggeration to say that between them they helped to create the terms in which modern autobiography has largely been written and appreciated. The Confessions and Poetry and Truth are thus normative for its emergence, development, and history; they represent its defining and definitive moment in the later eighteenth and early nineteenth centuries, when autobiography is in the process of constituting itself as a powerful and distinct genre. However, whereas Rousseau's psychologizing, subjective, egotistical, and at times rhetorically defensive confessional autobiography polarizes or juxtaposes the self against the world, Goethe's historicizing, objectivizing, world-embracing, and largely non-confessional and nondefensive life narrative unfolds his development as a progressive imbrication in the world in all its historical richness and circumstantiality. If Rousseau polemically opposes himself against a culture increasingly perceived as hostile and corrupt, Goethe sees a biological and even ecological relationship—a balance and interdependency—between the self and its world in his imaginative reconstruction of the history of his (richly informed) personality. Their two different yet in some respects complementary approaches adumbrate much of what will be pervasive in the genre for the next two centuries, and between them they map out the territory and lay the foundation for subsequent practitioners of the form.

The areas of commonality in their different approaches can also be seen as significant for the emergence of autobiography as a distinct and major genre during the past two centuries: the role of the imagination on the one hand, and the broadly anthropological conception of autobiography as a disclosure of the fundamentally human on the other. As to the first, the instrumentality of the imagination and of the presence of fiction that characterizes Romantic autobiography, which Paul John Eakin has also posited as a central feature of twentieth-century autobiography (Fictions), it is manifested in very different forms in Rousseau and Goethe. Whereas the author of The Confessions engages in the pleasures of the imagination covertly, defensively, and with considerable guilt as a mode of autoerotic fantasy, as I will argue in my analysis of the "dangerous supplement" (in chapter 2), the author of Poetry and Truth signals the consistent poeticizing of experience with his very title. What for Rousseau was a giving in to temptation was for Goethe a programmatic procedure throughout his self-presentation, a poetic heightening of experience to a symbolic and humanly representative level according to which, to invoke a remark of his (on the presentation of the Sesenheim narrative), he incorporated no trait that was not experienced, but no trait in the actual manner in which it was experienced.

Nearly a century ago, the German historian Hans Glagau signaled the importance of the fictive element of Rousseau's and Goethe's autobiographies and posited that "modern self-biography is a daughter of the novel" (58)—specifically, the Richardsonian psychological novel of the eighteenth century. Whereas Goethe emphasizes the novelistic, imaginative, and symbolic dimension of his life narrative from the outset (including the astrological constellation at his birth as a metaphor of the mutually implicated relationship of an individual identity and its world), Rousseau, in the strident insistence on his truthfulness and sincerity of his opening paragraphs, assigns the imagination a strictly circumscribed and subsidiary role as a function of the failure of memory ("if by chance I have used some immaterial embellishment it has been only to fill a void due to the defect of memory," 17). Only a decade later, in the apologetic hindsight of his *Reveries,* does Rousseau acknowledge that sometimes due to "a delirium of the imagination rather than an act of the will" he sometimes told more than the truth ("Fourth Walk," *Oeuvres* 1:1035). His version of the confessional "supplement" here is still causally linked to the failure of memory, for whose "lacunae" (1035) imaginary details furnish the fictional filler. These invented details, however, are never contrary to the truth, so that Rousseau can conclude his avowal of fiction and his defense of his essential truthfulness by still limiting the fictive or poetic dimension: "I have often retailed fables, but I have very rarely lied" (1038). However, the "very rarely" is a crucial concession, a crack in his defense through which (in the century of the hermeneutics of suspicion) one can march a whole army of fables. Thus even in his belated acknowledgment and attempt once more to circumscribe the play of the confessional imagination, Rousseau opens the door to a host of "innocent fictions" (1038)—fictions that (as I will show in chapter 2) are not so much innocent as they are self-serving.

The late Enlightenment anthropological and humanistic conception of autobiography common to both Rousseau and Goethe assumes the genre to be a privileged instrument of self-knowledge—although for Goethe one finds oneself primarily through activity (including literary activity) and not through passive introspection or "navel gazing"—as well as a vehicle for understanding and disclosing our larger humanity. As an adumbration and unfolding of what it means to be human, *The Confessions* and *Poetry and Truth* reflect the positive creed of the Enlightenment that there is such a bedrock and uniform humanity, something epitomized in Pope's famous epigram, "The proper study of mankind is man" ("An Essay on Man," Epistle 2). Even in its stress on individuality and, in Rousseau's case, on the singularity and uniqueness of the self asserted in his polemical opening, autobiography as life narrative and personal history attests to and discloses this larger, generic humanity. Such a quasi-hermeneutic conception informs Rousseau's canceled Neuchâtel preface (which I consider in chapter 1), and is also implicit in Goethe's "half poetical, half historic treatment of events" (*Poetry and Truth* 17).

For Goethe, however, writing in the early nineteenth century, the uniformitarian model of Enlightenment anthropology is adapted to a historicizing conception, according to which the human monad is always subject to and shaped by the particular contingencies of the historical moment, so that our individual identity is very much a function of our age and culture. Indeed, as I argue in chapter 4, Goethe's biological paradigm of a slow and steady human development came into conflict with and had to be revised in the light of the chaotic course of contemporary history. In Goethe's panoramic or epic vision as an autobiographer, individual development and personal history must always be seen in the larger context of an ongoing history and a rich and changing culture of which it is always a part and by which it is contextualized and defined. For Goethe, however, it is the mark of the creative individual or genius not only to be influenced by his age and culture, but also in turn to exert a reciprocal and even decisive influence on these. The Goethean self is thus at once acted upon and agential.

Unlike the historicizing Goethe, for Rousseau, writing a half-century earlier in the geographic and temporal heartland of the Enlightenment, there is an archetypal and authentic humanity, as it were, preceding and underlying history. This is the primordial realm of "nature" and the natural that he set out to identify, recover, and champion, first as a philosopher and then in the end as an autobiographer. Such a hypostatized and valorized "nature" or unalienated human essence is his philosophical touchstone, and his anthropological quest as *philosophe* and historian of the self is to uncover this authentic and original human substratum from underneath the layers of disfigurement and occlusion by the progressive corruption of society that for Rousseau is the course of history and the burden of civilization. That is why (as I posit in chapter 2) Rousseau's project as an autobiographer, that of recovering as a standard a lost or occluded human essence, is a fundamentally philosophical one. In Rousseau's secularized, Enlightenment version of the Judeo-Christian story, history is the story of the fall away from nature and the natural. The story of civilization is that of a growing inauthenticity, disguise, disfigurement, and corruption. Unlike the Christian paradigm, however, for Rousseau there is no chiliastic or millennial scenario of a return to innocence and transparency at a higher level. For the political theorist as well as the autobiographer, we can at best recognize and minimize the consequences of our fall into civilization and its discontents. In Rousseau's political theory, there can be no return to the individual freedom that prevails in the state of nature; at best, the social contract, through social institutions and the pressure of the general will, can *force* the citizen to be free (*On Social Contract* bk. 1, chap. 7, *Political Writings* 95).

In his *Confessions*, Rousseau seeks at the level of his life narrative to identify, celebrate, and invoke as a standard the wholeness, integrity, and transparency progressively lost in, covered over, or corrupted by history, individual and collective. Our lives in society rob us of our original integrity and goodness: that is the confessional and philosophical masterscript of Rousseau the autobiographer, for whom the story of his life is paradigmatic not so much of the formation as of the deformation of his character through the process of acculturation, which is also one of adulteration. The personal "reform" he undertook in the wake of his fame after the publication of his two Discourses is a quixotic and oxymoronic attempt to return to the standard of nature in modern society—a return that appeared to be a ridiculous affectation in the eyes of carping Encyclopedist friends like Denis Diderot and Friedrich Melchior Grimm, and that even in his pastoral retreat in the forest of Montmorency did not relieve him of the complicated social relations and intrigues with the high aristocracy at whose sufferance he was in fact residing at the Hermitage. One important lesson that Goethe the writer appears to have learned from the example of Rousseau championing the standard of nature—while simultaneously supported by and struggling against the silken threads of aristocratic patronage—is that in our advanced civilization the effect of the natural (as I argue in chapter 6 with respect to the Sesenheim idyll in *Poetry and Truth*), can only be achieved through the most artful means.

OVERVIEW OF BOOK

The assumption that informs the chapters that follow is that Rousseau and Goethe are foundational figures of Romantic and modern autobiography whose life narratives are instrumental and paradigmatic for the emergence of modern subjectivity in European literature and culture in the later eighteenth and the early nineteenth centuries. Their autobiographies are thus also decisive in the transformation of the genre of autobiography from a previously relatively marginal one to a central mode of Romantic and post-Romantic literature.

A number of things sets my book apart from other studies of the autobiographical writings of Rousseau and Goethe. There is no other book devoted to these two as the leading Romantic autobiographers, nor any study that parallels my sustained critical and psycho-biographical analysis of their narrative self-presentations. If in this introductory chapter I have attempted to situate and define the new genre of Romantic autobiography in historical and critical terms, the rest of this book examines Rousseau's and Goethe's conceptions of the genre and motives for writing, as well as their performance as autobiographers. More so than previous commentators, I explore the developmental patterning of their presentation of their early years. I consider in some detail the scheme of sexual development in Rousseau's *Emile* for the revealing light it throws on the covert play of the author's autoerotic imagination in his *Confessions,* and I demonstrate how Goethe positively exploits the element of fiction or "poetry" that Rousseau indulged in covertly but refused to acknowledge in the *Confessions.* I also argue that although Goethe never says so directly, *Poetry and Truth* is indeed written against the grain of *The Confessions,* as an autobiographical counter or corrective to the self-destructive pull of a solipsistic subjectivity that Goethe saw at work in Rousseau.

Chapter 1, my introduction to Rousseau, attempts an interpretive overview of Rousseau's philosophical conception and defensive practice of autobiography by analyzing the Neuchâtel draft preface as a template of his complex confessional aims and agenda. Chapter 2 is devoted to

Rousseau's pioneering autobiographical exploration of childhood and youth. This long chapter tries to do justice to his achievement here by considering all the major episodes of part 1 of *The Confessions* in the light of his philosophical writings as well as of the biographical record. In reading the autobiographer Rousseau through the lens of Rousseau the philosopher (especially his *Second Discourse* and *Emile*), I follow in the direction laid out by Christopher Kelly in his reading of *The Confessions* as political philosophy. While Rousseau's best critics have tended to focus on a few selected episodes of *The Confessions* to build global interpretations of the work, I attempt a close reading as well as an overview of part 1 in its entirety as the confessional *Bildungsroman* of Rousseau's youth. The focal point of that novel of (mis)education is the young Rousseau's search for a home and a mother he never had and that he tries to (re)constitute in a perverse family romance (two ménages à trois) with his female mentor, Mme de Warens. I conclude the Rousseau portion of my study with chapter 3, a short revisionary reading of Rousseau's largely unknown autobiography, his *Dialogues,* in order to analyze that forensic and defensive text as the author's final and manipulative attempt to justify himself to the world and to assure his posthumous reputation.

The second half of this study, the three chapters on Goethe, constitutes the fullest critical analysis of *Poetry and Truth* extant. Chapter 4, "Goethe and Autobiography," presents the biography, as it were, of Goethe's ambitious project for writing his autobiography in terms of the genesis of the project as well as its unrealizable goal (a life fully recorded up to the moment of writing). In this chapter I also consider the relationship of Goethe the autobiographer to Rousseau, analyze his view of the "fundamental" truth of autobiography as one allowing for the creative play of "poetry," and discuss his ideal of *Bildung* as it both informs and problematizes his life narrative. Chapters 5 and 6 focus on Goethe's presentation of his relationships with others: his family—specifically his conflicted relationship with his father and his self-serving and idealizing account of his sister Cornelia's short and tragic life—and the romantic relationships that play such a prominent role in Goethe's portrait of his early years and in the public legend of his life. Unlike Rousseau's autobiography, where romantic love takes the form of an explicit sexual history, in Goethe's we have a highly poeticized treatment of young love, beginning with the "New Paris" fairy tale as a symbolic reprise of the boy's sexual awakening.

I consider the Gretchen and Friederike sequences at length as sophisticated confessional narratives that present a merger of romance and history (in the former) and nature and art (in the latter).

In my reading of Rousseau's and Goethe's accounts of their relationships with others I point in different ways to how these are at times defensive or self-serving and indicate (as in Rousseau's narrative of the two famous spankings and Goethe's portrait of his sister), a truth more complex and ambiguous than they are willing to acknowledge. My probing of the family and romantic relationships in Rousseau's *Confessions* and Goethe's *Poetry and Truth* reflects the current interest in autobiography studies in the "relational self" that has come to the fore as a consequence of the revisionary feminist critique of the genre. I should acknowledge that this powerful critique has made me look at these canonical male autobiographers in a different light, that is, it has made me look beyond their admittedly looming egos to their connection(s) to the *alter,* or other.

From the perspective of this contemporary feminist critique, to quote Bella Brodzki and Celeste Schenk, "the masculine autobiography, from . . . Saint Augustine to Roland Barthes . . . assumes the conflation of masculinity and humanity, canonizing the masculine representative self of both writer and reader" (2). The charge that the those preeminent canonical male autobiographers, Augustine and Rousseau, are inappropriate as models for women's life-writing was spelled out two decades ago by Mary G. Mason. Her conclusion that "the self-discovery of female identity seems to acknowledge the real presence and recognition of another consciousness," and that female identity is thus relational (210), has become something of a truism in the feminist readings of the genre, although recently there has been a movement away from essentializing identity differences in autobiography, including those of gender.[8] As Eakin put it in the keynote address of a 1994 autobiography conference, "The serious and sustained study of women's autobiography . . . is the single most important achievement of autobiography studies in the last decade." "One of the consequences," however, "has been an unfortunate polarization by gender of the categories we use to define the life of the self" ("Relational Selves" 66). Anyone reading the autobiographies of Rousseau and Goethe can find in them plenty of evidence of the autonomous and imperial self common to the Enlightenment and Romanticism—from Rousseau's obsessive self-preoccupation to Goethe's magisterial presumptuousness—and of what Brodzki and Schenk call "the classic stance of the male autobiographer" as the representative of his age and his assumption of "the conflation of masculinity and humanity" (3). But as Eakin points out, one "consequence of the attempt to define women's autobiography has been the widespread acceptance of a concomitantly narrow definition of men's autobiography" (66).

His larger thesis that "all selfhood . . . is relational despite differences that fall out along gender lines" ("Relational Selves" 67) is amply borne out by Rousseau's *Confessions* and Goethe's *Poetry and Truth*. Even the two scenes of reading—one imaginary, one actual—that frame *The Confessions* by way of a beginning and an end are relational, drawing in as they do both a divine auditor ("my Sovereign Judge" 17) and fellow human hearers (the former is invoked only at the outset, the latter are scripted in both scenes). Admittedly, Rousseau's ego presides theatrically at the center of both scenes—but it is the ego of a man who is always looking over his shoulder to see how others see him, and who, moreover, sometimes seems to identify with the female or feminine role. However, by far the most important dimension of the relational self in *The Confessions* is Rousseau's complex relationship with the woman who helped to shape his adult identity, Mme de Warens.

For Goethe as well, *Poetry and Truth* is relational from beginning to end. At the outset he thematizes the larger and dialectical historical relationship between himself and his world, but he also shows with epic sweep and psychological depth how his protean—talented but unstable—character was shaped through an intricate pattern of human relationships, from his patrician family to his many friendships and romantic relationships. Indeed, for Goethe the ideal of the relational self takes in the full range of his human relationships but also aspires to nothing less than the totality of Western culture, from the Greeks and the Bible to the contemporary European literature to which he made such a decisive contribution. However, since, like Rousseau, he came of age in, was shaped by the ethos of, and in many ways came himself as a writer to embody the outlook of a fundamentally patriarchal culture, it is of course not surprising that his account of his relationships with others, like that of Rousseau, reflects the deeply embedded androcentric assumptions of this eighteenth-century European culture.

1 ❦

Rousseau and Autobiography

ROUSSEAU AND THE FUNDAMENTAL CHALLENGE OF AUTOBIOGRAPHY

Nobody in the world except for myself knows me.
—Rousseau, First Letter to Malesherbes

The work for which Rousseau is best known in our time, his *Confessions* (written 1765–70), is generally recognized as the first modern autobiography and the founding text of a genre that has continued unabated for two centuries, from major works of "high" literature down to the popular culture of the present day, with its flood of ghostwritten celebrity autobiographies and its ever more sensational talk show and tabloid confessions. Before Rousseau the autobiographer, however, there was Rousseau the celebrated writer of such influential and controversial philosophical works as the two discourses (*On the Sciences and the Arts* [1750] and *On the Origin of Inequality* [1755]), *The Social Contract* (1762), and *Emile* (1762). From his first, prizewinning *Discourse,* Rousseau's writings brought him an unprecedented fame, but they also embroiled him in polemical debates and bitter controversies. And they helped to generate a public image or legend of "Jean-Jacques" that he felt bore little or no resemblance to the man he knew he was. The famous but misunderstood writer turned in the final phase of his literary career to autobiography to give an account of himself and his motives. In fact, his first significant step toward becoming an autobiographer included an explanation of how he became a writer, given in the four letters he sent in 1762 to M. Chrétien-Guillaume de Malesherbes, "containing the true picture of my character and the true motives of all my conduct" (*Oeuvres* 1:1130). Ill and convinced that he was not long for this world, Rousseau penned his apologetic and lyrical self-portrait with uncharacteristic rapidity. His effusive letters to the French aristocrat at the head of the office of censorship offer a miniature version of what a few years later he set out to do in the full-scale treatment of his *Confessions*.[1]

Rousseau insisted that literature was never a profession for him, a way of earning his living. In his *Dialogues* he puts it with a pun: he wrote books (*livres*), but he was never a mere maker of books (*livrier*) (*Oeuvres* 1:840). Nor did he write, he asserts with a certain disingenuousness in the first letter, merely to shine and to make a name for himself. Unlike professional men of letters who write out of vanity and who give everything for their reputation in the world, Rousseau became a writer almost despite himself, because of his "passionate attachment to the truth" ("Second Letter," *Oeuvres* 1:1136). Indeed, at the height of his celebrity, Rousseau renounced all worldly success, choosing instead to earn his living as a mere copyist of music. He seems to have taken almost as much trouble to avoid becoming rich as most men put into the pursuit of material gain. Rather, literature was a vocation, a calling, and it came to him, as he tells us in the second letter to Malesherbes, in a baptism of fire, or more appropriately, of light, in the famous illumination of Vincennes (1749). He discusses this founding experience or epiphany in *The Confessions* and elsewhere, but never as vividly and fully as in this letter. The illumination is a "spot of time" (to use Wordsworth's phrase) crucial not only to Rousseau the thinker and discursive writer but also to Rousseau the autobiographer. He was walking from Paris to Vincennes, where his friend Diderot had been imprisoned for some of his too-unorthodox writings. As he walked, he read a literary journal and came across the prize question of the Dijon academy that came as a wake-up call to Rousseau the philosopher and brought him sudden celebrity with the publication of the first *Discourse:* "Has the progress of the sciences and arts done more to corrupt morals or to preserve them?" (*The Confessions* 327):

If anything has ever resembled a sudden inspiration, it was the agitation which took place within me during this reading; all at once I
felt my mind dazzled by a thousand lights and a confusion which
threw me into an inexpressible disturbance; I felt my head possessed by a giddiness resembling intoxication. A violent palpitation
oppressed me and uplifted my chest; no longer able to breathe
while walking, I let myself fall under the trees of the road, and there
I spent half an hour in such an agitation that when I got up I
noticed that the whole front of my vest was wet with tears without
my having noticed shedding any. Oh sir, if I could have written a
quarter of what I felt and saw under that tree, with what clarity I
would have exposed all the abuses of our institutions, with what
simplicity I would have demonstrated that man is naturally good,
and that it is through these institutions alone that men become bad.
All that I have been able to retain of this host of great truths which
during a quarter of an hour illuminated me under this tree, has been
quite feebly disseminated in my three principal writings [the two
Discourses and *Emile*]. . . (*Oeuvres* 1:1135–36)

In book 8 of *The Confessions* Rousseau epitomizes this pivotal experience as one in which he "beheld another universe and became another
man" (327). His language suggests a sudden conversion experience, like
that of Saul struck blind by God on the road to Damascus, but he does
not embrace any particular religion or creed, or argue for his as a metaphysical "illumination." In an age when the advanced thinkers were res-
olutely secular and antireligious, such an experience required a different
context. A friend and aspiring colleague of the Enlightenment *philosophes*
and contributor to Diderot's project of the *Encyclopedia,* Rousseau keeps
the mind-blowing "illumination" in the realm of the psychological and
intellectual, as a tremendous cognitive breakthrough that convulses his
being. The "inspiration" that dazzles him with "a thousand lights" on the
road to Vincennes does not put Rousseau in touch with God; rather, it is
the cathartic manifestation of impulses from within, his *daimon.* His
account does not contradict the rhetoric of the Enlightenment but goes it
one better by taking it to a new level—the ecstatic.

Although it has been ignored by poststructuralist critics, for whom in
any event, in the words of one of them, "selfhood is not a substance but a

figure" (de Man, *Allegories* 170), the Vincennes illumination is clearly decisive for Rousseau the writer and thinker, and, in the end, the autobiographer as well.[2] However, in the bleak retrospect of his *Confessions*, it is seen
as a mixed blessing at best, because it launched him on a literary career
that led from fame to infamy, and from celebrity to a persecution that cul-
minated in the banning of *The Social Contract* and *Emile* and that was
responsible for his flight from France (in order to avoid arrest), as well as
for his subsequent expulsions from Swiss territories. For Rousseau, his
unhappy stay in England under the sponsorship of Hume, his disastrous
quarrel with that philosopher, and his status in France as a maligned persona non grata are all consequences of the career initiated at Vincennes.
"When I reached Vincennes I was in a state of agitation bordering on
delirium. Diderot noticed it; I told him the cause. . . . He encouraged me
to give my ideas wings and compete for the prize. I did so, and from that
moment I was lost. All the rest of my life and of my misfortunes followed
inevitably as a result of that moment's madness" (*The Confessions* 328).
Although in hindsight Rousseau judges his first discourse a fervent but
feebly argued effort ("the art of writing is not learned all at once" 329), he
knows that the energies of the Vincennes inspiration fueled and sustained
the writing of his major works during the richly productive years that followed. He was a man on fire, an intoxicated idealist: "All my little passions were stifled by an enthusiasm for truth, liberty, and virtue; and the
most astonishing thing is that this fermentation worked in my heart for
more than four or five years as intensely perhaps as it has ever worked in
the heart of any man on earth" (328). In the concise summation of his later
Dialogues, the Vincennes illumination is again identified as the source of
his problematic career as the most controversial thinker and writer of his
age. "From the intense effervescence which then took place in his soul
emerged those sparks of genius which have been seen to shine in his writings during ten years of delirium and fever" (*Oeuvres* 1:829).

The original inspiration is a powerful psychological experience that
puts him in touch with his inner self and points out to him his vocation;
but it is also questionable and unfortunate in its results, because by turning him into a writer and philosopher it put him at odds with his world.
In Nietzsche's sense, it is at once the great health and the great disease. It
made him a kind of moral Don Quixote, or even a Gulliver measuring
men by the rational horses' impossible standard of virtue, "swayed by the

ridiculous hope of making truth and reason finally triumph over preju-
dices and lies, and of making men wise by showing them their true interest" (*Dialogues, Oeuvres* 1:829). Rousseau's motivating insight on the road
to Vincennes and the burden of his theoretical-critical writings is humanity's natural or inherent goodness and its progressive corruption in and
through civilization. The philosopher and culture critic caught up in controversy and polemic invokes the standard of nature, but the zeal with
which he pursues it, in his writings as well as in his own life, by way of his
personal "reform," is unnatural and extreme.

In book 9 of *The Confessions* Rousseau acknowledges that in the wake
of Vincennes he had become "intoxicated with virtue": "I was truly transformed; my friends and acquaintances no longer recognized me" (388).
The paradox is that the transformation of Rousseau into the outspoken
apostle of virtue is sincere—"I played no part; I became indeed what I
appeared"—yet it carries him out of, away from, his ordinary or "natural"
self. "No state of being could be found on earth more contrary to my true
nature than this one. If ever there was a moment in my life in which I
became another man and ceased to be myself, it was at the time I am
speaking of. But instead of lasting six days or six weeks it lasted nearly six
years" (388). He claims that only his move from Paris to the countryside
(to the Hermitage, in 1756), "restored [him] to Nature; out of whose
realm [he] had been trying to soar" (388). As with so many other areas of
his life, Rousseau's chronology of his period of "virtue" is tenuous and
inconsistent, but what I want to emphasize here is the larger paradox that
the continuing impact of the illumination of Vincennes is grounded in an
overwhelming experience of authentic selfhood that yet carries him
beyond his "true nature." The position of the philosophical champion of
nature became more and more unnatural and anomalous; Rousseau
reached an impasse where both he and his writings were increasingly subject to misprision and concerted hostility.

In the light of this unhappy situation, his turn to autobiography in his
sixth decade was in many ways a new beginning. Clearly, Rousseau
wanted to explain himself—to present his side of the story, his version of
himself, which he thought had been willfully preempted by the false public image or malign legend of "Jean-Jacques" fabricated by his detractors
and enemies, who after the traumatic shock of his flight from France
began to loom large in his increasingly paranoid imagination. They

included former friends and patrons with whom he had fallen out, among them Diderot, Grimm, and Mme Louise-Florence Pétronille d'Epinay, as well as public figures like the minister Etienne-François de Choiseul and Mme Jeanne-Antoine de Pompadour, the king's mistress, who he thought had been personally offended by his writings. By the time Rousseau wrote the second part of his *Confessions*, he was fully convinced that these and others had entered into a sinister conspiracy to blacken his reputation, to persecute, and to turn all of his contemporaries against him. They had somehow gotten wind of the shameful secret that burdened his life—a secret he had shared with only a few of his closest friends—and published it, along with scurrilous falsehoods about him and his mistress/companion Thérèse Le Vasseur, in an anonymous pamphlet of 1764, *The Sentiment of the Citizens*. (Rousseau was unaware that Voltaire had written the pamphlet.) It revealed that the author of the famous treatise on education, *Emile*, had placed his five children in the Paris Foundling Home upon their birth. The citizen of Geneva was exposed as a hypocrite, a bad man and a worse father.

While the need for self-justification and defense is prominent in Rousseau's turn to autobiography, it is, nonetheless, far from Rousseau's only motive in writing his *Confessions*. In a man as complex as he was, the reason for writing an autobiography can hardly be a simple one. Another important need, as he tells us repeatedly in *The Confessions*, was to recover the happy times of his past, to relive the best of the *temps perdu* before he became the unhappy celebrity, to escape into and seal himself off in his memories of a better past, like those of the rural retreat at Les Charmettes. Through these poetic recollections of his affective memory, he wanted to keep in touch with the best energies of his early years. But Rousseau also brought to the task of the autobiographer the full burden of the thinker and philosopher, and of the insights—psychological, political, educational, cultural—of his earlier theoretical writings. Ultimately as important as and perhaps more fundamental than the defensive and escapist motives—and more decisive for the genre of modern autobiography—are the cognitive and the philosophical: Rousseau wanted to unfold and lay bare his own humanity in a way that no writer or thinker before him—not even Montaigne—had ever done. For Rousseau, whose adumbration and disclosure of his humanity is meant to be as unreserved and as complete as possible, autobiography is ultimately an epistemology of the self. If

Augustine's religious confession, addressed to God, embodies a typological pattern of sin and conversion that can serve as a model for all Christians, Rousseau's exemplary secular confession, addressed to his fellow humans, is a psychological laying bare of the complexities of human personality and the individual self for their own sake. By making himself his subject, the celebrated *philosophe* wanted to achieve an unprecedented philosophical disclosure of what it means to be a human being. In this respect at least, and despite *The Confessions'* insistent rhetoric of his self's singularity, Rousseauean confession has a representative human purpose.

Rousseau was quite aware of the novelty and originality of his project, which had been on his mind for a long time before he set seriously to work on his *Confessions* in 1765. The first modern autobiography has a complex prehistory, one that includes his "earlier comings to write about himself" (2) in the occasional texts (including prefaces and texts) that Susan K. Jackson has analyzed in *Rousseau's Occasional Autobiographies*. Bernard Gagnebin and Marcel Raymond have traced its "long period of incubation" back a decade earlier, to Rousseau's move from Paris to the Hermitage (*Oeuvres* 1:xxiii, xvi–xvii), where he penned a fragmentary self-portrait that may haven been written at this time but that cannot be dated with any precision (*Oeuvres* 1:839–40). It already raises the issue of misprision and identity: "I see that the people who live with me in the greatest intimacy do not know me, and that they attribute the greater number of my actions, be they good or bad, to motives entirely different from those that produced them. This makes me think that most of the characters and portraits that one finds in the historians are but chimeras that a gifted author can easily render likely [vraisemblable]" (*Oeuvres* 1:1121). Far from being overtly defensive, this aphoristic reflection on and of his self attempts a moral and psychological anatomy of his character, including a frank avowal of his vanity: "I would prefer to be forgotten by the human species than regarded as an ordinary man" (1123). Still earlier, around 1749, Rousseau had attempted a highly stylized and witty verbal sketch of himself, "Le Persifleur" ("The Banterer"), for a projected journal to be edited by him and Diderot. Already the aspiring litterateur and *philosophe* is struck by certain "peculiarities of [his] character," and the contradictions that define it are aphorized as a paradox of personal identity: "Nothing is as dissimilar to me as myself" (*Oeuvres* 1:1108).

The psychological puzzlement and philosophical curiosity about his own character and identity and those of others, and about the difficulties that stand in the way of achieving a genuine understanding of these and of fathoming our own and others' real but often hidden or unacknowledged motives, is the epistemological heart of Rousseauean autobiography. Due to the pressure of his increasing sense of the public misunderstanding, hostility, and persecution that greeted his doctrinal writings, however, this fundamentally philosophical motive was more and more displaced or overlaid by his defensive strategy, including the stridently self-assertive opening and conclusion of *The Confessions,* which have turned off many readers. Despite the fact that the defensive and self-exculpatory impulse so prominent in that book invites a reading of it as *the* self-justifying autobiography par excellence, a view that has governed its reception in our century, this reading is incomplete, partial, and misleading if pursued too exclusively and in isolation from other approaches. Readers who reduce his text to a mere personal statement, a *plaidoir,* focus on something admittedly very prominent in it, but do so at the expense of the philosophical dimensions that played such an important role in the inception of Rousseau's project. Only recently have critics begun to explore this important aspect, most notably Christopher Kelly in his study of *The Confessions* as political philosophy.

Rousseau's conception of his autobiography as a pioneering and unprecedented act of human self-disclosure is not as pronounced in the text as his self-justifying rhetoric, but it does surface on occasion. The most prominent instance is in his discussion in book 10 of the genesis of the work, where he states,

> I decided to make it a work unique and unparalleled in its truthfulness, so that for once at least the world might behold a man as he was within. I had always been amused at Montaigne's false ingenuousness, and at his pretense of confessing his faults while taking good care to admit to likeable ones; whereas I, who believe, and always have believed, that I am on the whole the best of men, felt that there is no human heart, however pure, that does not conceal some odious vice. I knew that I was represented in the world under features so unlike my own and at times so distorted, that notwithstanding my faults, none of which I intend to pass over, I could not help gaining by showing myself as I was. (478–79)

In this excerpt from the latter portions of *The Confessions*, burdened as they are by his paranoid anxieties, Rousseau slides readily from the philosophical (disclosure) conception to his self-justifying or defensive mode. The larger significance of these two complexly intertwined motives is most comprehensively spelled out in a draft introduction or preamble, which unfortunately Rousseau chose not to use for the final version. The excerpt above, including the contrast between Montaigne and Rousseau as autobiographers, presents in fact a brief digest of some of the ideas enunciated in the canceled preamble of 1764, the so-called Neuchâtel Preface, Rousseau's most incisive and comprehensive statement of the philosophical and apologetic issues central to the final, autobiographical phase of his literary career.

For Rousseau the autobiographer, a crucial concern is the reader's arriving at a proper understanding and judgment of his life. The preface opens with a problematizing reflection on whether we can ever know ourselves or others:

> I have often remarked that even among those who pride themselves most on knowing men, each hardly knows himself, if it is even true that anybody knows himself. . . . Nevertheless this imperfect knowledge which one has of oneself is the only avenue one has to understanding others. One makes oneself the rule of everything, and this is precisely where the double illusion of self-love [amour propre] lies in wait for us: whether in falsely attributing to those we judge the motives which would have made us act like them in their place; or whether on this very supposition we delude ourselves about our own motives because we are not able to translate ourselves sufficiently into a situation other than the one we are in. (*Oeuvres* 1:1149)

He goes on to assert that he has been consistently misjudged by others: "Among my contemporaries there are few men whose name is better known in Europe than mine but where the individual is more misunderstood [ignoré]. . . . Everyone imagined me according to his fantasy, without any fear that the original would come to deny it. There was a Rousseau in the great world, and another in his seclusion who resembled him in nothing" (1151). The public's misprision of Jean-Jacques, however, is not only a function of the general difficulty of human understanding and communication, but of a concerted effort by his "personal enemies" to distort his image and blacken his reputation: "Nothing was more different from me than this picture" (1152). As in the excerpt above from book 10 of *The Confessions*, Rousseau here shifts readily from the philosophical to the defensive mode: "Here are not only the motives which made me undertake this project, but also the guarantees of my integrity in executing it. Since my name is bound to endure among men, I do not want it to bear a false reputation; I do not want to be given virtues and vices or to be endowed with traits I never had. . . . I prefer to be known with all my defects, so long as it is me, than with counterfeit qualities and a personality alien to me" (1152–53).

The Neuchâtel Preface also makes an argument for autobiography as a privileged mode of understanding a life that is an extension of Rousseau's earlier reflections on historiography and biography in *Emile*. In book 4 of *Emile*, Rousseau had called into question the accuracy of the historians' representation of human character. History "ceaselessly calumniates humankind" because "it is only the wicked who are famous; the good are forgotten or are made ridiculous" (309). The historian is like the historical novelist who "piles fictions on fictions to make reading him more pleasant" (310). Even when historians do not merely fabricate "personages who never existed and imaginary portraits" (310), they show men only "in their parade clothes" (312). History "exhibits only the public man who has dressed himself to be seen. It does not follow him into his home, his study, his family, the midst of his friends. It depicts him only when he acts a role." Biography would appear to offer a better avenue to "the study of the human heart" (312). Ideally, the biographer leaves his subject "no moment of respite, no corner where he can avoid the spectator's piercing eye; and it is when the latter believes he has hidden himself best that the former makes him known best" (312). But modern biographers, unlike "the ancients" (Plutarch in particular, who "excels in these details in which we no longer dare to enter"), do not practice such an art of telling exposure, for "men are as adorned by our authors in their private lives as on the stage of the world" (313). By the time Rousseau writes his Neuchâtel Preface, these facts have become for him a *donnée:* "Histories, lives, portraits, characters—what does all that amount to? Ingenious novels." Now autobiography emerges as the preferred mode of representing, understanding, and judging a life: "No one can describe the life of a man except that man himself. His manner of being inward, his veritable life is known only by him" (*Oeuvres* 1:1149).

Only the genre of autobiography, then, is adequate to the philosophi-cal-cum-psychological challenge of doing full justice to a life. But no auto-biographer so far has lived up to this challenge. Here Rousseau finds his confessional opening by scripting himself as the first authentic autobiog-rapher. In the language of the passage cited above from *Emile,* Rousseau will be the first modern writer to enter into "these details into which we no longer dare enter." He will be a kind of modern Plutarch. His subject will be himself: auto-biography. He will spy on himself, leaving himself "no moment of respite, no nook where he can avoid the spectator's pierc-ing eye." The result will be an unprecedented disclosure of humanity, an unpacking of consciousness. To drive home this point in his preface, Rousseau makes a polemical contrast between himself and Montaigne:

> [I]n writing it [his life] he disguises it; in the name of his life he writes his apology; he shows himself how he wants to be seen and not at all as he is. The most sincere are truthful at most in what they say, but they lie through their reticences; and what they hold back changes to such a degree what they pretend to avow that in telling but a part of the truth they tell nothing. I put Montaigne at the head of these falsely sincere who wish to deceive in telling the truth. He shows himself with his defects, but he gives himself only pleasing ones. . . . Montaigne paints himself as he appears, but in profile. Who knows if some scar on his cheek or an injured eye on the side which he has hidden from us would not completely have changed his physiognomy? (1149–50)

The profile-painting metaphor is really another version of the *mask,* a central motif in Rousseau's writings associated with the corruption of civ-ilized man, who artfully hides and disguises himself and his motives. In his insistent concern with transparency, of which Jean Starobinski has fur-nished the definitive study, the mask is associated with the *amour propre* of men in society, that inflamed self-love which makes us constantly compare ourselves with others in the spirit of envy and malice and which is the per-verted form of *amour de soi,* the innate self-love of humans, which is natu-ral and good. Rousseau the moralist claims in the preface that he is uniquely situated for seeing modern humanity as it is, since he has experi-enced all social conditions, having "lived in them all from the lowest to the most elevated, excepting the throne" (1150). Members of the different social classes are distanced from one another by these artificial barriers and cannot see their common humanity. But Rousseau, "careful to cast off [man's] mask," has "seen him everywhere" (1150).[3] As an autobiographer too, he will be without the mask that all previous autobiographers have worn because of their *amour propre*. His portrait, unlike Montaigne's profile, will be a full-face one: he will show and tell all.

With this rhetorical assertion Rousseau invites the obvious charge that he too, like Montaigne and the others before him, is writing his apology, showing himself how he wants to be seen and not at all how he is. And the obvious but too simple answer is that of course he did—a fact he goes halfway toward acknowledging in his final work, *The Reveries*, with the admission that while he never told anything less than or contrary to the truth, he sometimes told more: "carried away by the pleasure of writing," he filled the gaps of his memory with innocent fictions ("Fourth Walk," *Oeuvres* 1:1035, 1038). The larger and perhaps moot question is, can any autobiographer write his or her life without turning it into his or her apology? Clearly Rousseau's self-chosen confessional cachet—*vitam impendere vero* (dedicate life to truth)—is fundamentally self-interested and even ideological. He will present his own life in order to sway his readers away from the counterfeit versions of his person circulating in public and to substitute for it the genuine—genuine meaning as he sees it—account that will permit them to make the proper judgment. His self-disclosure will be in the interest of justice and truth, for "since my name is bound to endure among men, I do not want it to bear a false reputation" (*Oeuvres* 1:1153). The promise and appeal of the preface is that of full disclosure: "I shall tell all: the good, the bad, in short, everything" (153). The provocative epigraph of *The Confessions*, "*Intus, et in Cute*" (*Oeuvres* 1:5) actually subverts or deconstructs the persistent portrait-painting metaphor of the preface, because "inside and under the skin" signals a moral anatomy as well as a psychological journey from the outside to the inside. Rousseau's will not only be the first full-face self-portrait, unlike Montaigne's *Essays*, but it will also be the first one to take us fully and unreservedly inside the author's head, the theater of his consciousness.

The defensive and even vainglorious stance of Rousseau the "tell-all" autobiographer writing to restore his tarnished reputation, however, should not obscure the genuine philosophical motive of Rousseau the unmasker who is laying claim to a new way of understanding individual human beings, a new philosophy and even an anthropology—in sum, a new *science humaine* in the first person.[4] At this level, his autobiography is nothing less than "a piece of comparison for the study of the human heart, and the only one so far in existence." Thus, asserts Rousseau the Enlightenment *philosophe*, a book precious to philosophers (*Oeuvres* 1:1154). By making available for the first time such a basis for comparison, Rousseau is not only offering up his life "for the severity of [public] judgment," but also throwing the hermeneutic gauntlet down at his readers, challenging them to a secular *imitatio*, a type of introspective self-examination that will unmask the illusions of their own *amour propre* and unfold and reveal them to themselves for the first time as they really are. "Let each reader imitate me; let him enter into himself as I have entered into myself, and let him say at the bottom of his conscience, if he dare: *I am better than that man was*" (*Oeuvres* 1:1155). The challenge of the preface's final phrase, which reintroduces Rousseau's defensive motive, is retained for the opening of his *Confessions*.

With his philosophical conception of his autobiography, Rousseau offers his readers a vehicle for their own self-understanding and interpretation. The tempting but facile and ultimately dismissive reading of his book is to judge him without genuinely examining ourselves. It is all too easy for us to experience a smug, self-satisfied sense of our moral superiority over the author. We, of course, have never been forced to tell all—not to others, not publicly, and perhaps not even in the confessional of our most private thoughts. But Rousseau the moralist sets a subtle trap for the reader: *Let him who is without guilt cast the first stone.* Boldly yet cunningly Rousseau turns the issue of judgment back on his reader: Judge yourself as you judge me; judge me as you judge yourself.

Rousseau, who is convinced that his "name is fated to live" (*The Confessions*, book 8, 373) and that his full-disclosure gambit will serve his interests, insists repeatedly that his will be a good-faith effort to enable the reader's judgment without seeking to influence it. He will tell all—a utopian presumption, to be sure—and it will be up to the reader to make the determination. "The summing-up must be his, and if he comes to wrong conclusions, the fault will be of his own making" (book 4, 169). Despite such disclaimers, it is obvious that in his self-justifying mode he writes his autobiography as a public relations campaign. Because he has resolved, as he puts it in the Neuchâtel Preface, not to publish his memoirs during his lifetime (*Oeuvres* 1:1154), his target audience is a future one.

The focus of his campaign to restore his reputation is his standing with posterity, a concern first voiced in the fourth letter to Malesherbes (1145) that finds its culmination (as I argue in chapter 3), as the compulsive agenda of his *Dialogues*. Indeed, in the tour de force of megalomania that is the opening of *The Confessions*—"I am like no one in the whole world"— he projects his posthumous fame to the very end of time. Rousseau scripts himself at the final judgment with his book in hand—"Here is what I have done" (17)—proffering the supreme judge a presentation copy, and, as it were, enrolling him, along with "the numberless legion of [his] fellow men" (17) gathered to hear his confessions, in the Jean-Jacques Rousseau Fan Club. In this metatextual fiction of Rousseau preparing to read aloud from the book he is just beginning to write, we have a kind of conversion narrative, but one very different from the Augustinian model, for Rousseau through his confessional rhetoric seeks to win the reader over from indifference or hostility to acceptance, sympathy, friendship—and yes, even love. His object of making the reader an ally and intimate friend is the burden of secular, Rousseauean confession. It involves the transposition into a textual, reader-response key of an experiential hunger for an intimacy so radical, as he tells us in book 9, that "only two souls in the same body would have sufficed" (386)—a hunger that was never satisfied in his real-life relationships.

If Rousseau programmatically identifies his self with his book, he seeks in turn to get his readers to make the same self-identification. That is, if in Rousseau's philosophical conception the reader is challenged to a genuine self-examination, in Rousseau's defensive and apologetic scheme his ideal reader is a nonjudgmental, loving double of Jean-Jacques. As real readers of *The Confessions* discover soon enough, the author's claims of full disclosure and of having the reader judge are really a strategy of disarming the reader's judgment. Rousseau's most compromising confessions are always self-exculpating—his intentions were always good, even if his misdeeds cannot be excused in terms of their putative consequences, as in the framing of the servant girl Marion for the theft of the ribbon the adolescent Rousseau had himself stolen, the leaving of Jacques-Louis Le Maître in the lurch during his fit in a public street in Lyons, and even the abandonment of his children on the doorstep of the Paris foundling home. At worst, he is guilty of a momentary weakness, or errors of omission, or faulty reasoning that has misled his sound heart. Another means of tempering the reader's judgment of Rousseau's misdeeds, employed consistently throughout part 1, is his presentation of them in comico-picaresque key, as the misadventures of Jean-Jacques at which author and reader join in laughter or pity: the adolescent exhibitionist in Turin cornered by the offended servant girls, the composer Vaussore de Villeneuve who doesn't know any music, the Englishman Dudding who doesn't know a word of English.

In the darkened world of part 2 of *The Confessions,* however, the double of the ideal reader disappears progressively to be replaced by his evil twin, the unfathomable and labyrinthine conspiracy against Rousseau. From megalomania to paranoia is not a long journey, even for a writer who had real enemies and persecutions to contend with. As Rousseau succumbs to his mounting paranoia, he feels an increasingly desperate need to justify himself and to get out the true version of who he is and what he has and has not done. But as his enemies multiply in his alienated and masochistic imagination, and as the "league" arrayed against him has more and more control of his life and his reputation, this justification seems an increasingly impossible task. The close of *The Confessions,* like its beginning, is metatextual, save that in Rousseau's account of a real reading of his autobiography at the Countess Jeanne-Armande d'Egmont's, the response of his human audience is very different from the reaction anticipated in the fiction of the final judgment at the beginning of the work. He has broken his earlier promise (in the Neuchâtel Preface and in book 10) to reserve his book for a future audience, in order to seek the approbation and absolution of his contemporaries. In the manic fervor of his innocence, he protests too much and even ends by threatening his audience:

> I have told the truth. If anyone knows anything contrary to what I have here recorded, though he prove it a thousand times, his knowledge is a lie and an imposture; and if he refuses to investigate and inquire into it during my lifetime he is no lover of justice and truth. For my part, I publicly and fearlessly declare that anyone, even if he has not read my writings, who will examine my nature, my character, my morals, my likings, my pleasures, and my habits with his own eyes and can still believe me a dishonourable man, is a man who deserves to be stifled. (book 12, 605–6)

The silence that greets this stridently aggressive assertion at the conclusion of his reading means that his autobiographical project has not fulfilled his expectations, at least as far as his present audience is concerned. True, the situation is not entirely dismal, because there is one small sign that his audience has not failed utterly in giving him the response he sought: "Thus I concluded my reading, and everyone was silent. Mme d'Egmont was the only person who seemed moved. She trembled visibly, but quickly controlled herself, and remained quiet, as did the rest of the company" (606). It is significant that a female member of the audience manifests a suppressed sympathy, because it was always the women that Rousseau tried to move, from at least the time the runaway adolescent apprentice won Mme de Warens's heart with the story of his misadventures. The detail of the Countess d'Egmont's body language is a small but promising sign of the reception of Rousseau's *Confessions* by future readers. By incorporating this episode of a failed reading into the close of *The Confessions*, the author who may have already given up on his contemporaries is still seeking to win over his posthumous readers by implying that they will have a more sympathetic response than the unnatural silence of the select circle of aristocratic auditors who refused him his deserved tribute of understanding, sympathy, and love. The trembling countess seems to augur well for such a result.

The poignant yet highly contrived anticlimax of the end of *The Confessions* implicitly scripts a particular role for Rousseau's reader crucial to the author's scheme of posthumous vindication. In Rousseau's confessional scheme, the reader becomes instrumental in the author's textual salvation. As Huntington Williams has concluded in his rhetorical analysis of "the author-reader dialogue" in Rousseau, in Rousseau's "construction of a textual world," (74) the autobiographical pact functions so that "the reader 'outside' the autobiography enters Rousseau's pact only indirectly, reading and interpreting him through the image of the reader the author has constructed in the text" (201). But if "the actual reader" identifies with Rousseau's "narrataire" or constructed reader, "the reader 'outside' the text is no longer 'outside' it; he has stepped into the reader's role which the text has offered him, has become the author's advocate." What Williams does not mention is that Rousseau's attempt to control the reader's response is a strategy operative to some degree in all autobiographies. Rousseau simply goes much further in his attempt to seduce his readers. Williams concludes that "the subtlety and underlying outrageousness of Rousseau's image of the reader, like his image of himself, is a major reason why readers and even critics of him have either been so rebuffed or so enamoured, so willing or unwilling to take up his case; why his text continues to live" (201).

Williams here identifies astutely enough the reason for Rousseau's unabated and controversial appeal as an autobiographer, and the extremes, from love and identification to hatred and revulsion, that *The Confessions* continue to elicit—as any instructor who has worked his way through the text with a group of students can attest. The critical challenge for Rousseau's readers today is to appreciate the complexity of his autobiographical motives and the originality, richness, and manipulativeness of his philosophical conception of confession without unreflectively succumbing to either of these extremes. To meet this challenge, we must be, to use Williams's distinction, at once readers "inside" and "outside" the text—critical, resistant, detached, *and* sympathetic, attracted, attached. We have to be aware of, and resist being unreflectingly hostile to, his secular scheme of textual salvation, which is in a sense underway whenever we read him, without allowing ourselves to be manipulated by him and lose our integrity and autonomy as readers. By construing him both as he sees himself and as we see him, we liberate him and ourselves by saving his text from him and for ourselves.

THE CONFESSIONS AS PHILOSOPHICAL AUTOBIOGRAPHY

How much you have changed from what you once were! It is, so to speak, the life of your species that I am going to describe to you in accordance with the qualities which you received and which your education and habits could corrupt but not destroy.

—Rousseau, *Discourse on Inequality*

The author of a recent book on the system of Rousseau's thought has observed that Rousseau wrote "more autobiographically than any previous philosopher" (Melzer 280). This interesting assertion is equally true if turned around: Rousseau's confessional narrative is more philosophical than that of any previous autobiographer, Augustine not excepted. That his *Confessions* are not the merely idiosyncratic and sensational memoirs of his unusual—and for many, aberrant—life, but have a genuinely philosophical character and agenda rooted in his earlier theoretical writings, particularly the *Discourse on Inequality* and *Emile,* has not until recently been sufficiently acknowledged by students of Rousseau the autobiographer, who may in any case have little familiarity with the "other" Rousseau of the doctrinal works. Of course, some of his best critics, like Starobinski, have pointed to the multifarious and significant connections between his autobiographical and discursive works. But only lately have critics of *The Confessions* begun to stress the philosophical character of that work as a text in which the narrative of his life is also an exploration of larger truths that bear a significant relationship to the leading concerns of his earlier writings.[5] The fullest discussion of the philosophical dimension of Rousseau the autobiographer to date is Kelly's powerfully sustained reading of *The Confessions* as political philosophy. Kelly's book makes it clear that readings of *The Confessions* that do not take into account Rousseau's theoretical writings will be limited at best, because the narrative of his life and his vision of himself and his world are very much a function of Rousseau the thinker. The philosopher turned autobiographer may feel that he and his message have been misunderstood, but the former nevertheless brings to the latter the gist of his insights, reformulated or modified though they may be in the process of autobiographical intro- and retrospection. Conversely, Rousseau the autobiographer delineates the experiential and biographical ground from which grew the ideas of Rousseau the thinker. The philosopher and the autobiographer are thus mutually implicated and illuminating—and this is true even when they seem to be at odds.

The relationship between Rousseau the thinker and Rousseau the autobiographer is a rich field for reflection, and one open to many different approaches and interpretations. It represents a considerable opportunity for critics of *The Confessions,* as well as a complex challenge, because both the man and his thought are rife with paradoxes and contradictions, as Rousseau's commentators have not tired of pointing out. (Rousseau himself of course made a profession of emphasizing the puzzling contradictions of his character.) After all, the writer who gained sudden celebrity with the thesis of the *First Discourse* that the development of civilization and the arts are a function of the progressive corruption of human nature, and who in his *Second Discourse* champions the concept of man's natural goodness, was also the thinker who polemically asserted in the latter treatise that "if nature destined us to be healthy, I venture to affirm that the state of reflection is contrary to nature and that the man who meditates is a depraved animal" (*Political Writings* 13). And the man who became the most celebrated writer of the age is the same man who insisted that he was never a professional author and who at the height of his fame claimed to be abandoning literature altogether for the trade of music copying.

Rousseau's penchant for paradox and contradiction is apparent in *The Confessions* from the opening paragraphs. He claims that he will offer "a portrait in every way true to nature," but the suggestion of human representativeness that this description carries is immediately undercut by the assertion of his uniqueness: "I am like no one in the whole world" (17). If "nature," as he claims in the second paragraph, broke "the mold in which she formed" him, then how can his self-portrait be true to nature? "Nature" here seems to be an unstable or shifting concept, something that is even more apparent in his subsequent *Dialogues,* where Rousseau characterizes himself as "the historian of nature" (*Oeuvres* 1:936) whose great philosophical "principle [is] that nature made man happy and good but that society depraves him and makes him miserable" (934). But what is Rousseau's model of and norm for "nature" and the "natural"? As he frankly acknowledges in the *Dialogues,* it is his own "heart" (936). On the basis of an introspective self-examination, Rousseau found—or made—himself the norm of "nature," even though nature broke the mold and deviated from that very norm when she made him.

But Rousseau ignores this contradiction in the self-portrait of his *Dialogues,* where he presents himself as the modern sage who rediscovered a lost or hidden nature. "A retired and solitary life, a lively taste for revery and contemplation, and the habit of entering into himself and of seeking in the calm of the passions those first traits that have disappeared in the multitude permitted him alone to rediscover them" (936). In his *Discourse on Inequality,* he had accused other philosophers who had conceptualized the state of nature, like Hobbes and Locke, of having unwittingly "transferred to the state of nature ideas they have acquired in society" (*Political Writings* 9). If Rousseau's principal model of nature is his own heart, it is fair to say that he is guilty of a similar error, because his view of nature is as much a hypothetical construct as theirs. In his treatise, he had already neutralized such a criticism by acknowledging the difficulty of having "a clear understanding of a state which no longer exists, which has, perhaps, never existed, and about which it is necessary to have accurate notions in order to judge the present state properly" (5). However, the suspicion that the thinker modeled his view of nature largely on the shifting reflection of his own features is confirmed only in a reading of his autobiographical writings.

Rousseau's slippery invocation of "nature" is not the only questionable element in the opening of his *Confessions*, for his stress on his *sincerity* and *truthfulness* is equally problematic. The writer who challenges his fellow humans to "reveal" their hearts "with equal sincerity" (17) before the throne of the supreme judge does so in the context of a highly theatrical scenario in which he plays the starring role. The assertion of his sincerity is thus undercut by the melodramatic appeal of his self-serving imagination. We should not forget that in his *Letter to d'Alembert on the Theatre,* he had condemned theater as an unnatural and corrupting spectacle and the actor as a counterfeiter whose "art" is that "of appearing different than he is" (79). Rousseau's profession of sincerity here is framed in the context of a dramatic script, a kind of act or spectacle produced, like drama, by the author's literary imagination. As for his profession of truthfulness—"I have never put down as true what I knew to be false"—it is more directly countered and undercut by his own qualification, "if by chance I have used some immaterial embellishments it has been only to fill a void due to a defect of memory" (*The Confessions* 17). This acknowledgment already anticipates the confession of the Fourth Revery that where his recollections failed him he filled in the gaps of his narrative with innocent fictions—innocent because they never went against the facts as he knew them to be.

Nature, sincerity, truth—these are for Rousseau the thinker the primordial possessions and attributes of natural man, of our being in the state of nature. In society we become progressively unnatural, insincere, false, deceitful; that is the bitter truth taught in the *Discourse on Inequality* and *Emile*. Natural man has few needs—and no need for developed spectacles, for imagination, both of which are associated with the corrupting influence of civilization. Nature, sincerity, truth—these are for Rousseau, the first Romantic autobiographer, the great ideals and the lost gods to aspire to, to (re)capture in his text and in his life. In a word, authenticity of being is his dream and goal.[6] But can we modern, civilized humans, disfigured and deformed by the institutions of society, ever get back to the sacred possession of ourselves that was ours in the state of nature? Rousseau the thinker, writer, and autobiographer aspires to it, but his chosen vehicles, thinking and writing, are themselves instrumentalities of civilization. Rousseau the philosopher and author is by definition an unnatural man, and the more he thinks and writes, the more unnatural he will become. In this respect as in so many others, Rousseau is a man powerfully divided against himself, and in this he is a quintessential example of modernity.

For both Rousseau the philosopher and Rousseau the autobiographer, the most fundamental issue in determining who and what we humans are is the nature-nurture one. What is inherent and innate in human nature, and what is acquired through history and culture? At the outset of the *Second Discourse*, he posed his central question: "And how will man succeed in seeing himself as nature created him, through all the changes that the passing of time and events must have produced in his original constitution, and in separating what he owes to his own essence from what circumstances and his advances have added to or changed in his original state?" (*Political Writings* 4). In the Neuchâtel Preface, as we have seen, he reformulated this query as the hermeneutic challenge of understanding any individual: "To really understand a character it is necessary to see how it has been formed, to distinguish what is acquired from what is natural, what occasions have developed it, what secret chain of feelings has made it what it is, and how it modifies itself to produce sometimes the most contradictory and most unexpected results" (*Oeuvres* 1:1149). In the famous figure of the *Second Discourse*, modern humanity, "altered in the midst of society by a thousand constantly recurring causes," is "like the statue of [the sea god] Glaucus; which time, sea, and storms had so disfigured that it resembled less a god than a wild beast" (4). The author of *The Confessions* is himself such a Glaucus, whose original nature has been disfigured by the agency of the society and the age into which he was born. His autobiography is an attempt both to chronicle and analyze the career of disfigurement that is his life and to recapture his original or natural self. But the more he pursues that unadulterated self, the more alienated and unnatural he will become. Like the horizon, his original nature recedes as he seeks to approach it. Rousseau never seems to have allowed himself the profoundly unsettling thought that beyond some obvious biological givens, there really is no single, ahistorical, inherent, and clearly definable human nature or essence. He was a modern, not a postmodern, thinker. The nature he keeps invoking as his touchstone of value is meant to serve as the Archimedean lever of his critique of eighteenth-century European culture.

In the *Dialogues*, Rousseau summarized the view of natural man informing *Emile:* he was "better, wiser, and happier in his primitive constitution" (*Oeuvres* 1:934). But the culture critic and historian of social corruption also knew that there was no ready way back to this original condition. "Human nature does not retrograde and one can never return to the time of innocence and equality once it has been removed from it; this is one of the principles on which he has insisted the most" (935). Thus Rousseau did not uphold the ideal of the noble savage, a phrase never used by him, as a solution to the problem of advanced civilization, although that epithet and that solution have been foisted upon him in the popular misconception of his attack on modern Europe. In his own life and in the wake of his celebrity, however, he did seek to effect such a return, in the personal "reform" he undertook to have few needs and live a simple life of independence, and in his move from Paris to the Hermitage and the countryside—a return that increasingly put him at odds with and alienated him from his former colleagues, friends, and patrons. In his later incarnation as an autobiographer he also seeks to trace beneath the layers of his disfigurement and corruption by society the features of the original Jean-Jacques. He wants to limn these as a kind of standard against which to measure his fall into, and his undoing by, society. And he begins— where else?—with his childhood. We can't return to the childhood of the race, except in our imaginations, which according to *The Second Discourse* and *Emile* are very much a product of civilization. But we can return after a fashion, in and through memory, as the Romantics discovered, to our individual childhoods.

If in his earlier *Emile* Rousseau the philosopher had envisioned the ideal of the healthy development of an individual (from birth through childhood and adolescence to early adulthood), in a society that is fundamentally corrupt, in his later *Confessions* the autobiographer unfolds the sad reality of a child born into and growing up in such a world and being more and more contaminated by it. *Emile* indeed "is nothing but a treatise on the original goodness of man" (*Dialogues, Oeuvres* 1:935). Despite Rousseau's rhetorical stress on his personal uniqueness, *The Confessions* is meant to be a representative and even archetypal chronicle of how that "original goodness" fares in a fallen world, where the transparency of an innocent *amour de soi* is threatened by the various masks of a self-serving *amour propre*. And as his frank or "full-face" self-portrait, the book is also his literary attempt to purge himself of the layers of guilt and corruption attendant upon his life in society that had motivated his earlier (misunderstood and not very successful) "personal" reform. Rousseau's powerful and vivid narrative of his early years is at once that of a poet and novelist, a psychologist, a moralist, and a philosopher. It is his anthropology and psychology in the first person. As in the *Discourse on Inequality* and *Emile,* but now at the level of his own life narrative, Rousseau the philosopher is concerned with the refractory issue of what is original in human nature and what is acquired through acculturation and—as we shall see in the analysis of part 1 of his *Confessions* in the next chapter—at what price and with what dire consequences that acculturation comes.

2

Dangerous Supplements

A Reading of Part 1 of *The Confessions*

CHILDHOOD AND THE ROMANCE OF READING

At the age of six Plutarch fell into my hands, at eight I
knew him by heart; I had read all the novels.
—Rousseau, Second Letter to Malesherbes

The picture Rousseau paints of his early years is a strange mixture of light
and dark, of happiness and misfortune. Given the realities of eighteenth-
century life, his childhood is not all that unusual as far as the bare facts are
concerned—the death of the mother a few days after his birth, which he
characterizes as the first of his misfortunes, the happy-go-lucky and hapless father, who is more of an older brother than a parent figure, the loving aunts who spoil the half-orphan. The tone of the opening pages seems
heavily romanticized, however; as Jean Guéhenno has noted, the story
takes from the start the cast of a dream and an idyll (23). One doesn't need
the biographer's factual confirmation to guess that some of Rousseau's
more sentimental details are more poetry than truth, like the double wedding of his mother and father and of his mother's sister and father's
brother, which marriages took place five years apart. Rousseau's active
imagination is already at work at the outset, or perhaps he is merely

repeating family legend as it was handed down to him. Between the lines one gets glimpses of less than romantic realities: the great love and happy marriage of Rousseau's parents cannot have been all that great and happy if Rousseau's father was absent from home for six years before Rousseau's birth. The father's irresponsibility is already foreshadowed in the husband's evasion, and it comes as no surprise that the father leaves his ten-year-old son in the hands of relatives and flees Geneva rather than appear in court to face the consequences of a public quarrel with a leading citizen that seems to have been mostly his fault (Cranston, *Early Life* 28).

To say that Rousseau was born into a dysfunctional family would be an understatement, since his father's active involvement with and support of him came to an end after his flight from Geneva.[1] The older son, "neglected" and abused, eventually "ran away and completely disappeared" (*The Confessions* 21). Rousseau himself tries to put the best face possible on the fact, apparent in the opening pages and in subsequent references, that his father left a lot to desire. As Maurice Cranston has wryly put it, "Jean-Jacques, who was in time to abandon all his own children by sending them at birth to an orphanage, had the good grace not to blame his father for abandoning him at the age of ten" (*Early Life* 28). Rather than dwell on his father's shortcomings, Rousseau in his brief account of his early relationship with him stresses two important elements, both of which are decisive in the formation of his identity. The first is the guilt the father makes the son feel for the death of his wife ("he seemed to see her again in me, but could never forget that I had robbed him of her," book 1, 19), and the psychological pressure he puts on him to replace her ("Give her back to me, console me for her, fill the void she has left in my heart! Should I love you so if you were not more to me than a son?" 19). This strange family romance of the child burdened by guilt for his mother's death and pressure to replace her may account for some of Rousseau's later problems, especially his tendency to identify at times either literally or figuratively with the female role.

Rousseau does not seek to interpret the significance of this first element of his life. He is conscious however, of the importance of the second, that of his "earliest reading," back to which he traces "the unbroken consciousness of [his] own existence" (19). He makes it clear that his early identity was formed as much by literature as by life, and perhaps it is as far back as this that one should trace the origins of Rousseau the writer. His childhood reading shaped his character in two distinct but significant ways. The "romantic" influence came from the novels of his mother that he and his father would spend the nights reading aloud, and which they finished when he was seven:

> In a short time I acquired by this dangerous method, not only an extreme facility in reading and expressing myself, but a singular insight for my age into the passions. I had no idea of the facts, but I was already familiar with every feeling. I had grasped nothing; I had sensed everything. These confused emotions which I experienced one after another, did not warp my reasoning powers in any way, for as yet I had none. But they shaped them after a special pattern, giving me the strangest and most romantic [romanesques] notions about human life, which neither experience nor reflection has ever succeeded in curing me of. (20)

The "Roman" influence comes from Rousseau's subsequent reading of works of history and mythology, with Plutarch his "especial favorite":

> It was this enthralling reading . . . that created in me that proud and intractable spirit, that impatience with the yoke of servitude, which has afflicted me throughout my life, in those situations least fitted to afford it scope. Continuously preoccupied with Rome and Athens, living as one might say with their great men, myself born the citizen of a republic and the son of a father whose patriotism was his strongest passion, I took fire by his example and pictured myself as a Greek or a Roman. I became indeed that character whose life I was reading; the recital of his constancy or his daring deeds so carrying me away that my eyes sparkled and my voice rang. (20–21)

The reading of the novels is dangerous, because their romantic adventures and sexual intrigues precociously stimulate the boy's erotic imagination. The "Roman" influence also fuels his fantasy life, but in a different key, making him dream of the virtue of the citizen, forcing a passionate imaginative identification with the historical characters whose heroic lives he is reading. Both types of reading alienate him from, make him unfit for, the demands of "real" life.[2] This is Rousseau's version of "Bovaryisme" a century before Flaubert's heroine. But all this overheated reading is ultimately also the cradle of Rousseau the writer: the romantic novels plant the imaginative seeds of *The New Héloïse,* and the Roman influence comes to fruition later in *The Social Contract.*

Given Rousseau's analysis of the impact of his early reading, it is no wonder that in *Emile* the pedagogue recommends a very different approach to his pupil's exposure to books and literature. Rousseau's statement that as a child he had no reasoning powers reflects the teaching of *Emile.* Reason is a faculty that develops and must be cultivated only *after* childhood—or when childhood has ripened in the child, to use Rousseau's striking phrase in book 2 of *Emile* (113). Thus to immerse a child, or allow him to be immersed, in a world of erotic fantasy before he has any ratiocinative powers is a prescription for disaster, one that Emile's tutor will avoid at all costs. Because literature is such a dangerous supplement to life, it is one that Rousseau the educational reformer and moralist wants to control strictly. The philosopher of *Emile* knows only too well the price of such early reading from his own experience. Emile will not be allowed to repeat Rousseau's mistakes: not until the age of twelve will he be allowed to read a book (book 2, 145), and then only *Robinson Crusoe,* "the most fortunate treatise of natural education" (book 3, 239), with its exemplary lesson of how the shipwrecked hero survives on his island through the application of his practical intelligence. Fiction being the chief stimulus and food of the imagination, the adolescent Emile's "imagination remains still inactive" since "nothing has been done to animate it": "he sees only that which is" (book 2, 207). Even at fifteen his imagination still lies dormant (book 3, 271).

The strict control of Emile's reading is Rousseau's moralizing and prudential corrective to the precocious (over)stimulation of his libido as a child because of the novels he read with his father. As we see in the excerpt (from book 1 of *The Confessions*) quoted earlier, the boy was immersed in a hothouse atmosphere of adult passions without any understanding or explanation of the physical basis of these passions. The mental or libidinal and the physical dimensions of erotic experience were completely divorced, giving him a totally unrealistic view of human relations. For Rousseau the philosopher, the natural development of the sex instinct and its development in modern culture are two different things: "The instructions of nature are tardy and slow; those of men are almost always premature. In the case of the former, the senses awaken the imagination; in the case of the latter, the imagination awakens the senses; it gives them a precocious activity which cannot fail to enervate" (*Emile* book 4, 279). Because Emile will have to grow up in modern society, the tutor's task is to retard and control the emergence and development of his pupil's sexuality. He must neutralize his "nascent imagination by objects which, far from inflaming [his] senses, repress their activity." One way to do so is to keep boys at a distance from "the great cities, where the immodest attire of women hastens and anticipates the lessons of nature" (299). Indeed, it is obvious to Rousseau that women's clothing, even when it hides rather than reveals the body, stimulates the male erotic imagination. In describing Sophie, Emile's fiancée, Rousseau, in an access of voyeuristic rapture, writes, "She does not exhibit but covers her charms, but in covering them she knows how to make others imagine them . . . and one would say that all her so simple apparel is only there in order to be taken off piece by piece by the imagination" (book 5, 517).

Ironically, the moralist so intent on controlling the imagination of Emile succumbs to erotic fantasy in the novelistic description of the meeting of the young couple whose amours he will orchestrate and supervise. The boy reading novels all night with his father and the philosopher undressing the fictional Sophie in his imagination in an eighteenth-century striptease are of a piece. But the developmental script of an Emile whose libido will be retarded and repressed until he meets Sophie, and whose chaperoned courting will be conducted with a view to strictly controlling the budding romantic passion of the young lovers in order to assure their chastity until their wedding night, is really the idealized philosophical and pedagogic inversion of Rousseau's actual experience. It is an anti-autobiographical and ultimately unrealistic fiction par excellence. Through the tutor's cunning management, Emile's sex drive has been effectively delayed, "to the profit of reason and the progress of nature" (414), until the very end of adolescence. In what may strike the reader as absurd in the century of psychoanalysis and a highly commercialized age in which the media are constantly stimulating the libidos especially of the young, Rousseau the moralist insists that "one can at least extend to the age of twenty the ignorance of the desires and the purity of the senses" (book 4, 415). Since leisure and imagination are the fuel of eros, once Emile's natural sex drive finally comes into its own, he will be taken away from the tempting spectacles of Paris and subjected to strenuous physical activity—with hunting as a kind of substitute passion, for "Diana is the enemy of love" (420).

Finally, when Emile can no longer be put off with such deflections and sublimations, when his sex drive and budding imagination seek a direct outlet, Rousseau the psychologist will make use of the principle that "one can only control the passions through the passions" (418) to focus and govern his charge's libido. He will help him to conjure the saving fiction of an imaginary love object, Sophie: "It does not matter that the object I paint for him is imaginary; it suffices if it disgusts him with those which could tempt him" (430–31). The stratagem "of repressing his senses by his imagination" (431)—the paradoxical ruse of controlling the sexuality fueled *by* the imagination *with* the imagination—is morally acceptable because romantic love is fundamentally a "chimera, a lie, an illusion": "If one could see what one loves exactly as it is, there would be no more love on earth" (431). The saving fiction of Sophie will keep the tutor in control of Emile, because he will still be "the master of comparisons" that his pupil will make between the imaginary and idealized love object that is Sophie and "the illusion of real objects" (431).

CE DANGEREUX SUPPLÉMENT

There is, however, one danger to the control of Emile's sexuality so great that actual sexual intercourse would be preferable to succumbing to its temptation: the "dangerous supplement" ("ce dangereux supplément") of masturbation. Rousseau's vehement characterization of *le vice solitaire* registers the intensity and the personal nature of his concern with this issue. He makes the hyperbolic claim that "only through the imagination are the senses awakened" and speculates that "a solitary raised in a desert, without books, without instruction, and without women, would die there a virgin at whatever age he would have reached" (*Emile* book 4, 436). At this crisis in his development, Emile's worst enemy is himself: "Therefore carefully watch the young man; he can preserve himself from all the rest; but it is up to you to preserve him from himself. Do not leave him alone neither at night nor during the day: let him go to bed overcome by sleep and let him arise the moment he wakes up" (437). Rousseau then comes to his central admonition, one that carries a powerful autobiographical burden: "It would be very dangerous if it [Emile's sex instinct] taught him to deceive his senses and to supplement the occasions of satisfying them: if he once knows this dangerous supplement, he is lost. From then on he will always have an enervated body and heart; he will carry to the grave the sad effects of this habit, the most fatal to which a young man can be subjected . . . I will not allow the goal of nature to be eluded" (437). For Rousseau the puritanical moralist and citizen of the theocratic republic founded by John Calvin, masturbation is exclusively the activity of an inflamed erotic imagination; it is not a legitimate or acceptable expression of sexuality, but a perverted and sterile self-indulgence that saps one's energies and destroys one's mental and physical health.

Lejeune has argued convincingly that Rousseau's sense of shame and fear about masturbation is "not proper to Rousseau" but the "effect of the repression of sexuality which developed in Europe in the eighteenth century and in which Rousseau himself actively participated" ("Supplément" 1015). Lejeune offers a useful historical sketch (1015–20) of the repression of masturbation and sexuality from the later eighteenth to the beginning of the twentieth century. He explains how the "crusade" against masturbation was carried out in the name and with the authority of medical science. The most influential treatise here is Dr. Samuel-André Tissot's *Onanism, or Physical Diseases Produced by Masturbation,* first published in 1760 and reprinted until the beginning of our own century as the definitive study of the subject.[3] Thus the self-professed historian and polemical spokesman of nature who wrote the *Second Discourse* and *Emile* is voicing the narrow sexual mores of his own age when he proscribes masturbation as the most unnatural of activities. For Rousseau the moralist, as far as the sex drive is concerned, "the goal of nature" is heterosexual intercourse and presumably also procreation.[4] But for the autobiographer—and by extension, the novelist, for *The New Héloïse,* as Rousseau tells us in *The Confessions,* was written in a state of erotic "intoxication" (397) and "voluptuous imaginings" (405)—autoerotic fantasy was an essential component of his being, and he could never cure himself during the remainder of his life of the fatal habit to which he succumbed during his adolescence. Even as he tries to warn against it, and to unwrite or rewrite the script of his own life, the "dangerous supplement," whose confessional subtext in the passage above is Rousseau's guilt, is an essential part of his identity as a man and a writer.

Rousseau was quite aware of the contradiction within him between the austere moralist who produced the influential and controversial discursive writings (including the philosophical fable of the tutor-sage of *Emile*), and the autoerotic fantasist that he also knew himself to be. He acknowledges the absurdity of this incongruity or inconsistency in book 9 of *The Confessions* in connection with his rapturous writing of his famous novel of romantic passion in the wake of his much publicized personal reform and withdrawal to a reclusive life at the Hermitage (in 1755) in the forest of Montmorency. In a "delirium" and "seduced" by "all the fictions of [his] mind," he decides to turn these "into a sort of novel":

> My chief embarrassment was shame at so fully and openly going back on myself. After the strict principles that I had just proclaimed with so much noise, after the austere rules that I had so loudly preached, after so much stinging invective against effeminate books which breathed of love and languor, could anything more unexpected and more shocking be imagined than that I should suddenly with my own hand enrol [*sic*] myself among the authors of these books I had so violently censured? I felt my inconsistency in all its force. . . . But all this was insufficient to bring me back to reason. Being completely captivated, I was forced to submit. (404–5)

Characteristically, however, he seeks to justify and rationalize his self-indulgence in romantic revery and fiction by making *The New Héloïse* ultimately "beneficial to morality" (405). His readers will be instructed and edified by a moral exemplum, so that their absorption in the romance of reading will have the opposite tendency of that of the boy Rousseau undone by the novels he read with his father. The story of his heroine, Julie, "a young person, born with a heart both honest and tender," who succumbs to "love before marriage" but who "gather[s] sufficient strength, when a wife, to turn the tables and regain virtue," is a fiction conducive "to morality and marital fidelity, which are the root of all social order" (405). Only by the imagination is the danger of the imagination overcome: just as the fiction of Sophie preserves the purity of the adolescent Emile, the fiction of Julie is conducive to the virtue of its readers. In this self-serving sublimation of his elaborate libidinal fantasies, Rousseau the bourgeois preacher is a sort of male Pamela, indulging in the autoerotic delights of his imagination while claiming a moral purpose and benefit.

I have considered in some detail the issue of Emile's sexual development and the role of the imagination in *Emile* and *The Confessions* for the light it throws on Rousseau's autobiographical self-presentation. Read in the context of his pedagogic treatise, Rousseau's autobiography attests that in regard to his sexual development, as with so many other aspects of his character, he is undone by civilization and its products. Conversely, the educational program of *Emile* is to maximize the boy's natural abilities (including learning manual skills and trades), and to minimize the negative and corrupting influences of modern society. The awakening of Emile's libido is long delayed by his crafty and godlike tutor, who is really Rousseau's older and wiser self trying to correct and save his younger self, as it were, after the Fall; unlike that of his fictional counterpart, the libido of the boy of *The Confessions* is stimulated prematurely and causes him problems for the rest of his life in the form of intense but unfulfilled sexual desires and erotic fantasies.

The dangerous supplement of the hyperactive erotic imagination that has undermined his natural self but has helped to make Rousseau the writer he is actually appears much earlier in the text than its explicit and literal mention in book 3 of *The Confessions* (as a description of masturbation). It is the burden of "the first and most painful step in the dark and miry maze of [his] confessions" (28), the famous spanking by Miss Gabrielle Lambercier, that ignites the sexuality precociously fueled by his early childhood reading. Rousseau discovered "in the shame and pain of the punishment an admixture of sensuality" that made him eager for a repetition of the experience (25). "The second occasion, however, was also the last," because, as Rousseau adds with uncharacteristic discretion, Miss Lambercier "had no doubt detected signs that this punishment was not having its desired effect" (26). The maiden sister of the pastor who was also Rousseau's tutor must have noticed the physical signs of the boy's sexual arousal. Rousseau typically makes this famous episode of book 1 almost too decisive in its influence on his later development: "Who could have supposed that this childish punishment, received at the age of eight at the hands of a woman of thirty, would determine my tastes and desires, my passions, my very self for the rest of my life, and that in a sense diametrically opposed to the one in which they should have normally developed. At the moment when my senses were aroused my desires took a false turn and, confining themselves to this early experience, never set about seeking a different one" (26).

Rousseau and his spanker were both actually older—he was eleven, and thus on the cusp of puberty, and she was a matronly forty (Voisine, *Confessions* 17). For the moralizing author of *Emile*, the "degree of precocious sexuality in all this" (25) would clearly be traced back to Jean-Jacques's early novel reading, though the author of *The Confessions* does not make this connection explicit—at least not in the published version, for in the Neuchâtel manuscript he does speculate about it: "I do not know the reason for this precocious sensuality; *the reading of the novels had perhaps accelerated it*" (Voisine, *Confessions* 796, emphasis added). Rousseau does, however, emphasize how these arousing chastisements gave both impulse and direction to the life of his imagination.[5] Since he did not until "adolescence [have] any clear ideas concerning sexual intercourse" (27), he could not imagine any other pleasures than those experienced at the hands of Miss Lambercier: "In my crazy fantasies, my wild fits of eroticism, and in the strange behaviour which they sometimes drove me to, I always invoked, imaginatively, the aid of the opposite sex, without so much as dreaming that a woman could serve any other purpose than the one I lusted for" (27). Because as an adult he never found the courage to ask any woman to fulfil his masochistic desires, he "spent [his] days," as he puts it, "in silent longing in the presence of those [he] most loved." In any event, the dangerous supplement of his autoerotic fantasy can clearly be traced back to this first spanking:

I never dared to reveal my strange taste, but at least I got some pleasure from situations which pandered to the thought of it. To fall on my knees before a masterful mistress, to obey her commands, to have to beg for her forgiveness, have been to me the most delicate of pleasures; and the more my vivid imagination heated my blood the more like a spellbound lover I looked. As can be imagined, this way of making love does not lead to rapid progress, and is not very dangerous to the virtue of the desired object. Consequently I have possessed few women, but I have not failed to get a great deal of satisfaction in my own way, that is to say imaginatively. (27–28)

Actually, as a boy Rousseau did act out his "strange taste" to a degree with "a strange little person," a Miss Goton, who played the dominatrix with him in the guise of schoolmistress and to whom he was "submissive" in the compromising "liberties" she took with him (36–37). Their peers must have gotten wind of their not-so-childish games, for some time later Rousseau hears some girls teasing him that "*Goton tic-tac [beats] Rousseau*" (Voisine, *Confessions* 29).[6]

For a period during Rousseau's adolescence, the sexuality stimulated by his early reading finds an outlet—a kind of textual sublimation— through a renewed spell of reading that also permits the youth a temporary escape from his unhappy condition as an apprentice:

> My senses, which had been roused long ago, demanded delights of which I could not even guess the nature. . . . In this strange situation my restless imagination took a hand which saved me from myself and calmed my growing sensuality. What it did was to nourish itself on situations that had interested me in my reading, recalling them, varying them, combining them, and giving me so great a part in them, that I became one of the characters I imagined, and saw myself always in the pleasantest situations of my own choosing. So, in the end, the fictions I succeeded in building up made me forget my real condition, which so dissatisfied me. (book 1, 48)

As the boy in his "Roman" mode had identified with Plutarch's heroes, here in his "romantic" mode he identifies with and participates imaginatively in the fictions he is reading. Soon enough, however, this relatively innocent escapism yields to the more explicit mode of autoerotic fantasy that is masturbation. Referring in book 3 to his stay in Italy after his flight from Geneva and his apprenticeship at the age of sixteen, Rousseau mentions that he "had preserved [his] physical but not [his] moral virginity" ("J'en avois rapporté non ma virginité, mais mon pucelage" [*Oeuvres* 1:108])—the distinction between *pucelage* and *virginité* is that between physical and moral purity or chastity:

> Soon I . . . learned that dangerous supplement[7] which leads in young men of my temperament to various kinds of excesses, that eventually imperils their health, their strength, and sometimes their lives. This vice, which shame and timidity find so convenient, has a particular attraction for lively imaginations. It allows them to dispose, so to speak, of the whole female sex at their will, and to make any beauty who tempts them serve their pleasure without the need of first obtaining her consent. Seduced by this fatal advantage, I set

about destroying the sturdy constitution which Nature had restored to me. (108–9)

Because the multiple ambiguities and equivocations of this famous confession have already received close scrutiny from Rousseau's leading critics, Lejeune and Jacques Derrida among them, suffice it for my purposes to point out that from Rousseau's adolescent fall into this "vice" is born the moralist who wants to preserve Emile from the same fate by postponing and deflecting his sex drive well beyond his adolescence.[8] For the Enlightenment *philosophe* of *Emile,* the sensuous and novelistic imagination indulged in by the celebrated author of *The New Héloïse* and *The Confessions* is suspect and must be strictly controlled because it is erotically wayward and leads us fatally astray. Like Keats's demonic "La Belle Dame sans Merci," it can literally enthrall us. Reading, or at least the wrong kind of reading, stimulates and inflames it. "The imagination lights up and whets its appetite in the silence of the study" (*Emile* book 4, 283). Fueled by such reading, masturbation undermines our physical and moral constitution. The common adolescent practice that many developmental psychologists and sex educators today see as almost as natural as eating and breathing is characterized by Rousseau, here very much a creature of his age, as most unnatural. Nature may not change, but our perceptions of what is "natural" certainly do. Ironically, it was the "unnatural" Rousseau endowed with a powerful autoerotic imagination who ultimately gave rise to the famous writer who championed nature and the natural.

If there is an explicit connection between reading and masturbation in *The Confessions,* the implicit connection between writing and masturbation in Rousseau—inherent, as we have seen, in his account of the romantic fantasies that resulted in the writing of *The New Héloïse*—has not gone unnoticed by his critics. Derrida observes that "the supplement that 'cheats' maternal 'nature' operates as writing" (151), and Lejeune concludes that "there is in the work of Rousseau a sort of lyricism of masturbation. But then we have to discover it under other names: imagination, revery, writing, in texts that are carefully *disjoined* from the confession touching on masturbation" ("Supplément" 1021). As Rousseau tells us in book 3, because of his awkwardness in polite society and his lack of fluency and *esprit* in salon conversation, which often make people who should know better take him for a fool, writing for him is a substitute for and supplement to speaking: "I should enjoy society as much as anyone, if I were not certain to display myself not only at a disadvantage but in a character entirely foreign to me. The role I have chosen of writing and remaining in the background is precisely the one that suits me. If I had been present, people would not have known my value; they would not even have suspected it" (116).

The equation of absence and hiding with writing that Jean Starobinski has emphasized (*Transparency* 122–26) also links writing with the "dangerous supplement." As a solitary and secretive exercise of the imagination, both masturbation and writing are activities that supplement and compensate for the absence of a desired presence. In differing degrees, both can be debilitating; writing letters, for instance, is "a real torture" to Rousseau, and even penning one "on the most trivial subject" costs him "hours of weariness" (*The Confessions* book 3, 114); similarly, the "vice" of onanism undermines his "sturdy constitution" (109). Both activities are also privative: the supplement of one—writing—constitutes a withdrawal from social intercourse, while the supplement of the other cheats nature of its proper due. Masturbation is, as it were, an unauthorized withdrawal from the bank of nature, a misappropriation. Both writing and masturbation are analogous to theft, and stealing, as we know from what Rousseau tells us in book 1 (in connection with his petty larceny during his engraving apprenticeship), is always a correlative of desire—the desire for public recognition and validation of his worth, of which writing is the frustrated compensation and substitute, and the sexual desire for another, whose frustration results in the compensatory substitution of masturbation. "Unsatisfied desires always lead to that vice" (41), writes Rousseau of his adolescent stealing, but the phrase could just as well describe his lifelong indulgence in "ce dangereux supplément," which elsewhere in his autobiography he tellingly referred to as "the vice."9

CHILDHOOD AND THE GENESIS OF CHARACTER

Rousseau's first confession is a bold and painful exploration of the shaping of his character at the expense of his *amour propre:* "How much it has cost me to make such revelations can be judged when I say that though sometimes laboring under passions that have robbed me of sight, of hearing, and of my senses, though sometimes trembling convulsively in my whole body in the presence of the woman I loved, I have never, during the whole course of my life, been able to force myself, even in moments of extreme intimacy, to confess my peculiarities and implore her to grant the one favor which was lacking" (28). Because Rousseau's analysis of the spanking at the hands of Miss Lambercier establishes a causal connection between this punishment and his sexual proclivities as an adult, he deserves to be credited as an early progenitor of psychoanalysis. The other—and in the history of Rousseau criticism, equally famous—spanking at Bossey, that for Miss Lambercier's broken comb, and its larger impact on him, is thematically connected with the earlier punishment. "Who would imagine . . . that I owe one of the most vigorous elements in my character to the same origins as the weakness and sensuality that flow in my veins?" (28). The fact that these two spankings are psychological illustrations of the formative function of childhood experiences is more clearly spelled out in the Neuchâtel manuscript of *The Confessions:* "If I did not sense the difficulty of having to put up with so many puerile details, how many examples wouldn't I give of the strength that frequently the slightest facts of childhood have to stamp the most prominent features of the characters of men" (Voisine, *Confessions* 797–98). The second chastisement is decisive for Rousseau the philosopher and critic of society, because it is the source of his "indomitable aversion to injustice": "Who would believe that this invincible sentiment came to me originally from a broken comb?" (Voisine, *Confessions* 798).

The boy is falsely accused and punished by those he loves and respects for something he did not do. He did not break Miss Lambercier's comb, but he does not possess "sufficient reasoning power to realize the extent to which appearances were against [him]" (29–30). Nearly five decades later, the author still protests his innocence: "I declare before Heaven that I was not guilty. I had not broken, nor so much as touched, the comb" (29). The Lamberciers bring Jean-Jacques's guardian, his uncle Gabriel Bernard, into the case, but the boy refuses to own up to the infraction he insists he did not commit. "All I felt was the cruelty of an appalling punishment for a crime I had not committed. The physical pain was bad enough, but I hardly noticed it; what I felt was indignation, rage, and despair" (30). His hatred of injustice "was only a personal one in its origins, but it has since assumed such consistency and has become so divorced from personal interests that my blood boils at the sight or the tale of any injustice, whoever may be the sufferer and wherever it may have taken place, in just the same way as if I were its victim" (30). His sympathetic imagination, grounded in his own experience, provides the basis of the moral and political sentiments of the adult philosopher.

However, this tendentious and pathetic account of the second spanking, with its genetic grounding of his adult sense of injustice, is not the whole story, which seems to have the psychological resonance of family romance. Again Miss Lambercier is involved, and the significance of her role in Rousseau's account of his stay at Bossey appears to be overdetermined in the Freudian sense. Particularly for the modern reader, there is a curious and almost absurd disproportion between the object—a broken comb—and the physical and moral result. In our plastic world, a comb is a cheap and easily replaced commodity; in the eighteenth century, however (compare Belinda's toilette in Pope's *Rape of the Lock*), combs could be precious items made of ivory or tortoise shell. The comb also has an erotic and fetishistic significance, for, like the ribbon Rousseau later accused Marion of stealing (another seemingly trivial object whose theft again leads to extraordinary consequences), it is associated with female sexuality. The comb implicated in the second spanking in a sense symbolizes the erotic appeal of the woman who sexually aroused the boy during the first spanking. Rousseau's Bossey memories include mention of a comic episode of "Mlle Lambercier's unfortunate tumble at the end of a field, which caused her to display her full back view to the King of Sardinia as he passed" (book 1, 31). And also to Rousseau, we might add, whose memory zeroes in on this display, and who adds the suggestive statement, "an accident which, though comical in itself, filled me with alarm on behalf of one whom I loved as a mother, *or perhaps even more dearly*" (32, emphasis added).

The biographers can furnish no extratextual evidence of who might have broken the comb, or why. Rousseau does not even attempt to offer an explanation of what might have happened. He only protests his innocence, and perhaps it is interpretive bad faith to suggest that he protests too much. Had he intended to do what he in fact was punished for doing, as Lejeune speculates?[10] Or did he actually break the infamous comb in order to bring on another of those desirable spankings, and later hide that knowledge from himself? If Rousseau *did* damage the comb, it may have been an act of Oedipal desire and violation. To the boy who lost his mother at birth, Miss Lambercier was a mother figure, as he himself stresses, and her brother the pastor, his teacher, was a father substitute. And here biographical research does cast a revealing light, for this brother and sister seem to have had a curious relationship:

> Jean-Jacques Lambercier excited suspicion from his first arrival in Bossey, for he appeared to live in altogether unsuitable intimacy with his sister Gabrielle. He was observed through the window of the parsonage engaged in such indecent familiarities as helping her dress her hair and put the finishing touches on her *toilette*. Then again, as he could not afford two horses, he had his sister ride on the same saddle with him, a practice which shocked the villagers no less. The word 'incest' was not only whispered, it was alleged before the Company of Pastors, the disciplinary body of ministers. (Cranston, *Early Life* 33)

Given the peculiar configuration of this substitute or foster family, Jean-Jacques might have seen himself at some level as the rival of the father-priest for the love of the mother-sister. The comic episode of the walnut tree seems to be fraught with such Oedipal tensions. The pastor's planting of the tree (to provide some shade on the terrace) is mimicked by Jean-Jacques and his cousin, "who cut a slip from a young willow, and planted it on the terrace some eight or ten feet from the walnut" (32). In order to have their slip succeed, they surreptitiously dug "an underground tunnel which would secretly bring to the willow some of the water which was given to the walnut tree" (32). The "cutting" that is meant "to compete with a large tree" is very suggestive, as is the violent reaction of the minister to the boys' challenge to his masculine power and authority: "'An aqueduct! an aqueduct!' he cried, and rained down his merciless blows on every side. Each one of them pierced us to the heart. In a moment the boards, the runnel, the trench, and the willow were all destroyed, and the earth all round was plowed up. But, in the course of all this frightful business, the only words uttered were his cries of 'An aqueduct! an aqueduct!' as he knocked everything to pieces" (33).

In this highly stylized and novelistic episode, the patriarchal power that bears down on the boys is neutralized by the humor of Rousseau's presentation. Nevertheless, Rousseau had tried to steal or appropriate for his cutting the good pastor's water, intended for the walnut tree. As we have seen, Rousseau posits that theft is always a function of unsatisfied desires (*The Confessions* 41). If one layer of this ambiguous episode is the revelation of the boy's Oedipal wishes, the episode of the broken comb— *if Rousseau did break it*—also carries such an Oedipal charge: in the frustration of his desire, Rousseau may have tried to appropriate something symbolically and fetishistically associated with Gabrielle Lambercier. And if Rousseau was indeed innocent and did not take and damage the comb, the Oedipal tension still seems to inhere in Rousseau's narrative imagination in the way the autobiographer recollects and represents this crucial experience. If he did break the comb in order to elicit another spanking from Gabrielle, one can readily imagine the disappointment, frustration, hurt, and rage he must have felt when the punishment was administered not by her but by the stern figure of the pastor acting in concert with Jean-Jacques's guardian, who was sent for from Geneva. Jean-Jacques is made to feel the full weight of the patriarchy bearing down on him, as is his cousin Abraham Bernard, who is also unjustly "punished for what had only been a mistake but was taken for a premeditated crime" (30). The cousins' shouts of "Carnifex [torturer]" repeated "a hundred times at the tops of [their] voices" as they lay in bed may be, as Rousseau presents it, the visceral shock and outrage of persecuted innocence, or it may also be—at least in Rousseau's case—a frustrated shout of Oedipal rage. Intended to illustrate the origin of his sense of injustice, the second spanking, if analyzed in terms of the psychological significance in it of the Lamberciers as parent figures, tells a truth other and more complex than the history of character formation that Rousseau wanted it to exemplify.

PARADISE LOST

Once sexuality and social injustice have intruded into the natural paradise that is Bossey, there is only the Fall. "We stayed for some months longer at Bossey. We lived as we are told the first man lived in the earthly paradise, but we no longer enjoyed it. . . . No longer were we young people bound by ties of respect, intimacy, and confidence to our guardians; we no longer looked on them as gods who read our hearts; we were less ashamed of wrongdoing, and more afraid of being caught; we began to be secretive, to rebel, and to lie" (30–31). Rousseau's proto-Romantic version of the Fall is very different from the Christian, however, and reflects the viewpoint of Rousseau the modern philosopher. The Fall of Adam and Eve (like the adolescent Augustine's robbing of the pear tree, which recapitulates it), is a demonstration of original sin through their willful disobedience of the divine prohibition. The first couple brings about and is responsible for the Fall and its consequences. In the Rousseauean and Romantic-modern myth, unlike the Christian-Augustinian, however, the child is innocent: we turn out badly only if we are treated badly. To put it baldly, criminals are not born but made by society: so runs the modern and sentimental view, from Rousseau to Marx to the latest sociological tract. Unbeknownst to them, contemporary criminals who protest that they are not responsible for what they did because of what was done to them are apostles of Rousseau.

With its two famous spankings, the rural retreat of Bossey represents a crucial point of transition from the happiness of the indulged child to the misery of the put-upon apprentice. At Bossey, Rousseau is already aware of the existence of social class differences, but they do not as yet press down upon him. He mentions that his cousin "never abused his favoured position in the house as [his] guardian's son" (24). If the injustice of the second spanking planted the seeds of Rousseau the political philosopher and critic of society, so did "the brutality and unreasonable restraint" (30) imposed on him by the young engraver to whom he was apprenticed. The aptly named Ducommun "managed in a very short time to quench all the fire of my childhood, and to coarsen my affection and lively nature; he reduced me in spirit as well as in fact to my true condition of apprentice" (39). At its worst, Rousseau's characterization of his condition as an apprentice reads rather like the account of slavery in Frederick Douglass's *Narrative of the Life*. Both the romantic and Roman elements of Rousseau's character are stifled, and "the vilest tastes and the lowest habits took the place of [his] simple amusements" (39). His childhood experience of freedom and equality is replaced by a pervasive sense of frustration and privation under his master's repressive regime: "Everything I saw about me I grew to covet in my heart, only because I was deprived of everything" (40). The resentful boy's downfall is rapid and almost complete: "So it was that I learnt to covet in silence, to conceal, to dissimulate, to lie, and finally to steal—an idea that had never before come into my head and one that I have never been able entirely to rid myself of since" (40–41).

In sum, Rousseau presents an exemplary modern scenario of the child's innocence destroyed by a corrupt society. "It is nearly always generous feelings misdirected that lead a child into taking his first steps in crime" (41). Soon enough he becomes desensitized, and the frequent punishments seem merely to justify further infractions. The journeyman Verrat, who through flattery betrays the boy into stealing and selling the asparagus from Verrat's mother's garden ("Verrat" is German for "betrayal"), is a perfect symbol of the cynical corruption of this fallen world. Had Rousseau the tool been caught, he would have been left holding the bag by the sly Verrat: "So it is that in every situation the powerful rogue protects himself at the expense of the feeble and the innocent" (42). In this eye-opening experience, too, is a germ of the social criticism of *The Second Discourse* and *Emile*.

Rousseau's downfall, of course, is not complete, because, like the rebellious slave, he seeks an escape. He rediscovers reading, and this new passion replaces stealing. Reading, after all, like stealing, is a mode of satisfying unfulfilled desires, but a more productive one. And Rousseau also runs away, shortly before his sixteenth birthday, from the slavery that is his apprenticeship. He has recognized the bitter reality of his personal and social situation, but will not accept it. His discussion of his flight at the close of book 1 shows to what extent he has come to appreciate the significance of social class differences, which have destroyed the former intimacy between him and his cousin, who was being educated as an engineer and who was thus marked out for a higher sphere:

> Being somewhat estranged from him since I had entered on my apprenticeship I was seeing him less. Nevertheless for some time we had been meeting on Sundays. But little by little, each of us was altering his habits and we met now more rarely. . . . He was a lad of the upper town [where the upper classes lived]; I was a poor apprentice, a mere child of the Saint-Gervais quarter [the working-class area down by Lake Geneva]. There was no longer any equality between us despite our equal birth. It was demeaning for him to go about with me. (49–50)

Though he didn't know it at the time, Rousseau's flight, scripted by the teenager's romantic imagination as an act of freedom and independence and a confident leap "out into the world's wide spaces" (52), was also a declaration of war against his society and his century whose most effective weapons were to be his philosophical writings.

BOOKS 2–6: THE SEARCH FOR HOME IN THE FALLEN WORLD
Overview

It is no wonder that critics of *The Confessions* have tended to devote a disproportionate amount of their attention to the first book, especially the two famous spankings, because it is not much of an exaggeration to say that in it Rousseau created the terms in which childhood and even the development of character were to be discussed for the next two centuries. As Michael Sheringham has emphasized, Rousseau's "exploration of his history" in and through narrative is part of a larger pattern of *"enchaînement"* or psychological causality "central to the subsequent history of autobiography—to give expression to a historicized self, a selfhood inseparable from the twists and turns of its story" (42, 33). Thus when some two hundred years later Jean-Paul Sartre devoted his entire autobiography, *The Words,* to the first ten years of his life, he was both following in the footsteps of and taking to the extreme the autobiographical study of childhood adumbrated by Rousseau. In Rousseau's case, the narrative of the adolescent years takes some strange and even bizarre "twists and turns" that complicate if not frustrate his efforts to impose a coherent developmental pattern on his early years.

The sixteen-year-old apprentice's flight from his job, his native city, his religion, and what was left of his family marks a radical rupture in a life replete, both before and after this fundamental break, with a series of other ruptures. Indeed, the rest of part 1 depicts in a highly novelistic fashion a vagabondage both physical and moral, as the teenage runaway tries to live by his wits and by ingratiating himself with others—the strategy of the powerless—in order to find a place for himself in an indifferent or hostile world, only to fail repeatedly, whether the project is a toy fountain or the new scheme of musical notation with which he sets out for Paris at the close of part 1. Throughout, the disappointment of his youthful aspirations is seen in the ironic and poignant light of hindsight, beginning with the illusion of freedom attendant upon his flight from Geneva: "Now that I was free and my own master, I supposed that I could do anything, achieve anything. I had only to take one leap, and I could rise and fly through the air. I marched confidently out into the world's wide spaces. Soon they would be filled with my fame" (book 2, 52). Clearly, highly rhetorical passages like this one have an archetypal quality in their evocation of the perpetual illusions of youthful aspiration; they resonate with his readers' sense of their own youths' fond dreams.

The career of vagabondage attendant upon Rousseau's adolescent dreams of freedom and mastery does not bring him the independence and self-reliance that mark the adult philosopher's concept of the state of nature; rather, it exposes him to all the moral deficits—the hypocrisy and the corruption—of modern civilization that he had sought to put behind him when he fled the tyranny of his apprenticeship. The most dire consequence of Rousseau's entry into the world is that it begins to taint the posited goodness of his original nature. What is *outside* and around him begins to contaminate what is *inside* him: thus the falsely accused and punished (the second spanking) becomes the false accuser (the ribbon of Marion); the abandoned child becomes the boy who abandons his friend and charge in his hour of need (Le Maître in his epileptic fit in Lyons); and later the man who deposits his newborn children one by one on the doorstep of the Paris orphanage. If the degradation of the child's innocence by the fallen world of adults is a favorite motif of nineteenth- and twentieth-century fiction (and of contemporary popular culture), Rousseau's text strives to temper or mitigate his degradation even as it chronicles it so vividly. The author presents his youthful vagabondage as erring, errant, and even aberrant (the sexual exhibitionism), but he also emphasizes his attempts to hold on to his innocence even in the process of losing it (as in his account of his conversion to Catholicism).

In essence, the dialectically structured plot of part 1 enacts the homeless youth's search for a home, and for a family in which he will be loved as and for himself. The semi-orphan who has turned his back on his native city seeks to constitute the terms of a mother-son relationship he has never experienced. The wanderer's quest for family and for the love of a mother that he never had operates simultaneously on two planes—the past that is being recorded as well as the narrative desire at work in the moment of writing—and finds only temporary and imperfect embodiment in the idealized and heavily edited account of his relationship with Mme de Warens, which culminates in the lyrical-pastoral dream of childhood restored at Les Charmettes. The ideal of a reconstituted home and of a loving parent-child relationship as well as a genuine and serene self-possession is under-cut, however, within the text itself (by the two ménages à trois involving two other young male dependents of Mme de Warens), as well as by ample extratextual or biographical evidence. Finally, Rousseau's quest for an authentic selfhood and an Edenic family romance is bedeviled throughout by repeated failures or absences of self and haunted by episodes of inauthenticity that take the form of the bad faith to which he succumbs and the false roles and masks (including various aliases) he is too often forced to take on under the pressure of adverse circumstances. Like the hypothetical history of civilization in Rousseau's discursive writ-ings, the autobiographical narrative of the *development* of his character is also that of its *deformation*. It is this dialectic of home and homelessness, authenticity and inauthenticity, and the strange and varying mixture of confession and apology with which Rousseau presents it, that will be the focus of my extended analysis of the remainder of the picaresque *Bil-dungsroman* that is part I of *The Confessions.*

The young vagabond's search for love and family is so errant and con-fused because he does not know what kind of love—maternal or erotic or sisterly, or all of them at once and then some?—he is looking for, nor what to make of it when he encounters it, nor even at times what gender he belongs to and identifies with.[11] To say that Jean-Jacques presents himself as a very mixed-up young man would be an understatement. Yet one of the signal virtues of part I is the novelistic charm and intrigue with which his text presents this multiple confusion, and the degree of reader engagement, sympathy, and even identification it manages to elicit. Rousseau plays upon this sympathy effectively and in different registers throughout book 2 as he chronicles the various misadventures and faux pas that follow his flight from Geneva. An analysis of this book, from his running to the arms of the Catholic Church with which it opens to the infamous and much discussed episode of the ribbon of Marion with which it concludes, can demonstrate some of the larger issues indicated above, including the compromise, despite protestations to the contrary, of his integrity by his need to survive in a hostile world, and his confused search for love and a home.

Flirting with the Church

Like some of his other attempts throughout *The Confessions* to explain away acts of bad faith, Rousseau's account of his conversion to Catholicism is a remarkable feat of equivocation. Yet his self-exculpating strategy of blaming the church for having seduced him—by holding it responsible for his loss of innocence—is so transparent in the script he provides that he seems to invite the reader to see through his verbal charade. A Jean-Jacques we can so easily feel superior to is also one we can pity and even sympathize, if not identify, with. All of that costs us very little and flatters our vanity—our sense of our own generosity vis-à-vis the young man's misfortunes and the confessional sophistries of the author. Still, the way his account, including his figurative language, turns so obviously against him suggests a deeper confession within the transparent apologia. Perhaps Rousseau is also playing a confessional game of hide-and-seek, allowing the reader as well as himself the pleasure of being found out. The game is certainly an enjoyable one, beginning with Rousseau's account of his self-interested visit to the Catholic priest and nobleman M. Benoît de Pontverre, who keeps him to dinner. "I was too good a guest to dispute his theology; and his Frangi wine, which I thought excellent, argued so triumphantly on his side that I should have blushed to contradict so good a host. So I gave in, or rather declined the contest. To judge from my tactics, indeed, a casual observer would have thought me a dissembler. But he would have been wrong. I was no more than grateful, of that I am certain" (53).

So the initial step in Rousseau's conversion is simply the issue of good manners. "There was no motive of hypocrisy behind my conduct; I never thought for a moment of changing my faith." But the very analogy Rousseau uses to justify his behavior—flirting—is one that betrays him. He "wanted to cultivate [the] benevolence" of people in a position to do him some good who want him to adopt their creed: "My crime, in that respect, was like an honest woman's coquetry. For sometimes, to gain her ends she will, without permitting any liberties or making any promises, raise more hopes than she intends to fulfil" (53). Rousseau's figure of speech is revealing—it shows his willingness to cast himself in or identify with the female role that is a recurrent feature of his confessional imagination—yet it turns against him in several ways. First, an honest woman who uses coquetry is something of an oxymoron. Second, the honest woman will flirt but not sleep with the man seeking to seduce her, which is patently not Rousseau's case, who not only flirted with but succumbed to the blandishments of the church. Third, female coquetry is not present in Rousseau's state of nature, where sex is a very straightforward matter, the fulfillment of an instinct, but is a feature of civilization and the sexual games played in it: the very innocence he asserts is disconfirmed by the trope he invokes to support it and that implicates him in the corruption of life in society.[12]

Rousseau's account of how flirtation with the Mother Church led inevitably to his conversion rhetorically plays up his own disingenuousness at the expense of the Catholic authorities' cynical motives. The hypocritical couple charged with delivering him to the doors of the hospice for catechumens in Turin has exhausted the expense account allotted him and has "found means to strip [him] of everything down to a little piece of silver ribbon which Mme de Warens had given [him] for [his] small sword" (65)—an ironic harbinger of the ribbon stolen later by Jean-Jacques. The satirical characterization of his fellow converts emphasizes his good intentions in stark contrast to their corrupt ones and projects onto them the fact that he too turned to the Catholic Church as a meal ticket: "In this assembly-hall were four or five frightful cut-throats, my fellow pupils, who looked more like the devil's bodyguard than men who aspired to become children of God. Two of these scoundrels were Croats, who called themselves Jews or Moors, and who spent their lives, as they confessed to me, roaming Spain and Italy, embracing Christianity and having themselves baptized wherever the rewards were sufficiently tempting" (65–66). As for his "sister converts," with the exception of one whom he finds "pretty" but to whom he can gain no access, "they were the greatest set of sluttish, abandoned whores that ever contaminated the Lord's sheepfold" (66).

In terms of his motive for being at the hospice, he is essentially in the same league with these other converts. By making them look worse than they are, however, he makes himself look better. But the moral picture here is much more ambiguous than this satirical pastiche would indicate, for Rousseau complicates the situation by plainly admitting his guilt: "I could not pretend to myself that the deed of piety I was about to commit was in essence anything but scoundrelly. Young though I was, I knew that, whichever were my true religion, I was going to sell my own, and that even if I were making the right choice I should in the depths of my heart be lying to the Holy Ghost, and should deserve the contempt of humankind" (68). He continues in the vein of severe moral self-judgment for several paragraphs, although it is difficult to determine what measure of that judgment was passed by the adolescent on himself and what measure is the moral burden of the moment of writing. There is, however, no mincing of words or ethical extenuation in this severe self-condemnation: "So finally, as we tumble into the abyss, we ask God why he has made us feeble. But, in spite of ourselves, He replies through our consciences: 'I have made you too feeble to climb out of the pit, because I made you strong enough not to fall in'" (69). But immediately after this frank acknowledgment, he slips back into his earlier mode of equivocation: "I did not exactly resolve to turn Catholic. But seeing the date of my conversion so far off, I utilized the time to accustom myself to the idea and, in the meanwhile, imagined some unforeseen event that would rescue me from my difficulty. To gain time, I decided to put up the best defense I possibly could." Earlier, he was the honest woman who flirted with the church, and now he puts up real resistance to the attempted seduction: "They certainly did not find me as easy as they expected, either in the matter of receptivity or inclination" (69). When the old priest who gives the converts their lessons is confounded by Rousseau's clever theological objections, a younger and better-educated cleric is called in to overcome the young man's resistance. Rousseau claims that he held out for a month, "for my directors required all that time to win the honour of a difficult conversion" (73).

The surviving records of the Turin hospice do not support Rousseau's chronology, however, for they indicate that he entered the institution on April 12, 1728, abjured Protestantism on April 21, and was baptized two days later (Cranston, *Early Life* 52). According to the hospice register, what as told in *The Confessions* took about two months actually took less than two weeks. The fact that autobiographers' recollections of dates and chronology are notoriously unreliable may explain this discrepancy. One can also entertain the remote possibility, as Cranston does, that "the records are inaccurate" (53). Yet even without any extratextual evidence, it is apparent from Rousseau's narrative that after an initial frank acknowledgment of his culpability, he proceeds to temper it by exaggerating his resistance. What is very odd in all this moral juggling of accounts is that there really is no need either to judge severely or to excuse the succumbing of the sixteen-year-old runaway to the security offered by the church. Given his young age and his exposed situation, both the self-judgment and the self-exoneration seem equally unnecessary. It is as if a contemporary teenage runaway were to feel guilty for accepting the help of Covenant House or some other religious-cum-charitable organization. It seems that the later Rousseau, in chronicling the vagaries of his youthful self, is suffering from the severity of the superego, which demands both a strict self-judgment and also forces the corresponding psychological maneuvers of self-justification.

If Rousseau's characterization of his conversion to Catholicism places as much of the guilt on his own expedient motives as on the ideological pressure brought to bear at the hospice upon a helpless adolescent, his shocking account of the sexual attack on him by a fellow convert and the religious authorities' nonchalant reaction to his report of the offense allows Rousseau to reclaim the moral high ground, by playing up his own ignorance and innocence against their cynical corruption. Rousseau mentions that "one of the two cut-throats who called themselves Moors took a fancy to me" to the point that

> Finally he tried to work up to the most revolting liberties and, by guiding my hand, to make me take the same liberties with him. I broke wildly away with a cry and leaped backwards, but without displaying indignation or anger, for I had not the slightest idea what it was all about. But I showed my surprise and disgust to such effect that he then left me alone. But as he gave up the struggle I saw something whitish and sticky shoot towards the fireplace and fall on the ground. My stomach turned over, and I rushed on to the balcony, more upset, more troubled and frightened as well, than ever I had been in my life. I was almost sick. (71)

Other than the provocative if unspecified sex games he played as a boy with Miss Goton and the spanking by Miss Lambercier, this is Rousseau's first overt confrontation with sexuality. Interestingly, in this homosexual and pederastic attack he takes on the female role (the man takes liberties with him and seeks to guide his hand), both during and after the incident. Rousseau claims he "could not understand what was the matter with the poor man"—a profession of ignorance difficult to credit in our suspicious age—and is not just shocked but revolted by this overt display of male genital arousal: "And really I know of no more hideous sight for a man in cold blood than such foul and obscene behavior, nothing more revolting than a terrifying face on fire with the most brutal lust. I have never seen another man in that state; but if we appear like that to women, they must indeed be fascinated not to find us repulsive" (71–72).

Rousseau scripts himself as something of a male Pamela here, and indeed the whole episode turns on one of the favorite motifs of the eighteenth-century novel, both literal and figurative: the rape or attempted rape of innocence. Thus in a sense this particularly graphic episode rather effectively serves the larger self-serving rhetoric of his presentation of his conversion experience. His is the innocence, and the seduction or rape is sanctioned by the Catholic authorities. When Rousseau informs "everybody of what just happened," he is told to hold his tongue, but continues to blab until "the next day one of the principals came very early and read me a sharp lecture, accusing me of impugning the honour of a sacred establishment and making a lot of fuss about nothing" (72). Not surprisingly, the principal assumes more knowledge on Rousseau's part than he claims he had,

> For he believed that I had known what the man wanted when I defended myself, but had merely been unwilling. He told me gravely that it was a forbidden and immoral act like fornication, but that the desire for it was not an affront to the person who was its object. There was nothing to get so annoyed about in having been found attractive. He told me quite openly that in his youth he had been similarly honoured and, having been surprised in a situation where he could put up no resistance, he had found nothing so brutal about it all. . . . There was no reason to be alarmed about nothing. (72)

Rousseau takes his exposé of the church's corrupt morality one step further as part of his larger theme, in the opening books of *The Confessions,* of the child's innocence being undone in and by a fallen world. "The whole matter seemed so simple to him that he had not even sought privacy for our conversation. There was an ecclesiastic listening all the while who found the matter no more alarming than he. This natural behaviour so impressed me that I finally believed such things were no doubt general practice in the world, though I had so far not had occasion to learn of them" (72).

Rousseau's assumption that "such things were no doubt general practice in the world" is an ironic anticipation of his later rationalization (in book 7) for adopting Parisian "principles" in placing his newborn babies with the Enfants Trouvés: "I caught the habit, and modelled my way of thinking upon that which I saw prevalent among these very pleasant and fundamentally decent people. 'Since it is the custom of the country,' I told myself, 'if one lives there one must adopt it'" (322). In the hospice sexual harassment episode, the general practice of the world is clearly exposed as morally tainted; in his explanation of what he did with his children, such worldly practices are invoked, ironically, to justify or extenuate his reprehensible and unnatural behavior. If the two passages are placed side by side, the former condemns the latter, and serves as an index of Rousseau's own corruption or deformation by the Parisian "principles" he has adopted.

Insofar as Jean-Jacques's sexual mores are undermined by the hospice authorities, one could speak of this novelistic episode as that of a *Verbildungsroman* (novel of deformation) more than of a *Bildungsroman* (novel of formation). To what extent appearance and reality are at odds in this fallen world is also apparent in the fact that whereas Rousseau receives this stern talking to, his pederastic harasser is none the worse for his disgusting act, but "a week later [is] baptized with great ceremony, swathed in white from head to foot to symbolize the purity of his regenerate soul" (73). In a larger and ironic perspective, the only touch of purity to be found anywhere in Rousseau's multilayered and richly suggestive narrative of his conversion to Catholicism is in the symbolic white of the putative Moor's baptismal robe.

Rousseau's embrace of the Catholic faith is linked with his search for home and love through the figure of Mme de Warens, who emerges as the focal point of his quest throughout the remainder of part 1. Other than Rousseau himself, she is the most fully and complexly rendered individual in his autobiography; like Jean-Jacques, she is a runaway (from a marriage she entered into at the age of fourteen), and a convert to Catholicism; like the church of which she is an unofficial emissary, she combines high moral and intellectual ideals with a goodly measure of worldly corruption. She is the missing way station in the trajectory I have traced from Monsieur de Pontverre to the hospice for catechumens in Turin; Rousseau literally enshrines in his imagination his meeting with what the priest had euphemistically described as "a good and charitable lady, whom the King [of Sardinia] . . . has empowered to save other souls from the error under which she once labored herself" (54): "I should like to surround that happy spot [where he first met Mme de Warens] with railings of gold, and make it an object of universal veneration. Whoever delights to honour the memorials of man's salvation should approach it only on his knees"(55).[13] His witty description of his first sight of her captures graphically the suggestive nature of her appeal to him: "I had expected M. de Pontverre's 'good lady' to be a disagreeable and pious old woman. . . . But what I saw was a face full of charm, large and lovely blue eyes beaming with kindness, a dazzling complexion and the outline of an enchanting neck. Nothing escaped the rapid glance of the young proselyte. For in a moment I was hers, and certain that a faith preached by such emissaries would not fail to lead to paradise" (55). From the start, his powerful attraction to this extraordinary woman some twelve years his senior—here described half-seriously as a conversion experience—represents a mingling of the erotic and the spiritual, and turns on a sentimental "affinity of souls" (58). His subsequent conversion to Catholicism is connected with the impact of this first encounter, for when she sends him on to the church authorities in Turin, "since it was at Mme de Warens's command that I departed, I regarded myself as still living under her direction" (60). His goal for the rest of part 1 will be precisely to achieve and maintain that desirable status in the home of his dear "Mamma."

In the short run this wish is foiled, for after his official embrace of Catholicism, he finds not the solid support of the church that he had foolishly expected, but a twenty-franc parting gift with which to fend for himself on the streets of a strange city. His self-judgment here is uncharacteristically severe, although it does not disable further unrealistic hopes for the future. "Thus all my grand hopes were eclipsed in a moment, and all that had accrued from the self-interested step I had just taken was the memory of having become simultaneously an apostate and a dupe" (74). Cast forth into the streets of Turin by the church and unable to return to Mme de Warens or to his native city, Jean-Jacques in his homeless condition turns to the ladies for help, as he will so often in his subsequent career in the world. The ensuing romantic intrigue with Mme Basile should be seen in the larger context of his need to be taken care of by a woman stronger and more mature than himself. She listens to his story, gives him work, feeds him, allows him to spend time in her company. The pretty young Italian wife of a much older husband away on a business trip, the shy and embarrassed attraction between Jean-Jacques and the bride who is only a few years older than he, the jealous and suspicious clerk who is the husband's spy in his absence—all of this is delightful and seems to come from the pages of some eighteenth-century novel.

Sign Language

The particular power and charm of Rousseau's rendering of this episode resides in the elision of speech in the pair's mounting and apparently mutual desire, which is indicated by other signs, including sighs and body language. "All that I could do was to heave a succession of noiseless sighs, which were most embarrassing in the silence in which we so often sat. Fortunately Mme Basile was too busy with her work to notice them, or so I thought. Yet I quite often saw the lace on her bosom rise in a sort of sympathy" (78). The high or low point of this comedy of embarrassed attraction is the "lively dumb show" of Jean-Jacques at her feet in worshipful and suspended animation. He had followed her and entered her room without her perceiving it.

> Her whole form displayed a charm which I had ample time to dwell on and which deprived me of my senses. I threw myself on my knees just inside the door and held out my arms to her in an access of passion, quite certain that she could not hear me, and imagining that she could not see me. But over the chimney-piece was a mirror, which betrayed me. I do not know what effect this scene had upon her. She did not look at me or speak to me. But, half turning her head, she pointed with a simple movement of her finger to the mat at her feet. I trembled, cried out, and threw myself down where she had pointed, all in a single second. But what seems almost incredible is that I had not the courage to attempt anything more, or to say a single word. I dared not raise my eyes, nor even, despite my uncomfortable position, so much as touch her on the knee, to give myself a moment's support. I was motionless and dumb, but certainly not calm. (78–79)

This vivid scene forms an instructive contrast with the earlier sexual attack in the hospice, and seems to have the markings of a quintessential Rousseau wish-fulfillment scenario. The Moor's sexual advances were openly and brutishly lustful and Jean-Jacques was properly horrified; here we have the delicate charm of a shy and unspoken mutual attraction that manifests itself only in physical gestures that, unlike the Moor's advances, are the opposite of revolting. The Moor's desire was grossly displayed and transgressive, whereas the desire that animates this scene is innocent and within the limits of obedience stipulated by the object of desire. The scene also answers to Rousseau's erotic need (as shaped by Miss Lambercier's spanking) to be submissive to a woman older and stronger than he. Mme Basile points with her finger to the mat at her feet, and he, like a well-trained and loyal retainer, instantly obeys her silent command. The rest of this piquant little drama frustrates his fantasy of submission, however, because she, due to her inexperience, is unable to enact the commanding position, so that the result is a ridiculous yet poignant impasse. The episode remains stuck in the groove of mutual bashfulness, because the young wife is apparently as innocent as her hapless adolescent admirer: "If she had had a little experience she would have taken different measures to encourage a young lover" (79).

In his *Essay on the Origin of Languages,* Rousseau asserts that "although the language of gesture and that of voice are equally natural," the former is the earliest human form of communication, because gestures are "more expressive and say more in less time" (240). He speculates that love may "have invented speech" but is often frustrated by it: "Dissatisfied with speech, love disdains it: it has livelier ways of expressing itself." The ancients had a relationship to gesture we moderns lack, because what they "said most forcefully they expressed not in words, but in signs" (241). Rousseau proceeds to locate the origins of gesture in our physical needs and those of language in "the moral needs, the passions"—"not hunger, nor thirst, but love, hatred, pity, anger, wrung their first utterings [voix] from them" (245). In the light of these assertions, Rousseau's romantic interlude with the shopkeeper's wife is a sustained oxymoron in which the two participants are, as it were, suspended between two states. The mutual desire between the timid participants is communicated strictly in terms of sign and gesture—Jean-Jacques kneeling inside the door in an access of passion, Mme Basile pointing with her finger to the mat at her feet, Jean-Jacques throwing himself down—and the only point at which the dumb show approaches the level of utterance is when Rousseau cries out as he throws himself down. The two are in a speechless and primordial state of nature, where sexual desire is expressed through the immediate and original language of gesture.[14] But the "coquettish" attire of Mme Basile and the mutual embarrassment of the would-be lovers suggest that they are already beyond the state of nature and that the moral need of the passion they are experiencing requires the intervention of *voix* or utterance. Unable to make the transition from gesture to utterance, they are trapped in their "dumb show" until, significantly enough, the sudden entrance of a servant—a reminder of the society and the adult world in which they live, and by which their little scene would be judged as the prelude to adultery, which is how her husband views the relationship upon his return—forces Mme Basile to speak in order to bring the drama to its anticlimactic end: "'Get up,' she said, 'here is Rosina!'" (79).

Servants' Intrigues

After Jean-Jacques's dreams of romantic love and shelter are rudely disappointed by the return of Mme Basile's offended husband, he finds a temporary niche as a valet to the Countess Louise-Marie de Vercellis, in the hope that she might see his true merit and do something for him. With her aristocratic *hauteur* and her cool, "philosophical" detachment, she is in many ways the opposite of Mme Basile, the bourgeois woman of sympathy and sensibility. Rousseau was obviously hoping to win her over—as he so often did the ladies—with his "story," about which "she showed some curiosity" (84). As an aristocrat, however, she cannot see beyond the distinctions of class. Thus their exchanges are a one-way street; she wants his confidence but will not reciprocate. She is trapped within her classist outlook and thus is incapable of the heart-to-heart exchange that is Rousseau's ideal of personal relationships. If it is both naive and presumptuous of Jean-Jacques to aspire to such a relationship with her, his summary judgment of her contains the revolutionary gist of his critique of the ancien régime: "She judged me less by what I was than by what she had made me; and since she saw nothing in me but a servant she prevented my appearing to her in any other light" (85). The domestic intrigue of the servants who surround their dying mistress like vultures is also an effective index at another level of the inevitable corruption of a polity fissured by a strict class system that denies the young Rousseau his "true place." "I did not consider that in addition to serving our common mistress I must also be the servant of her servants. Besides I was the kind of person who made them uncomfortable. They saw quite clearly that I was not in my true place, and were afraid that their mistress might see it also and take some measures to put me there, which might diminish their share of the money" (85). It is doubtful that Rousseau ever came close to finding his true place in society, but there must have been a sweet sense of vindication for the most influential author of his age when writing this and similar passages, an author who at the height of his fame had the high nobility vying for his attentions.

Sadly enough, the famous confession that concludes book 2, and that rivals the two spankings in book 1 for the interpretive commentary it has received, shows Rousseau himself initiating such a servant's intrigue. What is so painful and shocking in the ribbon of Marion episode is that now he is not the innocent victim he likes to cast himself as, but the corrupt victimizer. One of the issues that this clearly overdetermined confession thematizes is his own fall in the fallen world. As such it takes on the aura of a parable of original sin, like Augustine's robbing of the pear tree, with which it can profitably be compared.[15] But even as he shows how his character has become deformed by the false morality of the world in which he lives, and how the *outside* has now become part of his *inside*, Rousseau seeks to mingle confession with apology, by a confessional ethic that seeks to temper his guilt by giving the intention behind his act greater weight in any final judgment than its unknown but potentially sinister consequences, which are fully acknowledged and which he claims have haunted his guilty imagination.

The confession of this "crime" figures as a portentous postscript to book 2 and is a *locus classicus* of The Confessions. Rousseau had stolen "a little pink and silver ribbon" (86) from a young lady in the Countess de Vercellis's household, and when an inventory is taken after her death the item is found in Rousseau's possession. When publicly confronted about his theft, he lies "with infernal impudence," shifting the blame to the servant girl Marion. Rousseau's description of Marion throws into relief the unblemished innocence of her nature ("She had that fresh complexion that one never finds except in the mountains, and such a sweet and modest air that one had only to see her to love her" 87), even as it emphasizes the heartless villainy of his slander. In a sense Rousseau's false accusation constitutes a rape of innocence and is a graphic measure of how far he has fallen. His description also forms an implicit and instructive contrast with his earlier account (in book 1) of having been made to steal asparagus by the journeyman engraver. Then the innocent Rousseau stole only "to please the man who made me do it. Yet if I had been caught I should have been exposed to all manner of beatings, abuse, cruelty, while that wretch would have disowned me" (41). Rousseau concludes the moralizing account with the striking observation, "So it is that in every situation the powerful rogue protects himself at the expense of the feeble and innocent" (42). In the case of the purloined ribbon and the slander of Marion, the shoe is on the other foot, for Rousseau stands exposed as the powerful rogue who betrays Marion's innocence in order to protect himself.

If Rousseau's narrative of his "crime" were to end here, its moral of lost (his own) and betrayed (Marion's) innocence would be perfectly clear. However, with respect to his behavior, motives, and memories, nothing is ever perfectly simple or clear. As in the earlier narrative of the conversion to Catholicism, so here Rousseau tries to reclaim his innocence after he has already admitted how he lost or sacrificed it for his own interests. What one might call his supplement of apology and excuse turns on a "deontological" ethics that privileges the intention of an act over its consequences (a "consequentialist" ethics). Rousseau's attempt to extenuate the gravity of his "crime" by explaining his "inner feelings" introduces a psychoanalytic dimension that considerably complicates his confession. "Never was deliberate wickedness further from my intention than at that cruel moment. When I accused that poor girl, it is strange but true that my friendship for her was the cause. She was present in my thoughts, and I threw the blame on the first person who occurred to me. I accused her of having done what I intended to do myself. I said she had given the ribbon to me because I meant to give it to her" (88). As Rousseau's critics point out, the ribbon, in the words of one of them, "'stands for' Rousseau's desire for Marion or, what amounts to the same thing, for Marion herself" (de Man, *Allegories* 283).[16] De Man pushes his reading of Rousseau's most famous confession beyond that of an unacknowledged desire for Marion, to see it in narcissistic terms as "the structure of desire as exposure rather than as possession" (286): "What Rousseau *really* wanted is neither the ribbon nor Marion, but the public scene of exposure which he actually gets" (285).

If the hidden erotic and even narcissistic motives of Rousseau's "crime" are buried in his confession, he himself places the stress on the role of shame [honte] as the chief factor in the mitigation, if not the extenuation, of his guilt. Sheringham's objection—"what is disturbing here is not so much the explanation as the fact that Rousseau thinks it excuses him" (51)—is telling, but for Rousseau the intensity of his shame serves a double purpose. It supports his innocence even in his impudent accusation of Marion, because by implication shame—the fear of shame—is something that will govern only a good person, not an inveterate villain. And his fear of public shame and embarrassment is also meant to make his slander of Marion, if not forgivable, then understandable in his readers' eyes: "I was not much afraid of punishment, I was only afraid of disgrace. . . . [M]y invincible sense of shame prevailed over everything. It was my shame that made me impudent, and the more wickedly I behaved the bolder my fear of confession made me. I saw nothing but the horror of being found out, of being publicly proclaimed, to my face, as a thief, a liar, and a slanderer" (88). His professed shame, ironically, is the psychological justification for his acting in an utterly shameless manner.

The intensity of shame posited here also has a narcissistic element, to the extent that it shifts the focus of the episode from the victim to the perpetrator and tries to gain sympathy for the latter—a characteristically modern move played out in our increasingly tabloid media coverage of crimes and criminals. Rousseau's focus on his fear of shame and of being found out may also be overdetermined in his narrative imagination to the extent that he may be retroactively rerouting to this particular "crime" other powerful charges of shame, and the attendant anxiety of being found out, associated with later shameful lapses in his life—most notably his abandonment of his five children.

Appearance and reality also undergo some strange permutations in this Byzantine confession. On the one hand, the innocent Marion is made to appear corrupt by Jean-Jacques's impudent slander (and doubly corrupt, since she stands accused not only of theft but also, by implication, of seeking to compromise the morals of the male servant to whom she gave the ribbon); on the other, the guilty Rousseau who actually stole the ribbon seeks publicly to prove his innocence by accusing Marion of having done what he did, which makes him doubly guilty and corrupt in the reader's judgment. But then the narrator Rousseau seeks to reclaim his standing with the reader and to point to the situational factors that make his slander not an act of infernal audacity but a kind of delirium—in panic, he blurted out the first name that came to his mind—so that his very attraction to Marion, ironically, is the cause of her downfall. The slander is not an act of positive betrayal but an act of negative selfhood, a lapse, a momentary absence of self. The French reads, "if I had been allowed to return to myself, I would have infallibly admitted everything" ("Si l'on m'eut laissé revenir à moi même, j'aurois infailliblement tout déclaré" [*Oeuvres* 1:86–87]). Thus what appears to be cynical corruption, the sacrifice of an another in order to save himself, is really a hapless lapse of innocence. As such, Rousseau's psychological explanation of his behavior is a strange repetition and inversion of the motif of the Moor shrouded in baptismal white: like him, he appears to be the innocent party but is inwardly corrupt as he slanders the poor Marion. Unlike the case of the Moor, however, what appears to be the cynical corruption beneath the pretended surface of his innocence is really another and genuine kind of innocence that his psychological explanation has sought to foreground.

However, what Rousseau's overelaborated and ultimately sophistic account of this shameful episode leaves unexplored is why Marion, the timid servant girl who is roughly his equal in social position and in age, was sacrificed, or perhaps had to be sacrificed, by the young man who preferred to allow his romantic feelings to come into play only with women above him in social position, older than himself, and in a position to exercise some authority over him. The servant's intrigue inherent in his attraction to Marion, as symbolized by the fetish of the stolen ribbon, did not fit this erotic and social script. Perhaps the saddest confession here is an unspoken one: he may have betrayed her, as he abandoned his friend and charge Le Maître when the choirmaster collapsed in a street in Lyons, because of his self-consciousness in public; the exposure of his private feelings about her would have been inconvenient and embarrassing.

Rousseau comes closest to acknowledging the social bias inherent in his romantic feelings about women in book 4, when he describes the circle of female friends of Anne-Marie Merceret, Mme de Warens's maid, whose hopes for a romantic involvement with him he dashes:

> [S]eamstresses, chambermaids, and shop girls hardly tempted me; I needed young ladies. Everyone has his fancies, and that has always been mine. . . . However it is certainly not pride of rank or position that attracts me. It is a better preserved complexion, lovelier hands, greater elegance in jewellery, an air of cleanliness and refinement

about a woman's whole person, better taste in her way of dressing and expressing herself, a finer and better made gown, a neater pair of shoes, ribbons, lace, better done hair. . . . I find this prejudice most absurd in myself; but my heart dictates it, in spite of me. (132)

In this blind spot in his text, Rousseau is clearly unaware of his own hypocrisy: while disclaiming that social position plays a role in his romantic preferences, his list of preferred attributes in a woman is clearly very much a function of her social class and position. Only with a self-deception verging on the perverse can he claim that his preference for refined and elegant women is natural, that is, a prejudice dictated by his heart. Perhaps the real confession of the ribbon of Marion is that it was on the altar of this unnatural "prejudice" that the poor servant girl for whom he felt an attraction was sacrificed.

Aristocratic ladies, on the other hand, fuel Rousseau's erotic imagination, early and late, from the adolescent's first glimpse of Mme de Warens to the older man's romantic raptures with Sophie d'Houdetot (now the younger woman to his older self), described in book 9. The exception to this rule would seem to be Rousseau's strange relationship with the lower-class and semiliterate Thérèse Le Vasseur, his mistress, companion, and in later years his nurse as well. But in the same book in which he describes in great detail his romantic intoxication with Sophie, he also assures us in all "sincerity . . . that from the first moment I saw her [Thérèse] till this day I have never felt the least glimmering of love for her." Rousseau goes on to explain what he means by this shocking statement: "[T]he sensual needs I satisfied with her were for me purely sexual and had nothing to do with her as an individual" (385–86). Their relationship is on the same level as the instinctual relations between the sexes in the state of nature, which have nothing to do with romantic love, a product of the imagination that arises in society and has its origins in *amour propre*. In the mirror of his most famous fiction, *The New Héloïse,* his preference for upper-class women is also dramatized in his alter ego's, the commoner Saint Preux's, passion for his pupil, the aristocrat's daughter, Julie d'Etanges.

Missteps on the Road Back to Mme de Warens

In light of the class bias of Rousseau's romantic desires, his relationship with Mme de Warens, the focal point of his aspirations for the remainder of part 1 of *The Confessions,* becomes even more complex and suggestive, since this titled lady holds out at once the promise of satisfying the boy's Oedipal wishes and the outcast-vagabond's confused search for home and social position. The movement back to her as the affective center of his young life begins in earnest in book 3, appears to be finalized at the close of book 4 when Rousseau settles permanently into her household in Chambéry, "after four or five years of vagabondage, follies, and hardships" (169), and achieves its complex consummation in book 5 in the idealized ménage à trois with "Mamma" and Claude Anet, only to disintegrate in book 6 when Rousseau refuses to accept the reality of a new triangle involving yet another young male protégé of Mme de Warens. Rousseau's sense of betrayal by his second, adoptive mother in the last book of part 1 repeats the trauma of his abandonment at birth by his biological mother, and the shock of his loss of a reconstituted and perverse family romance spells the end of a belated childhood, as it forces him out into the world and a renewed struggle to find his place in it.

His fantasy of a life with Mme de Warens also involves a rejection of other possibilities, a scenario of roads not taken. One of these is his promising position, at the beginning of book 3, in the service of Ottavio Francesco Solaro, Count de Gouvon, and his family, whose aim was to "mould in advance a man of merit and talents who, depending solely upon them, might eventually be received into their confidence and serve them faithfully." After an initial period of probation, Rousseau's "general reputation in the house was that of a young man of the highest expectations, who was not in his proper place but was expected to get there" (99). Rousseau claims he became "a sort of favourite in the house"; the count's well-educated son gives him private Latin lessons, and Jean-Jacques experiences a triumphant moment of public recognition when at a "grand dinner" he is the only one able to give, at the behest of the count, the correct translation of the French motto on the family's coat of arms (96). This recognition of his abilities is doubly gratifying and has all the marks of a wish-fulfillment fantasy come true, because it gains him the appreciation not only of the count but of his attractive young granddaughter: "That moment was short, but it was in every respect delightful. It was one of those rare moments that put things back in their proper perspective, repair the slights on true merit and avenge the outrages of fortune" (97).

His triumph, however, is short-lived and followed by a double anticlimax, because through his awkward behavior he immediately loses any advantage that he has gained with Mlle Pauline-Gabrielle de Breil, and he also proceeds to go out of his way to get himself dismissed from his promising position, despite the family's conciliatory efforts to keep him in it. There are different ways to read this willed failure, ranging from an abiding need for authenticity of self that rejects inappropriate roles and choices, no matter how advantageous by worldly standards (for example, his avoidance [in book 8] of a meeting with the king and the prospect of a pension after the highly acclaimed performance at court of *The Village Soothsayer*), to a character quirk that made him constitutionally unable to accept and enjoy certain promising situations at face value (for example, intercourse with the beautiful young Italian courtesan, Giulietta, in book 7). It is clear that his explanation of a sudden friendship with his fellow Genevan, Bacle, and the irresistible promise of a scenic foot journey back to his native city, shifts his willful refusal to follow through on the promise of a diplomatic career with the powerful Solaro family into a distinctly romantic register. Indeed, Rousseau affirms his impulsive decision with the rhetorical judgment of hindsight: "Only a fool would sacrifice such a prospect for ambitious plans, slow, difficult, and uncertain of fulfilment. And even supposing that one day they were to be realized, brilliant though they might be they would not be worth a quarter of an hour's real pleasure and liberty in my youth" (100). So much for the Protestant ethic of prudence and hard work; Jean-Jacques will not be a Benjamin Franklin or even a budding Henry Kissinger. The privileging of the present moment and its enjoyment is a recurrent Rousseau theme that finds its definitive statement in the famous Fifth Revery, but his explanation here of the immediate pleasure of the journey seems very much a pretext and a rationalization for a deeper need or motive that is allowed to surface in the course of the account: "In all this I could see nothing but the ineffable bliss of a journey, at the end of which, as a further joy, I could just glimpse Mme de Warens" (100).

Jean-Jacques's perverse sabotaging of his prospects with the Solaro family and his return to Mme de Warens are also a rejection of positive male role models, of which there had been a real dearth in his life, beginning with his own father. Both the benevolent count and his learned son had taken an interest in him and might have helped to form or at least steady his character. He also mentions "a Savoyard abbé, M. [Jean-

Claude] Gaime," who during Rousseau's time in Turin tried to impart to him "lessons in a sound morality and in the principles of common sense" (92). The wise abbé, the principal real-life model of the Savoyard Vicar of *Emile,* tried to get Jean-Jacques to take an objective look at himself and his abilities and drew him "a faithful picture of human life, of which [he] had only false ideas" (92). Although at the time these politic and paternal ministrations fell on deaf ears, they were not ultimately wasted, because in the long run "they planted a seed of virtue and religion in my heart which has never been choked, and which only required the tending of a more beloved hand to bear fruit" (93). The "more beloved hand" is a veiled reference to "Mamma," and it is significant that a woman is thus given the credit for successfully completing the work of forming his character abortively begun by the Savoyard abbé. Conversely, the men who successfully appeal to or influence Rousseau at this period of his life are often negative role models because they appeal to his irresponsible side and lead him astray in one way or another: his sudden friendship with Bacle, which is correlated with his parting of ways with the Solaro family, and, in the next book, his position with the fraudulent Archimandrite of Jerusalem and his infatuation with the ne'er-do-well Venture de Villeneuve.

Of course, the adolescent Jean-Jacques is capable of being morally wayward strictly under his own power. Even though book 3 moves with a certain inevitability to his return to Mme de Warens—the first of several such emotional reunions with which part 1 is punctuated—it is framed by significant episodes of waywardness or dereliction in which Rousseau's character is shown taking a bizarre turn: the exhibitionism at the beginning and the "disgraceful confession" (128) of the shameful abandonment of Le Maître at its close. In the latter episode Rousseau acknowledges the seriousness of leaving his friend in the lurch, as the poor man lies "foaming and insensible in the middle of the street" (128). The avowal of his failure here at least rights the moral balance. The same cannot be said about his exposing himself to the young servant girls fetching water in a courtyard, a "disturbance of mind" (90) whose seriousness Rousseau seeks to deflect by turning it into a comic episode. With his "romantic excuse" to the man invested with phallic authority ("a big moustache, a big hat, and a big sword" 91), who saves Rousseau from the offended women who have cornered him, we are back in the world of eighteenth-century fiction: "I begged him in the humblest of tones to take pity on my youth and condition, claiming to be a young stranger of noble birth and to be suffering from a mental derangement" (91). Yet even the fantastic excuse repeats the earlier motif of an extreme "disturbance of mind." The way the entire episode is so neatly packaged and wittily rounded off (with the man's sarcastic repartee when he subsequently runs into Rousseau on the street, 92), points to the defensive handling of a complex not worked through or fully explored.

Some of the significant details of his exhibitionism are also left ambiguous or are oddly suggestive and revealing. Rousseau introduces the sequence by informing the reader that "the heat in [his] blood incessantly filled [his] mind with pictures of women and girls," but that "not knowing the true nature of sex [he] imagined them acting according to [his] own strange fantasies, and had no idea of anything else" (90). Too timid to ask any female to enact these fantasies with him, he resorts to "exposing [himself] to women from afar off in the condition in which [he] should have liked to be in their company." The text is unclear about exactly what is exposed, but based on the nature of his fantasies, one is inclined to guess that it was his back, and not his front: "What they saw was nothing obscene . . . it was ridiculous. The absurd pleasure I got from displaying myself before their eyes is quite indescribable" (90).

In a sense, his symbolically charged narrative repeats his pleasure, even as it contains it within the comic frame ("this folly led to a catastrophe almost equally comical, but less entertaining for me" 91).[17] The account of the servant girls at the well has the aura of romantic legend or mythology (compare the Nausikaa episode in the *Odyssey*, when the shipwrecked hero encounters the king's daughter and her servants as they fetch water). That the poetic motif of girls fetching water from a public well is invested for Rousseau with erotic significance is also apparent in his explanation in the *Essay on the Origin of Languages* of how "the first meetings between the sexes took place" when "young girls came to fetch water for the household." At a later stage "the first festivals took place" at these communal wells, and thus "from the pure crystal of the fountains sprang the first fires of love" (271). The description that follows in *The Confessions* of the "subterranean passages . . . long and pitch black," which lead to a dead end where Rousseau is trapped, seem to take us inside his mind as an anticipation of those metaphoric labyrinths and tunnels which are the trope of Rousseau's mounting paranoia in part 2. The detail of the "four or five women each armed with a broom handle" (91) who have cornered him is also intriguing, since at one level it seems actually to serve the masochistic desires grounded in his spanking by Gabrielle Lambercier; at another, however, those incensed servant girls may be the symbolic partisans of the slandered servant girl Marion—the confession of the stolen ribbon comes only a few pages earlier—appearing in a nightmarish scenario of revenge scripted by his guilty imagination.

The Perverse Family Romance of Annecy

Rousseau's account of his return from Turin to Annecy in 1729 to rejoin Mme de Warens idealizes their relationship as an Oedipal romance, but without any rivalry with a threatening father figure, or even any overt sexuality:

> From the first day the sweetest intimacy was established between us, and it continued to prevail during the rest of her life. 'Little one' was my name, hers was 'Mamma.' . . . The two names, I find, admirably express the tone of our behaviour, the simplicity of our habits and, what is more, the relations between our hearts. To me she was the most tender of mothers, who never thought of her own pleasure but always of my good. And if there was a sensual side of my attachment to her, that did not alter its character, but only made it more enchanting. I was intoxicated with delight at having a young and pretty mamma whom I loved to caress. (book 3, 106–7)

Claude Anet ("a valet from her own district," 106) is mentioned in passing as part of her staff, but not the fact that he was also her lover. There is a certain amount of narrative artifice here: Rousseau didn't discover this intimacy until later, but of course in writing book 3 he knows but keeps this knowledge from the reader.

It is clear that in seeking to account for the most important and formative relationship of his early years, Rousseau is ultimately unclear and confused about its sexual aspect. The latter is evident in his "outbreaks of tenderness," his "burning desire to spend [his] days beside her" (107), and in the "follies" and extravagances that his love for her made him commit. He kisses the bed in which she has slept, he greedily devours the morsel of food she spits out on her plate: "In a word, there was but one difference between myself and the most passionate of lovers. But that difference was an essential one, and sufficient to render my whole condition inexplicable in the light of reason" (108). The perplexity at his own behavior and motives is that of the renegade *philosophe* for whom the complexities and perversities of the human heart cannot be fathomed by reason. But Rousseau goes further than this acknowledgment of being perplexed, because he seeks to neutralize and to redirect for the purposes of morality the very erotic obsession he has just confessed. What further complicates his explanation is the introduction of the "vice" of the "dangerous supplement," which he claims he has acquired in Italy. His relationship with "Mamma" would seem to offer the imaginative fuel that is the basis of his newfound habit. Instead, in Rousseau's ambiguous and bizarre (non)explanation, his passion for "Mamma" inoculates him against sexual indulgence, both autoerotic and with actual women:

> Added to my temptations . . . were the circumstances in which I lived, in the house of a pretty woman, fondling her image in my secret heart, seeing her continually throughout the day, and surrounded at night by objects to remind me of her, lying in a bed where I knew she had lain. How much to stimulate me! Let the reader imagine my condition, and he will think of me as already half-dead! But I was far from it. What might have been my undoing was in fact my salvation, at least for a time. Intoxicated with the pleasure of living beside her, and burning with desire to spend my life with her, I saw in her always, whether she were absent or present, a tender mother, a beloved sister, a delightful friend, and nothing more. . . . For me she was the only woman in the whole world; and the utter sweetness of the feelings she inspired in me, leaving my senses no time to be roused by others, safeguarded me against her and all her sex. In a word, I was chaste [sage] because I loved her. (109)

Rousseau knows that the "state of things" he is describing is "extraordinary" and admits, "I cannot easily describe her effect upon me" (109). There seems to be a combination of sophistry and denial in his claim that the woman who is the single focus of all of his passionate feelings keeps him pure. He wants to unsay or undo the sexual attraction in the very act of inscribing it. "A tender mother, a beloved sister, a delightful friend, and nothing more" is inconsistent with "for me she was the only woman in the whole world" (uttered in almost the same breath), because if she is indeed the *only* woman in the world for him, then the relationship would have to include "something more." And even the linking of mother, sister, and friend is incongruous, since these are far from synonymous, but signify very different kinds of relationships. In the reconstituted family romance scripted by his imagination, Rousseau is something of a totalitarian, because he wants a single woman to play all these roles, plus the role of the lover, which, paradoxically enough, is at once inscribed and erased.

The missing or hidden factor in Rousseau's attempted unsaying here of his obvious sexual attraction to "Mamma" is the specter of the incest taboo, which does rear its ugly head when Rousseau's relationship with Mme de Warens becomes an explicitly sexual one (in book 5). In his *Essay on the Origin of Languages,* Rousseau states that in the earliest stage of civilization incest was not prohibited: "Each family was self-sufficient and propagated itself from its own stock alone" and "people became man and wife without ceasing to be brother and sister" (272). He does not mention parent-child incest but points to the sibling incest ("the first men had to marry their sisters") that was to prove so attractive to the Romantics as an imaginative ideal.[18] This pattern of sibling unions was the norm "even after the most ancient peoples had come together" (272). Clearly for Rousseau the incest prohibition is neither natural nor divinely ordained; nevertheless he holds that "the law that abolished it is no less sacred for being by human institution" because "in view of the intimacy between the sexes that inevitably attends upon domestic life," the continued practice of incest would corrupt morals and "soon cause the destruction of mankind" (272). These assertions of the philosopher provide a helpful context for the confusions, ambiguities, and doublespeak that characterize the passage cited above in which he attempts a provisional summary of his relationship with "Mamma." I would suggest that the pressure of the "sacred law" of the incest prohibition (*Essay* 272) internalized by Rousseau has a great deal to do with his equivocal feelings about Mme de Warens, both when he lived with her and when he wrote about the relationship decades later. In the innocence of the state of nature, intrafamilial eros is the norm, but in the civilized modern world, which Rousseau has already entered by way of sexual shame and guilt (exhibitionism, masturbation), a single woman cannot be a man's whole world—his mother, sister, friend, and lover.

Vagabondage and Impersonations

After giving this idealized yet conflicted and problematic summary of his first reunion with Mme de Warens, Rousseau shows himself losing her again when he returns after his abortive journey to Lyons with Le Maître to find that she has left for Paris on a mysterious trip.[19] "I came and found her gone. Judge of my surprise and my grief" (130). So opens book 4, which initiates the most sustained sequence of vagabondage and errant behavior in *The Confessions*. Once more without home and family or even means of support, Jean-Jacques has to fend for himself as best he can. Near the close of book 3, by way of preface to his confession of the abandonment of Le Maître, Rousseau had stated that "there are times when I am so unlike myself that I might be taken for someone else of an entirely opposite character" (126). The vagaries of the fourth book, at the close of which he is once more reunited with "Mamma," show this unlikeness at a literal level, as Rousseau assumes false identities and becomes an impersonator and confidence man. In book 3 he had become "infatuated" with the "charming rake" Venture de Villeneuve and his "witty" and "seductive" conversation; and finding "Mamma" gone, Rousseau "proposed to him that [he] should share his lodgings" (123–24, 131).

According to Guéhenno, Rousseau's infatuation with the roguish and voluble adventurer is a function of his perceiving him as a romanticized alter ego: Venture "was everything that Jean-Jacques could not be, but everything he dreamed of being" (46). His adolescent idealization of Venture (which is rudely dispelled when he meets him again many years later, in book 8), may also have a homoerotic element and reflect a latent bisexuality, since, as his description indicates, Venture put Jean-Jacques into something of a girlish swoon.[20] That this character, who seems to have stepped right out of the pages of one of the novels Jean-Jacques read as a boy, is exactly the wrong kind of male role model for the unsteady and impressionable young man is clear in the judgment of hindsight, in which his worship of the romanticized rake ("meditating upon his great virtues, admiring and envying his rare talents, and cursing my unlucky stars for not summoning me to a happy life like his"), is severely deflated ("Oh, how little I knew myself!" 131). When (in book 4) the penniless Jean-Jacques arrives in Lausanne, he decides to emulate "Venture arriving at Annecy"—nothing ventured, nothing gained, as it were. "I took it into my head to play the little Venture at Lausanne, to teach music, of which I was ignorant, and to say that I came from Paris, where I had never been" (144). As Rousseau puts it wittily, he "*venturized*" himself and became (anagrammatically) the composer Vaussore de Villeneuve. Although presented as a comic episode, his assumption of a false identity, which ends in the debacle of a humiliating public performance of a piece of music by the impostor composer, is yet another of those repeated failures or absences of self that punctuate Jean-Jacques's early life: "I have already noted certain moments of incomprehensible delirium in which I was not myself. Here is another extreme instance" (144).

The "delirium" in which Rousseau assumes another identity is very different from those instances of playful impersonation that Goethe chronicles in his autobiography. Whereas Goethe's incognitos are assumed in the spirit of an entertaining and harmless prank, Rousseau's false identities appear to be grounded in a psychic compulsion as well as in the survival instinct of the down-and-out vagabond. What Rousseau sees as his failure or absence of self by way of impersonation continues with the episode of his becoming the companion and interpreter of the fraudulent Greek Orthodox priest who passes himself off as the Archimandrite of Jerusalem on a fund-raising mission. In this sequence, Jean-Jacques becomes a lesser fraud serving a greater one, who is also a kind of substitute father figure, offering the vagabond Jean-Jacques food and shelter. Ironically, in assuming a role, Rousseau, whose shyness and social awkwardness made public speaking and polite salon conversation an ordeal, is able to hold forth successfully in public precisely because he is not discoursing *in propria persona*. His fluent address to the senate of Berne on behalf of the Archimandrite's mission is well received: "This is the only time in my life that I have spoken in public and before a ruling body, and perhaps the only time too that I have spoken boldly and well" (151–52).

In experiences of impersonation and playacting like this one, we may also discern the seeds of Rousseau's complex and ambivalent attitude to the theater and theatrical entertainments. Himself an avid playgoer in Paris and a lover of the Italian opera (since his short-lived diplomatic career in Venice, described in book 7), as well as a playwright and the composer of a highly successful opera, he nevertheless (in *Letter to M. d'Alembert on the Theater*) argued polemically against the project of instituting a theater in Geneva and launched an attack on actors that, read in the light of his impersonations in *The Confessions,* can also be seen to have a confessional element of covert self-judgment. "What is the talent of the actor? It is the art of counterfeiting himself, of putting on another character than his own, of appearing different than he is . . . of forgetting his own place by dint of taking another's. What is the profession of the actor? It is a trade which he performs for money . . . and puts his person publicly on sale. I beg every sincere man to tell me if he does not feel in the depths of his soul that there is something servile and base in this traffic of oneself" (*Letter* 79).

After Rousseau is separated from the Greek priest by the French ambassador at Soleure, he is sent on to Paris by the ambassador to be the companion of the nephew of a Swiss colonel, a scheme that, like so many others in this book, falls through after Rousseau has spent several weeks in the French capital. Paris does not live up to his unrealistic expectations, and in what can be seen as a minor parallel to the famous spot of time in book 6 of *The Prelude*, when Wordsworth discovers that he has crossed the Alps without realizing it, Rousseau too bears witness to the Romantic syndrome of reality falling short of high expectations. "Such is the fruit of an over-lively imagination, which exaggerates beyond the common measure and always sees more than it is told to expect" (155).

Three other aspects of Rousseau's narrative of vagabondage and impersonation in book 4 deserve brief mention: his further encounter with homosexuality, his vivid realization of social injustice, and his enjoyment of nature and landscape, which was to prove so influential for the emergence of Romanticism. He mentions that on one of his journeys to Lyons he is joined outdoors in the evening by a man "who suggested that we should have some fun together" (161) and proceeds to demonstrate to Jean-Jacques what he has in mind. "All that he wanted . . . was to have his fun and for me to have mine, each on his own account; and this seemed to him so natural that it had not even occurred to him that it might not seem the same to me. I was so alarmed at his beastliness that I did not reply, but got up precipitately and ran off as fast as I could go, imagining that the wretch was at my heels" (161). As in the hospice episode, Rousseau is again shocked by the overt display of male genital arousal, which, ironically, is the inverted mirror of his own indulgence in the "dangerous supplement": "I ran in the direction of the river-bank . . . trembling as if I had just committed a crime. I was addicted to the vice [masturbation] myself, but the memory of this incident cured me of it for some time" (161). The fear and guilt produced by the stranger's proposition may have emanated from sources deeper than Rousseau is willing to explore here. Given his bisexual tendencies, he may have been shocked not only because the stranger presented him with the graphic mirror of his own "vice" but also because of the homoerotic element of the stranger's proposition—so shocked that he can deal with it only by flight.

The test case for this hypothesis may be the night Jean-Jacques ends up spending with the homosexual priest, who accosts the down-and-out vagabond and offers him "for that night, the half of his [bed]" (162). If this had been the adolescent's first such encounter, the episode might be credible as it stands. But given his experience at the hospice and his more recent meeting with the phallic stranger, Rousseau's account of his night in bed with the priest has a disingenuous air that smacks of bad faith. "I accepted his proposal, for I had already hopes that I had made a friend who might be useful to me" (162). When inevitably the sexual advances come ("this man had the same vice as my Jew at the hospice, but did not display it so brutally"), Jean-Jacques comes across as a male Pamela: "[H]e did not venture to propose what he wanted openly but tried to excite me without alarming me. Less ignorant than on the previous occasion, I quickly realized his purpose, and shuddered. Not knowing in what sort of house or in whose hands I was, I was afraid that if I made a noise I might pay for it with my life. I pretended not to know what he wanted, but by showing that I much disliked his attentions and was determined to put up with no more of them, I succeeded in compelling him to control himself" (162). When Rousseau accepted the priest's offer to share his bed, he must surely have known what was in store for him. Since in the light of his previous experience he can no longer plead innocence or ignorance, his accepting the priest's offer and then being shocked by and refusing his advances leaves the whole episode in a questionable light, open to various unflattering constructions, from latent homosexual desires to his enjoyment of having men come on to him, of teasing them only to deny them.

Like his encounter with the predatory priest, Rousseau's experience with (or more accurately, perception of) social injustice comes when he is down and out. Having lost his way and "dying of hunger and thirst," he enters "a peasant's cottage, which did not look too fine but was the only dwelling [he] could see in the locality" (159). The peasant offers the young beggar "some skimmed milk and coarse barley bread, and said he had nothing else." When the host sees that the famished young man devours this miserable fare with obvious "delight," he decides he is not a spy of the tax collectors, opens a trap door, and returns "with a nice brown wheaten loaf, a ham . . . and a bottle of wine." "He gave me to understand that he hid his wine on account of the excise and his bread on account of the duty, and that he would be a lost man if they suspected for a moment that he was not dying of hunger" (159). If the punishment of the broken comb and his abuse by his engraving master had sensitized Rousseau to the issue of social injustice, the realization that this man "dared not eat the bread he had earned by the sweat of his brow" planted the seed "of that inextinguishable hatred which afterwards grew in [his] heart against the oppression to which the unhappy people are subject, and against their oppressors" (160, 159). Rousseau's explanation here strikes the opening note, as it were, of the French Revolution, and grounds in his own experience the republican values he was to champion in his political writings.

Equally important for later cultural developments are Rousseau's *plein air* enjoyment of nature, which is acknowledged in this book and surfaces periodically throughout *The Confessions,* particularly in the lyrical celebration of his life at "Charmettes" at the beginning of book 6. His invocation of the solitary pleasures of nature strikes a countertone of authenticity in a sequence replete with the false identities and masks associated with his (marginal) life in society: "[N]ever have I been so much myself . . . as in the journeys I have taken alone and on foot. . . . The sight of the countryside, the succession of pleasant views, the open air, a sound appetite, and the good health I gain by walking . . . the absence of everything that makes me feel my dependence . . . all these serve to free my spirit . . . to throw me, so to speak, into the vastness of things. . . . I dispose of all Nature as its master" (157–58).

His landscape description at the close of book 4, when he has finally heard from "Mamma" and is en route to join her in her new residence at Chambéry, anticipates the Romantic rhetoric of the sublime:

> The wandering life is what I like. To journey on foot, unhurried, in
> fine weather and in fine country . . . that is of all ways of life the one
> that suits me best. It is already clear what I mean by fine country.
> Never does a plain, however beautiful it may be, seem so in my
> eyes. I need torrents, rocks, firs, dark woods, mountains, steep

roads to climb or descend, abysses beside me to make me afraid. . . .
At a place called Chailles . . . there runs boiling through hideous
gulfs below the high road . . . a little river which would appear to
have spent thousands of centuries excavating its bed. The road has
been edged with a parapet to prevent accidents, and so I was able to
gaze into the depths and make myself as giddy as I pleased. (167)

What we witness here in passing is the same geography and sensibility
that Wordsworth celebrated in book 6 of *The Prelude*, when some six
decades after Rousseau's trip from Lyons to Chambéry, the Cambridge
student made a foot journey to the Alps.

The Ambiguous Presentation of the Happy Ménage à Trois

When Rousseau was reunited with "Mamma" late in 1731 in her new residence in Chambéry, he had come back home to stay for good. At the time
he was nineteen and she thirty-two. Chambéry remained his home base,
and Mme de Warens the emotional center of his life for almost a decade,
until he accepted a position as a tutor in Lyons in 1740. This period com-
prises the remainder of part 1 of *The Confessions,* until his departure for
Paris in 1742 to make a name for himself with his invention of a mathemat-
ical scheme of musical notation. Life in his new home was not as idyllic as
Rousseau would have liked it to be in the romantic script of his imagination. Though he tries to idealize his relationship with Mme de Warens as
much as possible, books 5 and 6 show how his dream of the perfect mother
was rendered problematic by her taking the initiative to make him her
lover, as well as by his involvement in two troubled ménages à trois, one of
which led to a tragic outcome while the other effectively put an end to the
happy romance of "Mamma" and "the Little One." What further complicates his account of his relationship with Mme de Warens is his inability,
despite a real interpretive struggle, to get an objective purchase on this
most "paradoxical" of women, (Cranston, *Early Life* 80) and what appears
to be a self-serving distortion of what really happened, including an unreliable presentation of facts and chronology.[21]

Even without any independent biographical information, a careful
reading of the text suggests that Rousseau is using autobiography here to
cover some of his biographical tracks, as well as to paint as positive and
generous a portrait as possible of his benefactress. In creating his memo-

rial portrait of her several years after her death in 1762, he does not deny some of the compromising character traits of her moral physiognomy—particularly her unconventional sexual mores—but he always presents these in the best and most attractive light possible. What is also striking is that while his interpretation of her character and conduct seems to err fairly consistently on the side of generosity, his narrative is so artfully arranged as to allow the reader to draw different and less generous conclusions. The interpretive benefit of the doubt that he so liberally applies to his presentation of her extends also to himself, his conduct, and his motives in the two ménages à trois. In many ways his characterization of "Mamma" is a masterful but ultimately open-ended tribute that gives us Rousseau's own biased—sanitized and nostalgic—interpretation without preventing us from reaching very different conclusions. Rousseau struggles in his portrait with the dilemma of the autobiographer to be fair to, but not to speak ill of, the departed.

Rousseau reveals the relationship between Mme de Warens and her steward, Claude Anet, at the beginning of book 5, at the time he himself claims to have discovered it—that is, when Anet attempted suicide by swallowing opium and "Mamma" called on Jean-Jacques to help revive him, revealing in the process that Anet was her lover (172). If it seems naive of the adolescent not to have guessed at the nature of their relationship earlier, when he lived with her in Annecy, it is downright misleading to present Anet's suicide attempt as having nothing to do with Rousseau's reappearance on the scene. In this case, the reader's *post hoc, ergo propter hoc* inference about Anet's attempt may not be a fallacy. Perhaps this circumspect but passionate retainer, unlike his younger rival, already saw what was coming and impulsively gave in to the despair of seeing himself as a supernumerary presence in the household he effectively supervised. Some eight years Jean-Jacques's senior, Anet must have known from his own experience of Mme de Warens's penchant for younger, socially inferior men in a position of dependence on her.

The gardener's son from Vevey had already been in Mme de Warens's employ when she, who had been a child bride at fourteen, abandoned her husband and her Protestant faith some thirteen years after her marriage by crossing Lake Geneva to the Catholic kingdom of Sardinia and throwing herself dramatically on her knees before the Bishop of Annecy as he was entering the cathedral with the king.[22] Her theatrical and well-timed embrace of Catholicism gained her the personal protection of the bishop and an annual pension from the king, which in the short run saved the prodigal young woman, who in fact ruined her husband by leaving him to face the creditors for the considerable debts she had run up. The young Anet, who may already have been her lover then (Cranston, *Early Life* 77), followed his mistress into Sardinia and embraced her new religion as well. Obviously Anet cannot have been too pleased when Mme de Warens took such a lively interest in this young runaway and recent convert and in the end made him a permanent member of her household.

We do not know if Rousseau discovered or guessed at the nature of the relationship between his benefactress and her servant any earlier than he asserts he did, or if he ever came to know its full history. Nor does he claim to have had any awareness of her intention to make him her lover (an "idea, which all the time I had been living with her had never once come into my head," 187). The attractive young woman who had made such an artful spectacle of her dramatic conversion ("In manus tuas domine commendo spiritum meum," she said to the bishop), also took theatrical measures to seduce "The Little One," probably on his twenty-first birthday (Cranston, *Early Life* 107). Rousseau presents her initiative in this matter as part of her larger scheme of forming his character, which is part of the theme of education that surfaces repeatedly in the last two books of part 1. In many ways Rousseau's view of women is the conventional one of his age and culture, including the notion, expressed in book 5 of *Emile,* that women should receive a limited education primarily geared to pleasing and serving men. However, perhaps due largely to the impact of Mme de Warens, in his *Confessions* (unlike in *Emile,* where the boy's all-controlling tutor is male), he is willing to assign a significant pedagogic role to women. In book 4 he observes that "there is no doubt that interesting and sensible conversation with a good woman is more capable of forming a young man's mind than all the pedantic philosophy in books" (166), and in book 5 he acknowledges the benefit of his intimate conversation with her after he has become her lover. "[A]ll the moralizing of a pedagogue will never be as good as the affectionate and tender chatter of an intelligent woman for whom we feel an affection" (192). Thus the rigid patriarchal view of education that informs *Emile* is in effect revised and feminized in his autobiography through the role he credits "Mamma" with playing in his *Bildung.*

Rousseau takes seriously "Mamma's" pedagogic professions in her proposal that they become lovers, that is, her resolve to "treat [him] like a man" in order to save him from "the dangers of [his] youth" inherent in the schemes of predatory and manipulative women who have taken an interest in the young music tutor. "[A]nd this she did, but in the most singular fashion that ever occurred to a woman in like circumstances. I found her expression more serious and her conversation more moral than usual" (186). Her unusual program of sex education reverses traditional gender roles, since she takes the active and Jean-Jacques the passive role, and it also seems cleverly to establish a genuine female counter-seduction ploy to the arts that men have traditionally been accused of using to seduce women. In her own way, "Mamma" is a liberated woman before her time. Although Rousseau fully credits her avowed motives, his narrative allows the reader to draw different conclusions, among them Guéhenno's tart observation that she had a "self-indulgent and vulgar soul and was an excellent comedienne" (56). "She suggested a walk in the little garden for the next day; and early in the morning we were there. She had made arrangements for us to be left alone all that day, which she employed in preparing me for the favours she intended to grant me, not as any other woman would, by artifices and provocation, but by conversation full of feeling and good sense, better calculated to instruct me than to seduce me, and addressed to my heart rather than to my senses" (186). The education of the heart here is crucial, because Rousseau seeks to attenuate or circumscribe the physicality of their coming intercourse. The teacher's lesson, however, is not very effective for her student, because he "only thought of her, but did not listen to her" (187). As a pedagogue, "Mamma" commits the same error Rousseau himself admits to as a theorist of education: "To try and make young people attend to the lesson you wish to give them by dangling in front of their eyes the prospect of something very interesting to follow is a most common mistake in teachers, and one that I did not myself avoid in my *Emile*" (187).

Mme de Warens gives Rousseau eight days to think over her proposal, an interval for which he is grateful, because "I dreaded what I desired, to the point of sometimes seriously searching my brains for some honorable excuse for evading my promised happiness" (187). It is when Rousseau seeks to account for his sense of "dread" that he comes up against an interpretive wall: "How was it that instead of the delight which should have intoxicated me I felt almost repugnance and fear?" (188). He is at pains to dismiss the suspicion of "the reader, already disgusted," that "as she was already the mistress of another man, she degraded herself in my eyes by dividing her favours" (188), and claims in what sounds like a bravura piece of sophistry that he was fully convinced of the disinterestedness of her behavior: "I knew her chaste heart and her icy disposition too well to believe for a moment that the pleasure of the senses had any part in this surrender of herself. I was perfectly certain that only her anxiety to preserve me from the dangers otherwise almost inevitable, and to preserve me entire for myself and my duties, forced her to infringe a law that she did not look upon with the same eye as other women" (189). What then is the impediment, the pain, the fear, the dread? It is only now that Rousseau's emotional resistance to sexual intercourse with "Mamma," despite all his accumulated passion and desire for her, forces him into a perplexed encounter with the hitherto largely unconscious and internalized incest taboo. "By calling her Mamma and treating her with the familiarity of a son, I had grown to look on myself as such; and I think that is the real cause of my lack of eagerness to possess her, even though she was so dear to me. I remember very well then my first feelings for her, though no stronger, were more voluptuous" (189).

Having come directly up against the incest prohibition, however, Rousseau fails to process its significance fully and instead throws up his hands in perplexity, in a repetition and modification of his earlier formula ("a tender mother, a beloved sister, a delightful friend, and nothing more," book 3, 109). "She was to me more than a sister, more than a mother, more than a friend, more even than a mistress; and that is why she was not a mistress to me. In short I loved her too much to desire her; that is the clearest idea I have on the subject" (189). Unable to fully fathom, analyze, or explain his feelings for her, he mystifies her figure in a sort of hermeneutic impasse. And when he finally has intercourse with the embodiment of the dominating and maternal woman who has been the erotic focus of his fantasy life since at least the spanking by Gabrielle Lambercier, "the day more dreaded than desired" is a disappointment. "I tasted the pleasure, but I knew not what invincible sadness poisoned its charm. I felt as if I had committed incest and, two or three times, as I clasped her rapturously in my arms I wet her bosom with my tears" (189–90). The lover in her arms is transformed into the weeping child at her bosom. Was this sexual experience with Jean-Jacques as much a failure for her as it was for him, and did either of the two roles enacted by the child-man give this childless and rather promiscuous woman any pleasure or satisfaction? And was Mme de Warens still *acting* in the intimacy of her bed? "As she was not at all sensual and had not sought for gratification, she neither received sexual pleasure nor knew the remorse that follows" (190).

The sexual history of "Mamma" that Rousseau presents in the next two pages is a masterpiece of diplomatic understatement and damage control. The bottom line is that while he acknowledges her essential promiscuity, her motives are seen as never less than honorable. "[T]hough she did not rate her favours at their true worth, she never made a common trade in them; she conferred them lavishly but she did not sell them, though continually reduced to expedients in order to live" (191). In his paradoxical attempt to excuse her "less excusable qualities," Rousseau turns the Enlightenment rhetoric of reason on its head: "[I]nstead of listening to her heart, which gave her good counsel, she listened to her reason which gave her bad" (190). Her feelings are always "true," but "false principles led her astray"; "she prided herself on her philosophy, and the morality she invented for herself corrupted that which her heart dictated" (190). One suspects that Rousseau is getting in some digs here at the *philosophes* with whom he had broken—although in the paradoxical assertion of the *Discourse on Inequality*, which Diderot and d'Alembert admired and defended, reason is already equated with depravity. According to Rousseau, Mme de Warens's morals were corrupted by the specious reasoning of her first extramarital lover and philosophy tutor, who "succeeded in persuading her that adultery in itself was nothing, and was only called into existence by scandal, and that every woman who appeared virtuous by that mere fact became so. Thus the wretch achieved his purpose by corrupting the mind of a child whose heart he could not corrupt" (190).

The child bride has been compromised by a false education. Thus by Rousseau's own sentimental standards—the values of the "heart"—she stands before us essentially still unblemished, despite all her questionable sexual morality. She is also vindicated on the grounds that she does not even enjoy sex. "She could not imagine that so much importance could be attached to something which had none for her; and never dignified with the name of virtue an abstinence which cost her so little" (190). Because Rousseau knows that this portrait, rife with contradiction, will not pass unchallenged by his readers, he himself anticipates their objection without effectively answering it, a purely rhetorical move. "By ascribing to her a sensitive character and a cold nature, I know in advance that I shall be accused, as usual, of being contradictory, and with no more reason than usual. It is possible that Nature was at fault, and that such a combination should not have existed; I only know that it did exist" (191–92). So after having sought to defend her by blaming her conduct on a false social morality, he is now even willing to impugn his chief criterion of value, nature itself. Rousseau ends his elegiac tribute with a generous compliment that he again feels called upon to support with a defensive gesture. "[S]he knew only one true pleasure in the world, and that was to give pleasure to those she loved. Nevertheless anyone is at liberty to argue the matter as he will, and prove learnedly that I am wrong. My function is to tell the truth, not to make people believe it" (192).

The portrait of this fascinating woman must remain forever an enigma, because we can really never obtain her point of view, although her behavior as reported by Rousseau allows for a very different construction from the generous and euphemistic one placed on it by her erstwhile protégé. It may well be that this woman of "heart" also had not only a sensitive but a passionate temperament, and that she sought out sexual relationships with younger men precisely because she enjoyed them. Perhaps they allowed her to mingle her maternal and her libidinal impulses. We do know that the religious current of Pietism played a crucial role in her early education and was perhaps "the most decisive influence" (Cranston, *Early Life* 69). The emotional intensity and the hothouse atmosphere of belief in the spiritual authority of intuitive feeling and of the passionate, inward justification of faith that defined this revolutionary eighteenth-century German religious movement may have conditioned Mme de Warens's adult cultivation of the values of sensibility and the "heart" (as we see it, for instance, in a very different key in the confession of the Pietist "beautiful soul" in Goethe's *Wilhelm Meister's Apprenticeship*). In the case of Mme de Warens, this cultivation of intense feeling may have readily crossed over from the religious into the erotic sphere. As an eighteenth-century woman of passion, she must have known only too well that an open display of enjoying sex with different partners was utterly unacceptable for a respectable woman; thus, perhaps, the pose or cover of having an icy disposition and deriving no pleasure from intercourse — a selfless and benevolent giving of herself, a pastoral task even, like those she undertook for the Catholic Church on a semiofficial basis.

Such a scenario, of course, is pure speculation. Did Rousseau ever suspect it, despite what he writes? It would have been uncavalier, an act of ingratitude, even of betrayal of the woman who benefited him in so many ways. In characterizing the happy ménage à trois (consisting of "Mamma," himself, and Claude Anet), Rousseau momentarily and wittily entertains such a perspective (significantly, one credited to the suspicious female reader), only to dismiss it out of hand in the name of the "heart." "How many times did she melt our hearts and cause us to embrace in tears, by telling us that we were both necessary for her life's happiness! And let not any woman who reads this give a malicious smile! With a temperament such as hers, there was nothing dubious about this need; it was simply that of her heart" (194). The romance of the happy threesome sounds too good to be true for this flesh-and-blood world, though Rousseau tried to capture it in some sense in the sublimated fiction of St. Preux, Julie, and Wolmar in the earthly paradise of Clarens in *The New Héloïse:* "Thus between the three of us was established a bond perhaps unique on this earth. Our every wish and care and affection was held in common, none of them extending outside our little circle" (194). This is clearly a sentimental fiction, especially since, all too soon, Claude Anet was dead.

What went wrong? Rousseau's biographers are inclined to believe that the facts are doctored and that his account of Anet's sudden demise is deceptive as well. Even though he is in a subservient position as Mme de Warens's steward, Anet is described as "mature and grave" (193) and invested in her household with a considerable amount of "authority" (198). Within three pages of Rousseau's idyllic characterization of their *ménage,* Anet is reported dead from an illness resulting from "an expedition to the mountain-tops in search of genipi" for a local doctor (197)—in March 1743, when the genipi would still have been under a blanket of snow. The biographers suspect a different cause; Guéhenno guesses at "a silent small-town drama" (56), and Cranston conjectures "that Anet's fatal illness was of psychological origin, brought on, like his earlier attempt to poison himself, by jealousy of Rousseau" (*Early Life* 110).

Given Rousseau's characterization of Anet as older and wiser, it is plausible that at least in his imagination this love triangle had the configuration of a family romance, with Anet scripted as the Oedipal father/older brother (compare Wolmar in *The New Héloïse*). Even though the text fails to acknowledge the true cause or nature of Anet's untimely death, perhaps because of Rousseau's guilty role as the rival who replaced him, Rousseau can at least be generous in his downfall. Thus Anet is eulogized as "a rare and estimable man . . . who, though in the position of a servant, possessed all the virtues of a great man, only lacking, perhaps, in order to prove himself one to all the world, some more years of life and a suitable post" (197)—in sum, a sort of double or precursor of Jean-Jacques. One loaded clue that Rousseau provides for such a psycho-biographical reading is his confession that on the day after Anet's death, in the middle of a conversation with Mme Warens, "the vile and unworthy thought came to me that I should inherit his clothes, and particularly a fine black coat which had caught my fancy. No sooner did it occur to me than I gave utterance to my thought; for in her presence thought and speech were to me as one" (197). The "thought" that he fails to censor may not be so much the heedless selfishness and greed that he thinks he is confessing to, but the unconscious wish to take Anet's place—which is, ironically, precisely what happens. "When he was gone, I was compelled to take his place, but I had neither the taste nor the aptitude for it, and filled it badly" (198). Rousseau of course means Anet's place as the manager of Mme de Warens's domestic affairs, "which never ceased to deteriorate" after his death. But there is surely also an unintentional pun here on taking Anet's place as her lover, which is a reading that gains plausibility in the light of his conflicted attitude about his sexual relations with "Mamma."

Charmettes and the Great Betrayal

Rousseau's failure to effectively take Anet's place in Mme de Warens's affairs sets up the second ménage à trois, which is not a happy one even on the surface, and which is also presented with an obvious *ressentiment* as well as what appears to be an artful arrangement of facts. Between these two triangles, however, lies the romantic dream or idyll of Charmettes, the exact dates and the veracity of Rousseau's account of which have occasioned a good deal of scholarly controversy.[23] Whatever the exact dates of his stay in this pastoral retreat or even the actual facts of his life there with and without "Mamma," Charmettes clearly occupies a privileged place in Rousseau's nostalgic imagination, as a kind of extended "spot of time" that along with the Fifth Revery has done much to create the romantic image of Rousseau, the lyrical poet of the timeless moment and of the plenitude of being. In the service of affective memory, Rousseau wants to stop or suspend his narrative, through a rhetoric of celebratory recollection that makes it clear that the pleasure given by Charmettes resides as much in the moment of writing about it as in the actual experiences recollected. Rousseau's idealizing and hyperbolic language creates the effect of an emotional tautology:

> Here begins the short period of my life's happiness; here I come to those peaceful but transient moments that have given me the right to say I have lived. Precious and ever-regretted moments, begin to run your charming course again for me! Flow one after another through my memory, more slowly if you can, than you did in fugitive reality! What shall I do to prolong this touching and simple tale, as I should like to; endlessly to repeat the same words, and no more weary my readers by their repetition than I wearied myself by beginning them for ever afresh? (215)

The famous lyrical overture of book 6 foregrounds the theme of paradise regained. The paratactic sentences and the quasi-biblical rhythms add up to a prose poem commemorating Rousseau's newfound joy and innocence. "I rose with the sun, and I was happy; I went for walks, and I was happy; I saw Mamma, and I was happy; I left her, and I was happy; I strolled through the woods and over the hills, I wandered in the valleys, I read, I lazed, I worked in the garden, I picked the fruit, I helped in the household, and happiness followed me everywhere; it lay in no definable object, it was entirely within me; it would not leave me for a single moment" (215).

The nostalgic merging of memory and imagination in the lyrical movement of writing is a compensatory strategy for his lack of happiness in the present: "My imagination, which in my youth always looked forward but now looks back, compensates me with these sweet memories for the hope I have lost forever" (216). But how happy, really, was he at Charmettes? Not very, as the precipitous descent of his prose into the prosaic (after his famous description of the periwinkle [pervanches] incident) indicates: "However, the country air did not restore me to my former health. I was languid, and became more so" (216). Already at the close of book 5

Rousseau had retreated from his troubled role as lover. Through hypochondriac illness, he had sought to regress into an infantile dependence with which he could monopolize the attentions of "Mamma": "I became entirely her concern, entirely her child, and more so than if she had been my real mother" (212–13). "Mamma" even prescribed milk for him, and it was at his request that they had retired from the town and its social demands to the "pleasant solitude" of the country. But once ensconced at Charmettes, Rousseau's hypochondria deepened into the mania that "[he] had not long to live" (217)—an obsession or delusion that haunted him periodically throughout his life. In one sense, his expectation of impending death was productive, for it stimulated his "taste for study" (222). Rousseau in his mid-twenties undertook an impressively disciplined and systematic course of self-education in the liberal arts. But his health, he claims, continued to deteriorate. The heart palpitations and the "vapours" ("being the malady of happy people" 235) point to neurosis and depression—perhaps due in part to his unresolved feelings about "Mamma"?

At this juncture in book 6 Rousseau seems to depart significantly from the actual facts of his situation. He has just mentioned a trip to Geneva in 1737 in which he successfully claimed his share of his mother's fortune. It was apparently upon his return from this trip that he discovered that another young man—like himself a Protestant convert to Catholicism and soon enough also the lover of Mme de Warens—was very visibly ensconced in the household of his benefactress (Guéhenno 84, Cranston, *Early Life* 127–28). Were "Mamma" and Jean-Samuel Wintzenried already lovers, and did Rousseau discover this fact then? We do not know, but it is clear that the appearance of this strapping and boisterous young man threatened his relationship with "Mamma" and his privileged position as the pampered man-child in her home. Rousseau, however, presents his discovery that he has been displaced by Wintzenried as coming *after* his return from his trip to Montpellier for a medical cure, when in fact the presence of his new rival may have been the real motive for his departure. Rather than acknowledge this motive, he claims that he went to Montpellier because his study of anatomy and physiology had convinced him that he was suffering from a "polypus of the heart" (236). Thus his alleged reason for the trip is an imaginary disease.

Once again homeless and adrift, Rousseau relapses into his old vagabond's tricks. As in the Vaussore de Villeneuve sequence, he seeks to transform a new bout of impersonation into a novelistic episode. The romance on the road with Mme Suzanne-Françoise de Larnage, in which he takes on the identity of a Jacobite Englishman, Mr. Dudding (although he speaks no English and thus risks easy exposure of his ridiculous alias), is entertaining enough, stylized as it is and punctuated with relevant literary allusions to signal its comic and picaresque character (the comedies of Marivaux, Scarron's *Roman comique*). Stripped of its novelistic trappings, his affair with the forty-five-year-old mother of ten children is also quite sordid, even if it is understandable: again it is a maternal and older woman who takes the initiative and goes out of her way to seduce him. His summary of this process is one of the wittiest passages in *The Confessions:* "[S]he undertook my conquest, and it was good-bye to poor Jean-Jacques, or rather to his fever, his *vapours,* and his polypus. It was good-bye to everything when in her company, except certain palpitations which remained and of which she did not wish to cure me" (237). As in his seduction by "Mamma," there is something of a reversal of traditional gender roles in this adventure, with Jean-Jacques playing the shy or coy feminine part to the dominating role enacted by the sexually predatory female. Ironically, it is in his fictional identity as Mr. Dudding that Rousseau claims, "for once, I was myself" (239) in his lovemaking. This traveler's romance—as intense at it is temporary—is untroubled by the sadness and guilt that cloud his sexual relations with "Mamma." "With Mme de Larnage . . . I was proud of my manhood and good fortune . . . I shared the sensuality I roused in her, and was sufficiently master of myself to look on my triumph with as much pride as pleasure, and thereby to derive the wherewithal to repeat it" (241). An unacknowledged element of his pleasure in this affair may have been the need, as Guéhenno suggests (85), to revenge himself on "Mamma" for her betrayal.

After his medical vacation in Montpellier, where he is properly diagnosed by the doctors as a hypochondriac (245), Rousseau presents his decision to return to "Mamma" as an act of moral strength, because he is passing up Mme de Larnage's offer to spend the winter in her home. But he also makes it clear that he has gotten cold feet about resuming his affair. His expressed fear at falling in love with her daughter seems a pretext for his concern that he will not be able sustain the sexual ardor he successfully demonstrated on the road. In this equivocal context, his reasoning—that by returning to Mme de Warens, who has sacrificed financially for his trip and whom he has deceived "most disgracefully," he is "putting duty before pleasure" (246)—seems specious. By thus occupying the moral high ground, he will make her seem that much more uncaring and guilty when he describes himself returning to find his place taken by Wintzenried. He sets up the anticlimactic scene of his homecoming to resemble that of a latter-day prodigal son. But there is no rejoicing at his repentant return, only indifference, even though he had "written to Mamma . . . announcing the day and hour of [his] return" (247).

Rousseau plays the traumatic little scene for all it is worth. Why does the autobiographer rescript the biographical sequence of his life to relocate the discovery of his displacement at this juncture? Perhaps in part for dramatic purposes; it makes a better story. And probably also because it makes him look better and "Mamma" worse; it glosses over the charge of getting even that may have been part of his affair with Mme de Larnage; and it also shows him loyally returning to "Mamma" after his fling with another woman, ready to put duty before pleasure. It is a heartwarming scenario. And what is his reward? Her nonchalant betrayal:

> The maid seemed surprised to see me; she did not know that I was expected. I went upstairs and saw my dear Mamma at last, whom I loved so tenderly, so deeply, so purely. I ran to her, and threw myself at her feet. 'Oh, so you have come, little one,' she exclaimed and embraced me. 'Have you had a good journey? How are you?' This reception set me back a little. I asked her whether she had received my letter. She answered, yes. 'I should have thought you had not,' I replied, and the explanation ended there. There was a young man with her. I recognized him, for I had seen him about the house before I left. But now he seemed to be established there, and he was. In short, I found my place filled. (247–48)

Rousseau's sense of betrayal by his foster mother is surely unconsciously linked in his imagination with the first and most traumatic abandonment in his life, the death of his mother. Wintzenried, his successful rival, becomes something of a whipping boy for Mme de Warens's moral frailty. His attempt to be fair to Wintzenried despite his obvious dislike of him leads to the most unintentionally funny characterization in *The Confessions:* "He was vain and stupid, ignorant and insolent, but in other ways the best fellow in the world" (248). Rousseau's unflattering portrait of his betrayal by his adoptive mother may also be intended to get back at her decades after the fact, in a kind of final reckoning. Perhaps this is the reason for his explicit apology to her for having shown her in such a questionable light. Again he seeks to occupy the moral and rhetorical high ground: "[P]ardon me, dear and honoured shade, if I have been no kinder to your faults than to my own and reveal them both alike to the eyes of my readers! I must and will speak as truthfully about you as about myself" (248). In his attempt at a final judgment he gives her the same benefit of the doubt that he consistently demands for himself: "You made mistakes, but you were never wicked. Your behaviour was culpable, but your heart was always pure" (248). In a sentence omitted in the English translation, he asks the reader for a balanced judgment: "[O]ne should put the good and the bad in balance, and one should be equitable" (*Oeuvres* 1:262). In Rousseau's defensive morality, "equitable" really means that both he and "Mamma" should be judged not by their conduct but by their good intentions. Thus his judgment of his mistress-mentor-mother is also self-reflexive and anticipates the apologetic gambit of his *Dialogues* (subtitled "Rousseau Judge of Jean-Jacques").

The casual betrayal by "Mamma" is the darkest moment in part 1 of *The Confessions,* the most fundamentally painful because it repeats the trauma of his first loss; it reactivates it and makes him reexperience its inexplicable shock. "Suddenly my whole being was thrown completely upside down. To judge of it, let my reader put himself in my place. In one moment I saw the happy future I had depicted for myself vanish for ever. All the sweet dreams I had indulged with such affection disappeared; and I, who even from childhood had never contemplated my existence apart from hers, found myself for the first time alone. It was a frightful moment; and those which followed it were just as dark" (249). The motif of darkness anticipates the later portions of part 2 of *The Confessions.* It can be argued, of course, that Rousseau betrayed Mme Warens more than she betrayed him. He proved a hapless lover and a worse manager of her household affairs; he helped to deplete the very finances that he should have helped to shore up; he had an affair with another woman that he never even told her about. She needed a more effective live-in companion and helper and chose the physically robust Wintzenried to fill the part. But all of that fundamentally does not matter. What does is the psychic script, which is what

Rousseau re-creates in his autobiography, and in that script he is unequiv-
ocally the one who is betrayed and abandoned.

The worldly Mme de Warens, naturally, did not see it that way. To
Rousseau's threat, which allies him with the fate of the fallen Anet—"this
will kill me, but you will be sorry" (249)—she replies that he was "a child,
that no one died of such things" (250). She offers him the bargain that
Anet had to swallow earlier and apparently found impossible to digest:
"She gave me to understand . . . that all my rights remained unaltered, and
that by sharing them with another I should in no way be deprived of
them" (250). Rousseau plays his last card when he rejects this offer of a
continued sexual relationship as degrading for her, opting instead for the
role of chaste son in a sanitized ménage à trois that is clearly not the one
she had envisioned. "From that moment I never saw my beloved Mamma
again except with the eyes of a true son" (250)—but from that moment
also her interest in him seems to have steadily declined to the point of
indifference. Jean-Jacques tries to hang on and to make the best of a bad
situation, even cultivating "disinterestedness" and banishing "from [his]
heart . . . all feelings of hatred or envy against [his] supplanter" (250). He
seeks to play the part that Anet, at least on the surface, enacted so gener-
ously with him, but of course the new rival proves an unworthy subject:
"I wished . . . to form him, to work at his education, to make him realize
his good fortune and, if possible, to make him worthy of it; in a word, to
do for him what Anet had done for me under like circumstances" (250–51).
Actually, what Anet had done was to exit the unmanageable scene by
dying. It takes Rousseau some time to realize that he too is a supernumerary presence: "At length this illustrious personage [Wintzenried] succeeded in making himself all important in the house, and in reducing me
to a cipher" (251). Because "this life soon [becomes] absolutely unbearable
to" (252) him, he decides to accept a position in Lyons as a tutor.

What goes around comes around: as Jean-Jacques replaced Anet, Jean-
Jacques is in turn replaced by Wintzenried. There is a pattern of ironic
reversal in part 1 that Rousseau's narrative enacts but of which Rousseau
the narrator does not seem to be fully cognizant. The innocently accused
(the broken comb) becomes the accuser of innocence (the ribbon of Marion); the younger man who displaces an older rival is in due course himself dislodged by a younger rival. But Rousseau cannot quite accept this
latter development and tries one more emotional homecoming to

"Mamma" at the end of his year in Lyons. "I departed, I flew to her, and arrived in all the rapture of my early youth. Once more I was at her feet" (256). He returns only to discover that he cannot go home again, and it is on this note of loss and disillusionment that part 1 draws to its melancholy close. "How frightful are the illusions of human life! She received me once more with that kindness of heart which would be hers for so long as she lived. But I had returned to discover a past which no longer existed and which could not be reborn" (256).

Jean-Jacques's protracted and delayed adolescence, during which he tried to live out the fantasy of a restored family romance and home, is finally over. The *Bildungsroman* of his youth—which is also a *Verbildungsroman* (novel of deformation) and an *Einbildungsroman* (novel of imagination)—is achieved. From now on he will have to stand on his own two feet, enter the arena of society, and struggle for a place in the world. The successes and ultimate failure of that struggle are the confessional burden of part 2, which begins with so much hope and youthful energy of genius, only to founder in the dark passages of despair and the tightening meshes of the straitjacket of his mounting paranoia. But as Rousseau turns his back on "the errors and the faults of [his] youth" (257) in the hope of making his fortune in Paris, he wittily frames the aspirations inherent in his departure with the infinite pathos of ironic hindsight gained through bitter experience: "I left Savoy with the system of [musical] notation as once I had set out for Turin with my heron-fountain" (257).

In its multilayered psychological complexity, its sophisticated and sometimes genuinely perplexed confessional self-probing deployed in the service of both self-understanding and self-justification, and finally, in the narrative virtuosity and sophistication with which it creates a memorable and vivid portrait of Rousseau's early years, part 1 is an extraordinary and pioneering achievement in the autobiographical exploration of childhood and youth. Without it, Romantic autobiography as we see it flourishing in Wordsworth and Goethe, and in the *Bildungsroman* as it reaches its consummation in Stendhal (*The Red and the Black*) and Dickens (*David Copperfield* and *Great Expectations*) among others, would be literally unthinkable.

3 ✣

Autobiography as Resurrection

The *Dialogues*

What does it matter to me if men want to see me as other than I am?

— Rousseau, *Dialogues*

Rousseau's *Dialogues*, written between 1772 and 1776 in the wake of the perceived failure of his *Confessions* (completed in 1770), might be described as his unknown autobiography. If the latter is by far his most widely read and influential autobiography, the former, although still "the least read of Rousseau's important works" (Kelly and Masters 239), has recently been gaining some belated recognition as a major, if difficult and problematic, autobiographical text. Indeed, only during the past decade has it been translated into English[1] and begun to receive a measure of serious critical attention.[2] Unlike the sensational and frequently entertaining *Confessions*, the *Dialogues* are not reader-friendly. Repetitive, longwinded, and written in distracted fits and starts, as Rousseau acknowledges in his preface (*Oeuvres* 1:665–66), the *Dialogues* have traditionally been slighted as the product of Rousseau's descent into madness, even if some of his more sympathetic critics have granted that "although the work for the most part reads like a paranoid nightmare, it is occasionally illuminated by remarkable flashes of insight" (Grimsley 160). While deconstructive readings of the *Dialogues* look beyond the issue of Rousseau's paranoia to bring out the intricacy of his textual strategies, they see these as self-canceling in their inability to accomplish Rousseau's central apologetic purpose.[3]

Even so astute and subtle an interpreter of Rousseau as Starobinski was willing to reduce the *Dialogues* to the terms of a crass contradiction: they are caught up in an unproductive antithesis, because in them "there is no way of overcoming the conflict between immediacy and reflection" (*Transparency* 207). The *Dialogues* are a logical impossibility, "a reflection aimed against reflection" (211), and the "Rousseau who speaks to us is absolutely *alien* to the image that he constructs of himself. Therein lies his true alienation, in the psychiatric sense of the word" (212). Implicit in Starobinski's harsh diagnosis is the assumption that a man so alienated from himself cannot produce a viable autobiographical text, which in the classic (Gusdorfian) view of the genre is underwritten by a coherent identity. Starobinski's insistence on Rousseau's self-alienation and the fact that his "mind is divided into two warring camps, which no path joins together" (212) virtually characterizes the *Dialogues* as an anti-autobiography.

My reading of the *Dialogues,* conversely, is informed by the assumption that they represent a powerful and fundamental autobiographical impulse—and do so in a highly unusual and ingenious manner, and with a measure of burdened brilliance that perhaps can be appreciated only in the wake of such modernist nightmare fictions of pervasive persecution, paranoia, and alienation as Kafka's *The Trial* and *The Castle,* and in a postmodern age less unsettled by and more receptive to the "hall-of-mirrors" setting of Rousseau's text and the strategy of fictional "doubling," the effect of which "is to disorder the text and disorientate the reader" (O'Dea 142). In essence, the *Dialogues* are autobiography written in extremis, for they pose in radicalized form a problem faced by all autobiographers: How can they succeed in communicating to anybody—to any *other* human being—who and what they are, what they have been, thought, done? How can they ever get others to understand their sense of themselves, their experience of being in the world? The *Dialogues* are a special and extreme instance of this larger problem; the work is Rousseau's desperate and brilliantly manipulative attempt to communicate how he perceives himself to others. Given the tremendous obstacles and impediments that he feels are placed in the way of such a clarifying self-explanation, Rousseau chooses a strategy of stepping outside himself and writing autobiography in the third person, as a means of getting across or through to an audience that he is convinced is biased against him and cannot be reached by any other means. As he informs the reader in his preface to the work, the bind in which he finds himself necessitates that "I say how, if I were someone else [un autre], I would view a man such as I am" (*Oeuvres* 1:665).

The author of the *Dialogues* is a man suffering from a persecution mania, but one originating in and fueled by the actual persecution and misfortunes he experienced as a result of his unprecedented celebrity as a writer and thinker.[4] His influential books on politics and education, *The Social Contract* and *Emile,* were banned in Paris and Geneva, and Rousseau had to flee France to avoid an order for his arrest. The secular and religious authorities had combined to teach this too famous irritant of a philosopher a lesson. After his flight, he was expelled from various Swiss territories, including the island of Saint Pierre, where he had planned, as he tells us in his *Confessions,* to be able to spend the remainder of his days quietly. Even the house in Motiers where he resided for some time was stoned. To add insult to injury, Voltaire, offended by the powerful anti-Enlightenment polemics of the renegade *philosophe* and probably also jealous that Rousseau's star shone even more brightly than his own in the firmament of literary fame, published an anonymous pamphlet revealing to the public the dark secret of Rousseau's abandonment of his children to an orphanage upon their birth—a secret he had shared with only a few close friends. For Rousseau, the triumphs of his celebrity had turned into a terrible curse, and in his self-torturing imagination, the trials that might shake even a strong and stable personality took on the monstrous proportions of an all-encompassing conspiracy against him.

The paranoid conviction of a conspiracy already darkens the second half of *The Confessions* and expresses itself in strikingly metaphoric language that one might call his confessional gothic. At the beginning of part 2 he voices his somber suspicions: "The ceiling under which I live has eyes, the walls that enclose me have ears. . . . I know that despite the huge barriers which are ceaselessly erected all round me, they are always afraid that the truth will escape through some crack. How am I to set about piercing those barriers?" (book 7, 263). And in book 12 he describes his situation as hopeless: "Here begins the work of darkness in which I have been entombed for eight years past, without ever having been able, try as

I might, to pierce its hideous obscurity. In the abyss of evil in which I am sunk I feel the weight of blows struck at me; I perceive the immediate instrument; but I can neither see the hand which directs it nor the means by which it works" (544). He leaves to his "readers" the task of probing the "mysteries" of the "intrigue" against him, and of tracing it back to "the prime movers of it all." "I am absolutely certain what the results of their researches will be, but I lose myself in the obscure and tortuous windings of the tunnels which lead to it" (544). Rousseau writes much of part 2 of *The Confessions* distractedly, in a hurry, trying to emerge from his sense of imprisonment and obstruction, trying to get out of the labyrinth by finding the light at the end of the tunnel. As we saw in chapter 1, the work concludes on a note of disappointment and frustration, with an episode of a reading from it (in Paris in 1771) that fails to elicit from his aristocratic audience the sympathetic response that would release the author from his sense of isolated enclosure and cursed selfhood. Only silence greets the narrative of his misfortunes: The autobiographer's fate is that of Coleridge's Ancient Mariner.

By the time Rousseau writes the *Dialogues,* the darkness is complete, the barriers are insurmountable; there is apparently no way out of the labyrinth. All of his contemporaries without exception have been enrolled in the vast and mysterious conspiracy against him, a work of sublime and almost infinite proportions. The tropes of what might be called his confessional gothic are, as James F. Jones has observed, "pivotal images" (323) of the work: "[T]hey have raised around him walls of darkness impenetrable to his gaze; they have buried him alive among the living" (*Oeuvres* 1:706). Paris itself has become "a solitude more frightful than caverns or woods, where he finds in the midst of men neither communication nor consolation, nor counsel nor light, nor anything which could help him to find his way—an immense labyrinth where he is allowed to perceive in the darkness only false paths which mislead him more and more" (*Oeuvres* 1:713). The ground on which he walks is "undermined"; he is hemmed in by "triple walls of darkness" (*Oeuvres* 1:752), "shut up alive in a coffin" (827), "plunged" into "an abyss of shadows" and of "subterranean paths" (840). The metaphors of this congealed paranoia, which anticipate De Quincey's spectacular account of his opium-induced nightmares, focus sensationally Rousseau's sense of his fallen condition. He is completely manipulated by *them,* his unspecified and unspecifiable persecutors.

Rousseau, then, is the autobiographer buried alive and entombed. He is locked in a Piranesian prison of his own alienated imagination. That is, the conspiracy has systematically taken charge of his public image, disfigured it, hidden his genuine self under layers of lies, slanders, disinformation. His light is extinguished by their concerted campaign of darkness. This grotesque distortion, this monstrous fabrication, bears no relationship to the person he knows he is, to his sense of himself. The outer, perceived Rousseau, and the inner, virtual Rousseau are totally at odds. Because of the nature of the prejudice against him, appearance and reality have been divorced, so that his contemporaries see what they believe and not what they actually see.[5] In an orgy of self-flagellation, Rousseau takes to the limit the Romantic polarization of self and society, the dismal sense of being an alien and an outsider "without support, without parents, without help, without belonging to any part, and whose savage temperament tended by itself to isolate him" (*Oeuvres* 1:709). His self, as in the opening of his earlier *Confessions,* is still unique, but now sealed in a sinister celebrity that singles him out from all his fellow humans, past and present. Rousseau's rhetoric of persecution and martyrdom knows no restraint in its secret consummation of his megalomaniac impulse of self-exaltation. Not since the world has existed has any mortal found himself in a similar position.

If the *Dialogues* express with a powerful if obsessively repetitive insistence Rousseau's sense of being buried alive by his contemporaries, they also seek a way out of his impasse. In his earlier *Confessions,* Rousseau had written his defense and apology in the form of a first-person narrative of his life. In claiming to reveal everything about himself, even the most sordid details, he had hoped to reestablish his good faith and to gain the understanding and sympathy of his readers, only to discover that he had furnished his enemies with more ammunition. Having played into the hands of his persecutors, he needed a new strategy—not a narrative of his life, but a defense in which he could bring to bear the formidable dialectical skill that had made him famous as a discursive writer and *philosophe.* Thus his turn to the dialogue form, with which he was familiar from his reading of Plato and which was still practiced in the eighteenth century by major writers and thinkers (among them Diderot, *Rameau's Nephew;* Hume, *Dialogues Concerning Natural Religion;* Berkeley, *Dialogues between Hylas and Philonous*).[6] As a mode of argumentation and rhetoric since the

Greeks, the dialogue is a genre both philosophic and literary, and open to the voice of reason as well as that of emotion. The use of this form allows Rousseau to impart a semblance of logical order and dialectical argumentation to his paranoid obsession—it allows him at once to rationalize and give a tangible shape to his mounting anxieties, and to neutralize these in a complexly articulated defensive scheme.

One of the central apologetic motives of *The Confessions* is carried over into the *Dialogues:* to write autobiography as a public relations campaign. But in the alienated and masochistic imagination at work in the *Dialogues,* the scripted fans at the opening of *The Confessions,* "the numberless legion of [his] fellow men" (17) gathered to hear his confessions, have, by a nightmarish reversal, all turned into antagonists. The public image of him, which they believe to be the true Rousseau, is a sinister fabrication. In dialogue form, Rousseau will seek an accommodation, to regain or reconvert his lost fans. In the programmatic confessional and apologetic dialectic of the *Dialogues,* Rousseau will take the impossible plunge from the *je* to the *autre* and try to see himself as the hostile others see him, so that they in turn will come to see him as he sees himself.[7] His forensic and defensive strategy shows a remarkable lucidity of purpose in a text that too often has tempted its few readers and critics to write it off with a clinical judgment of mental derangement. But then Rousseau's madness, to paraphrase Wordsworth on Lord Byron, is more interesting than the sanity of most people. At the discursive level, Rousseau's *Dialogues* are by far his best and most impressive *apologia pro vita sua* by way of a complexly layered self or *autoportrait* (to use Michel Beaujour's term), that is much more effectively and coherently elaborated than anything in his more famous and influential *Confessions.* Even though he wrote another major autobiographical text at the end of his life, *The Reveries,* it is his last word to the public with respect to his career and his writings; it is the difficult but definitive confessional *summa* of his contributions as probably the most influential thinker and author of his age.[8]

The opening "Dialogue" sets up schematically Rousseau's apologetic dialectic in the conversation about "J. J." between the two speakers who are called "Rousseau" and "the Frenchman." "J. J." never appears and speaks *in propria persona* in the *Dialogues,* but his character, writings, and conversation are reported on and quoted at length in the work. The interlocutor "Rousseau," who like "J. J." hails from Geneva, and who like the author has grown increasingly disenchanted with a corrupt world and has turned for solace to his inner self, has formed a clear impression of the character of "J. J." strictly on the basis of his books. It is that of a noble soul dedicated to truth, virtue, and justice—which is of course the author's ideal self-image. He discerns in all the writings of "J. J." always the same maxims, "the most sweet, pure, and most energetic language of virtue" emanating from that "inner voice" that "all our philosophers" have tried so hard "to stifle" (*Oeuvres* 1:687). "The Frenchman," however, has a diametrically opposed view of "J. J." because he is the kindly but unsuspecting dupe of the conspiracy. He represents the hoodwinked French public vis-à-vis the "league" that has controlled public opinion in Europe and thus the reputation of "Jean-Jacques," which is that of a cunning scoundrel and hypocritical villain. The discrepancy between the perceptions of the same legendary person by the two speakers is such that "Rousseau" comes to the paradoxical conclusion that "the author of the books and that of the crimes are not the same man" (*Oeuvres* 1:690). To resolve this contradiction, "Rousseau" will visit the author he has only read, and "the Frenchman" will read the writer he has only heard about from others. The end result of this double movement is that the negative image of "J. J." will be erased and only the positive will remain.

After setting up at the outset this Manichean chiaroscuro of the saintly sage and the infernal villain, Rousseau offers in the second dialogue, by way of the speaker "Rousseau's" report to "the Frenchman" of his visit to "J. J.," a masterfully developed self-portrait. Unaffected by the slander that has sullied the public image of "J. J.," the unbiased "Rousseau" observes and reports on "J. J." as he really is—such is the rhetorical ploy with which, under the guise of complete objectivity, Rousseau elaborates his subjective and self-idealizing impression of himself by way of autobiography in the third person. Thus the gist of the central panel of the dialogic triptych is the author's *unburying* of himself and his reputation, and his attempt to make good on the failed apology of the earlier *Confessions* (which had met with the auditors' silence at its conclusion). As in the earlier autobiography, Rousseau here seeks to disarm the reader's judgment by insisting on his personal uniqueness, which is also the foundational claim of Romantic and modern autobiography and of the secular self's scripture of its irrefrangible and unrepeatable individuality: "[T]his man does not resemble any others that I know; he demands a separate analysis designed only for him" (*Oeuvres* 1:774). The complex and multilayered self-presentation in the second dialogue of Rousseau the man and the writer offers an anatomy of his larger character that presents in analytic form most of the material presented in the loosely structured, rambling, and picaresque life narrative of his earlier *Confessions*.[9] As a comprehensive disclosure of who and what he is, including all the contradictory and clashing elements of his personality, it affirms his strengths and virtues as a writer, thinker, and critic of modern culture in touch with the depths of his own being and of nature, but it does not eschew some harsh self-judgments, particularly the failure of the citizen of Geneva to live up to the standard of civic virtue, a weakness emphasized at the start of the second dialogue. "[H]e is a man without malice rather than a good man; a sound but feeble soul, who adores virtue without practicing it, who ardently loves the good but who hardly ever does it" (774). Balancing and complementing this self-criticism is the assertion, thematized repeatedly in the earlier narrative of the self-exculpating *Confessions*, that "all his faults, even the most serious, are but sins of omission" (825).

It is ironic but perhaps appropriate that Rousseau's most memorable, insightful, and balanced discursive self-assessment and analytic unpacking of his complex personality should take the form of an autobiography in the third person. This account, an interview or series of in-depth interviews by an informed reporter of his famous—or in this case infamous—subject, in some ways uncannily anticipates the mass media public relations "image" and even the tabloid culture in which we have become so immersed in our century. The motive behind Rousseau's concerted attempt to "unbury" himself and resurrect his reputation is his acknowledged passion—"the strongest and the most vain"—of "being loved" (*Oeuvres* 1:873). Conversely, the conspiracy that has sprouted in his estranged imagination from a few seeds of real persecution to gigantic proportions of sheer paranoia is also an expression of Rousseau's self-hatred. Thus at one level the *Dialogues* are the confessional psychomachia of the author's conflicted feelings about himself, of which the interlocutors "Rousseau" and "the Frenchman" are the fictional projections.

In this forensic exchange, "Rousseau" wins out over "the Frenchman," because in the third and concluding dialogue the latter's now laudatory view of "J. J." ends up mirroring that of "Rousseau." On the basis of an intensive reading of the writings of "J. J.," "the Frenchman's" unreflecting hostility has given way to an informed admiration for and sympathy with "J. J." and his ideas. In fact, in the overall conversion script of the *Dialogues*, "the Frenchman" has become his disciple and defender and presents a clear, concise, and valuable overview of Rousseau the philosopher's basic system available nowhere else in his writings.[10] In the first and second dialogues, the speaker "Rousseau" had already cited some possible motives for the conspiracy against the famous author: (1) professional envy—"the celebrity of an author whose past successes hurt the self-esteem [*amour propre*] of those who could not obtain similar results" (*Oeuvres* 1:733); and (2) the resentment of the high and mighty—his outspoken exposé of "that false social order which in fact covers the most cruel disorder" (887–88) had offended those in power. At the outset of the third dialogue, "the Frenchman" follows up on the second motive by quoting excerpts from the writings of "J. J." to demonstrate how his frank criticisms have earned him the resentment of various professions and parties: "[H]e knew that the great, the viziers, the lawyers, the financiers, the doctors, the preachers, the philosophers, and all the members of factions who make of society a veritable brigandage, would never forgive him for having seen and revealed them such as they are" (926). Thus, through the voice of the converted "Frenchman," Rousseau presents a concentrated apology and brief for his subversive philosophical writings, as well as a powerful explanation of the concerted hostile reaction against them and their author by a politically, intellectually, and religiously corrupt eighteenth-century establishment.

If this be madness, yet there is a method to it. As a powerfully orchestrated and highly polemical public relations campaign to "unbury" and restore his good name through a vigorous analysis of his character and his writings, Rousseau's *Dialogues* are a virtuoso autobiographical performance. In the wake of the perceived failure of *The Confessions,* he presents a confessional brief in the third person of who and what he is. In the first person he has failed to make his case; now his dialogic puppets will speak for him. Yet even as he speaks at length through the masks of the two interlocutors to save himself in this life, as it were, there is a Kafkaesque sense of futility at the difficulty of the task and the insurmountable obstacles placed in his path. He knows that his contemporaries are lost to him, yet he persists in writing in the face of that knowledge. He writes to save himself for the future, for posterity. In the last part of the third dialogue and the dramatic postscript to the work, his concern shifts explicitly to the issue of his posthumous reputation. "J. J." is reported to be interested in the reversion of the future, "the re-establishment of my memory and the return of the public esteem which was due to me" (*Oeuvres* 1:953). He is confident of his posthumous vindication because justice always prevails in the end and because it is "an axiom generally admitted that sooner or later the truth is revealed" (954). "The Frenchman," however, now no longer naive, is skeptical of this outcome, for it is impossible for us to know if truth always triumphs in time, and "it is more believable that effacing step by step its traces, time more often makes the lie triumph, particularly so when men have an interest in perpetuating it" (957).

While Rousseau voices through the pessimistic prognostications of "the Frenchman" an anti-Enlightenment suspicion about time as the instrumentality of truth, the assertion of "the Frenchman," targeted against Rousseau's enemies, could in the spirit of dialectic be turned against Rousseau himself. His public relations image is as fabricated and one-sided as that of the monstrous "J. J." circulated by his detractors. That Rousseau is not unaware of the possibility of such an antithetical reading of his *Dialogues* is evident in the ambivalent hopes and fears, expressed through his speakers, about the posthumous fate of his reputation. Included in the autobiographer's anxieties is the fear that his own writings will be falsified and disfigured, and, what is more, that under the guise of eulogy, prejudiced biographers will carry into the future the conspiracy's project of falsification and slander (*Oeuvres* 1:957–58). Autobiography as a preemptive strike against biography is one of the final motives behind the *Dialogues,* one founded in Rousseau's long-standing suspicions, expressed in book 4 of *Emile* (309–11), that historiography and biography are actually disguised and debased modes of fiction. In this work, Rousseau will leave a record for the future to counteract the continuing efforts of his enemies. Although Rousseau's two speakers agree that they are unable in the lifetime of "J. J." to combat a conspiracy impenetrable and totalitarian in its sinister articulation, they will dedicate themselves, "in the interest of justice and in the service of truth," to the work of redeeming for the future the defamed reputation of "a persecuted innocent" (974). They will leave to posterity "the trace of all the maneuvers" against "J. J." in order to "guide" those who come later through "this labyrinth" (973). They see this as not only an issue of justice but as "the work of providence" (973) itself. Thus, in the mania of his persecution, Rousseau scripts his ultimate vindication through the fiction of his two speakers.

Rousseau's dramatic postscript to the *Dialogues* recounts his desperate attempt to force the hand of providence by placing the manuscript of the work on the high altar of Notre Dame cathedral. When that effort is blocked, significantly enough, by the unexpected obstacle of a grill surrounding the altar that he had never noticed before on his many visits to the cathedral, and when, moreover, he is unable to find a trustworthy human depositary, he is reduced to his final, desperate public relations gesture—a leafleting campaign on the streets of Paris "to all Frenchmen who still love truth and justice" (*Oeuvres* 1:984). When this last, desperate act of self-justification also fails—not a single Parisian passerby accepts one of his handwritten bills—Rousseau has to let his hopes repose with and in the manuscript of the *Dialogues* and to place his trust for the future prospects of his name in the divine providence that had already appeared to rebuff his plea in the cathedral. With this final resolution, the text rounds back on and folds into itself. The metatextual sequence of the postscript has dramatized in acute form Rousseau's concern about the work's reception and its larger efficacy in persuading any audience other than himself. As an agonized revelation of his anxiety about himself and his singular position in the world, the postscript is not supplementary to but an essential part of the confession of who he is and how he views himself that is the *Dialogues*.

With the failure of his last campaign of self-justification, Rousseau throws up his hands and assumes a posture of complete passivity. He *almost* transcends his paranoia by taking it to its limit. His "last resolution" is no longer to do anything to combat his persecutors; he will "even abandon to them the honor of [his] name and [his] reputation in the future" (*Oeuvres* 1:989). Without taking any further initiatives, the martyred philosopher will trust in divine providence for a just judgment. In this concluding sentiment we already hear the attenuated rhetoric of the lyrical *Reveries,* where Rousseau's final autobiographical stance is that of someone utterly alone on earth, supposedly reconciled to his status as a recluse and outcast. Unlike Montaigne, he writes only for himself, for the pure joy of writing, and as a kind of barometer of his soul. Now he is completely at peace, entirely self-sufficient. But all the while that he insists in the *Reveries* that he is beyond others and their judgments, he is writing—posing, acting, posturing—before them. For Rousseau, autobiography is always one of the performing arts, and the writer he is, the social man of *amour propre*, cannot do without some sort of audience, even if an imaginary or future one. His fundamental need is to live in the regard—if not sympathetic, then hostile—of others.

In the second dialogue, the speaker "Rousseau" reports that "J. J." has written "in the form of a dialogue a type of judgment of them [his persecutors] and of himself which is quite similar to that which may result from our discussions" (*Oeuvres* 1:836). Speaking through his two confessional alter egos, the autobiographer watches himself in the mirror of his own imagination writing his autobiography. In what Williams characterizes as a textual *mise en abîme* and a "proliferation" of "discursive frames" (156), the text self-reflexively reports on itself. But where Williams sees "a loss of control and a disappearance of the author" (156), I see a hyper-Narcissus, as the author spies on himself—like the "league" of conspirators who have him constantly under surveillance. As he observes and doubles back on himself in his text, he also by implication watches us across the centuries, as and when—and if?—we read him. His specular hope is that we will confirm or legitimize him in his own eyes, and validate the version of himself created in an autobiographical text (the *Dialogues*) that is his most consequent and sophisticated rendering—by way of multiple personae—of his subjective mode of being in the world.[11] Like "the Frenchman" inside the text, the reader outside the text will be converted from a view of "J. J." as a corrupt man (the slanderous version of the first dialogue), to one of him as an exemplary but unjustly persecuted human being (the view of "J. J." of the second and third dialogues). Such at least is the author's hope and rhetorical strategy, which, if successful, would effectively import the reader outside the text into it. The hinge of this strategy is the device of autobiography in the third person, which is meant to make the reader's view of Rousseau coincide with Rousseau's self-image. In fact, his scheme is that of a totalizing if not totalitarian unity, a textual system that combines author and readers and merges their perceptions of "J. J." into a single identity. It is in this sense that the autobiographer in extremis of the *Dialogues,* who is seeking his own resurrection by making his future readers share his own sense of himself, is but a special case of the larger quest of all autobiographers to get others to see them as they see themselves.

"What does it matter to me if men want to see me as other than I am? Is the essence of my being in their looks?" (*Oeuvres* 1:985). Apparently it is. For Rousseau, to be is to be perceived, and his image meant everything to him. He was obsessed with a celebrity fueled by the legend of the natural sage utterly indifferent to celebrity. The rhetoric of his protracted self-writing moves from the bravado of a naked confessional appeal in his *Confessions,* to the intricate forensic puppet play of his *Dialogues,* to the posture of serene indifference of his *Reveries,* in which he claims to forget his detractors even as he reinscribes them within the system of his resentment, with his larger project of controlling his posthumous reputation still very much intact.[12] From first to last, the essence of his being was a function of how others looked at him, and his three autobiographies are a thoroughly calculated attempt to control and manipulate their views.

4 ❧

Goethe and Autobiography

The individual is lost; our memory of him disappears, and yet he is concerned that it should be preserved.

Each of us is himself only an individual and can really as such only interest himself in the individual. . . .

We love only the individual; thus the great joy in lectures, confessions, memoirs, letters and anecdotes of deceased and even insignificant individuals.

The question whether one should write one's own biography is highly improper. I consider him who does so the most polite of human beings.

So long as one communicates one's self it does not matter what one's motives are.

—Goethe, "Concerning Autobiography"

GOETHE'S PROJECT OF AN AUTOBIOGRAPHY

As is evident from the manuscript fragment above, Goethe's view of autobiography was a broad and generous one. And properly so, for autobiography, defined in the widest sense, was a pervasive mode and informing impulse of all of his prolific writings, which, in the famous formulation of book 7 of *Poetry and Truth,* are but fragments of a great confession (214). According to a recent estimate (Müller 259), the material that can be considered primarily autobiographical takes up some twenty of the forty volumes of the last collected edition supervised by Goethe himself (*Ausgabe letzter Hand*, 1830). The confessional impulse as such cuts across the different genres of Goethe's vast opus—poetic dramas, prose fictions, poetry—and even appears in his extensive scientific writings, whose aim was not only to express his view of nature but also "to reveal, as far as that is possible, my self, my inner world, my manner of being" ("Significant Help through a Single Witty Word," HA 13:37). Thus his writings on morphology include a chapter in which "The Author Communicates the History of His Morphological Studies" (HA 13:148–68), and his treatise on the theory of colors concludes with "The Confession of the Author," in which Goethe states that after having chronicled the scientific careers of others, he wishes to trace "how I arrived at these physical, and especially chromatic, studies" (HA 14:251).

Goethe had a compulsive need to register his experiences, to record himself as well as to leave a record of his life and the complex essence of his protean personality. Hence his prolific, multifarious, and increasingly interdisciplinary writings over the course of a long career are in one sense an ongoing serial process of self-reflection—of self-revelation as well as self-questioning, of self-recording as well as self-fictionalizing and poeticizing (*Dichtung*). His confessional activity is an expression of the fundamental formative and educational drive (*Bildungstrieb*) that he identified as "the central point and basis of his existence" ("Self-Description," HA 10:529), a dynamic and productive instinct whose most dramatic and profiled symbol is Faust's endless striving. This drive could also take the form of an egotistical will-to-power, as in the final act of part 2 of the play (in Faust's incarnation as a land developer). In Goethe's autobiographical mode, this *Bildungstrieb* manifests itself as a complex need at once to understand, express, and form himself in and through the act of self-writing. Even in his last letter (17 March 1832), sent several days before his death and at the end of "a so long, productive and reflective life," he is still trying to fathom the "secrets" of this unusual life, subsuming the career of his "inborn individuality" into a larger human paradigm inherent in his favorite concept covering all life forms, *Steigerung*, which (untranslatable word) includes the meanings of ascension, heightening, and intensification: "I have nothing more important to do than to intensify [*steigern*] wherever possible that which is and has remained part of me and to purify my characteristic singularities" (*Briefe* 4:481).

For Goethe, however, the goal of self-understanding is not to be pursued or achieved through the passive and protracted introspection of a self withdrawn from its world, which he dismissed as sterile self-absorption, but by exploring the dynamic and dialectical relationship between self and world. His most paradigmatic statement on this issue comes in a late essay (1823): "I here confess that the great and significant demand, 'know thyself,' has always appeared questionable to me as a ruse of secretly allied priests who wish to confuse humans with unattainable demands and to misdirect us from an active involvement in the outer world to a false inner contemplation. Humans know themselves only insofar as they know their world, of which they only become aware in themselves and of themselves in it" ("Significant Help," HA 13:38). The "world" includes the natural cosmos, which he studied in his scientific investigations and of which our individual monad is a part. Goethe in fact believed his poetic and creative talent was an emanation of that greater and mysterious nature to whose laws we are all subject. But the "world" includes as well the sphere of human culture—history, society, the arts—that constitutes the horizon of our individuality and that at any given point in time defines our limits and our opportunities.

If Goethe's confessional career can be seen under the auspices of his unceasing productive drive and his perennial need to express as well as heighten, intensify, and purify his individuality as it is embedded in and defined by a larger objective (*gegenständliche*) reality, to study the confessional mode in the huge and heterogeneous body of his writings would be an unmanageable if not impossible task, although Stephan Koranyi's study of the relationship between autobiography and science in the thought of Goethe is an impressive contribution to our understanding of the larger continuity of the confessional mode, from the scientific to the poetic poles of his thinking and writing. In practice, even a single, detailed, and in-depth critical consideration of his "four major autobiographical works . . . *Poetry and Truth,* the *Italian Journey,* the *Campaign in France 1792* and *Siege of Mainz,* and the *Annals*" (Saine "Introduction," *Poetry and Truth* 1), has been beyond the scope of students and critics of Goethe the autobiographer.

No doubt this is due in part to the differences in approach, method, style, subject, and treatment of these diverse works, as well as to the epic length of the first two, which together run to nearly fourteen hundred pages. A more important reason is that only *Poetry and Truth* meets the traditional generic expectation of autobiography as a retrospective presentation and narrative interpretation of a significant portion of a life (in this case, Goethe's first twenty-six years). In this it differs fundamentally from the other three: *Journey* is based on Goethe's letters and journals during his two-year stay in Italy; *Campaign* and *Siege* combine the forms of memoir and autobiographical essay in Goethe's observations and reflections in the context of specific military episodes of the revolutionary upheavals of the 1790s; and the *Annals* (*Day and Year Notebooks as a Completion of My Other Confessions*) offer in shorthand form a mostly factual and discontinuous record of his life up through 1822. While some of the later years are covered in some detail in the *Annals* and at times offer developed personal reflections as well as vivid accounts of Goethe's involvement in the outer world (such as his encounter with the overbearing Madame de Staël [Anne Louise Germaine Necker] on her visit to Weimar in 1804), others are barely touched on; the first twenty years of his life are encapsulated in two short paragraphs.

Probably the most important reason why Goethe's four major autobiographical works are not usually given detailed analysis as a group is the preeminence of *Poetry and Truth*. Just as the figures of young Werther and Faust are the only two from Goethe's fictional works that have entered into the pantheon of world literature, so *Poetry and Truth* is the only Goethe autobiography that has achieved truly canonical and exemplary stature. It has come to be recognized as the culmination and high point of eighteenth-century German autobiography (153), one that takes a marginally literary kind of writing (such as Pietist and scholarly life narratives) and transforms it into a high literary form, while also furnishing a model for the structural forms and representational modes of subsequent German autobiographies (Aichinger 33).[1] Indeed, in the German-speaking world, *Poetry and Truth* has since the early nineteenth century had a kind of hypercanonical standing, even though this—in some ways so formidable and monumental—work does not appear in our own time to have a significant readership beyond that world. Even contemporary students and theorists of autobiography seem to know the book more by reputation than through actual reading. With the publication in 1994 of Robert

Heitner's translation (in the Princeton edition of Goethe's works), the obstacle of John Oxenford's stilted Victorian English has been removed, and perhaps the door is open to a more informed appreciation by English-speaking readers of *Poetry and Truth* as, in the enthusiastic words of one of its critics, "probably the greatest autobiography *as out-and-out work of art* there has ever been and probably will ever be" (Bowman 151).

The later Goethe's decision to write his autobiography has traditionally been explained as a function of his interest in history and of his growing awareness of his own life as historical (see Erich Trunz's commentary, HA 9:599, 623–27). Goethe's intermittent but intensive studies in various fields had convinced him that relevant phenomena can only be understood in a historical context. In Rome, surrounded by a wealth of art from so many different periods and under the continuing influence of the art historian Johann Joachim Winckelmann, he concluded with respect to art apprecia-tion "that every one who is serious can readily see that in this field too no judgment is possible unless one can develop it historically" (*Italian Jour-ney*, HA 11:167). Several years later he generalized on the basis of his inter-mittent study of the history of physics that "only through an explanation of the past can the present be understood" (*Annals*, HA 10:510). This way of thinking also defines Goethe's approach to autobiography. As Weintraub stresses in his history of the concept of individuality in Western autobiog-raphy, for Goethe "the formative process can only be given . . . as history" (367), and his "unattainable goal" was "to write biography as if it were cul-tural history" (347). Like other scholars, Weintraub sees a direct connec-tion here between Goethe and European historicism: "*Dichtung und Wahrheit* represents the moment in the history of autobiography when the self-understanding and self-presentation of an individual parallels the emerging historicist understanding of human life" (368).[2] More recently, Koranyi has pursued the thesis that Goethe the autobiographer first emerged from his "intense preoccupation" with science (12–13). The "Con-fession of the Author," a narrative account of his interest in the phenomena of color and light and his epiphany that the Newtonian explanation was fundamentally wrong, is Goethe's "first genuine autobiographical work" and formative of his "subsequent autobiographical endeavors" (13). Even in this revisionary account, however, the historical connection is still deci-sive, because it is Goethe's immersion in the *history* of science that is identi-fied as the preparatory stage of his turn to autobiography.

Goethe started working on *Poetry and Truth* at the age of sixty. On the threshold of old age, he took on the Herculean labor of reviewing his life and career in the context of his world and times. A journal entry of October 1809 mentions the "scheme of a biography" (Trunz, HA 9:599), and his initial plan was to take his life story close to the time he set out to write it—an early four-part outline (the so-called Karlsbad scheme of May 1810) takes the narrative up to 1803 (Trunz, HA 9:746–47). The composition of the first three parts of the work proceeded rapidly. Part 1 (books 1–5) was completed in July 1811; part 2 (books 6–10) was finished in November 1812; part 3 (books 11–15) appeared in May 1814. Part 4 (books 16–20), which concludes dramatically with Goethe's decision at age twenty-six to go to the court of the Duke of Weimar, was published only after his death. He worked on it intermittently over the decades, making a major effort near the end of his life, and left it an almost finished fragment that was given final form, its rough edges smoothed over, by his literary executors.

Even though, contrary to his earlier scheme, the narrative of *Poetry and Truth* takes Goethe only into his mid-twenties, he never abandoned the hope that his autobiographical project would encompass his entire life history. In an 1826 notice of the final edition of his works, he still envisioned a separate volume dealing with the important period (1775–86) prior to his Italian journey, during which he functioned both as a companion and a minister of the Duke of Weimar. And as Saine has recently reiterated, *Italian Journey* and *Campaign in France* were, like *Poetry and Truth,* "conceived as individual parts of that original autobiography which was never to be completed" ("Introduction," *Poetry and Truth* 3). As continuations in a different key, they too carried the generic title *From My Life,* with the year by year chronistic entries of the *Annals* a last-ditch effort to connect and complete the three other autobiographical works. Thus, even if one leaves out of consideration the confessional impulse at work in his poetry, fiction, and drama—where, in any event, it appears in poetically veiled and universalized form—Goethe's autobiographical oeuvre as I have briefly reviewed it represents a totalizing if unrealized attempt to offer a narrative and chronological reprise of his entire life.[3] For the author who turned to autobiography when his life had become historical to himself, the elusive end of his autobiographical obsession was to leave a fully historicized account of his own existence. He probably came closer than any other autobiographer to achieving that impossible objective.

Like Rousseau's *Confessions, Poetry and Truth* has a long prehistory. No autobiographer before Goethe, not even Rousseau, was so well prepared and so superbly positioned to write his own life. Not only did he think about it and ready himself for it for a considerable period, but when he finally committed himself to writing *Poetry and Truth,* he approached it in the spirit of a biographical, historical, and cultural research project, one undertaken in an interdisciplinary and even collaborative spirit. When Goethe began to make serious plans late in 1809 to write his life, he had a long-standing interest in and familiarity with biographical and autobiographical writings and with the European memoir-literature that had developed into a popular vein of writing since the Renaissance. In fact, Goethe's first real literary success, the Shakespearean drama *Götz von Berlichingen,* is based on the sixteenth-century memoirs of the historical figure who is its title hero. In the second half of the eighteenth century, autobiography (both secular and religious) had become an increasingly well-established kind of literature, particularly in England, France, and Germany, with Rousseau of course providing the most influential instance. Goethe was conversant with a significant amount of this literature, including Rousseau's *Confessions,* which he read in 1782.

Although Goethe obviously knew Augustine's *Confessions,* given his fundamentally this-worldly outlook, his interest in autobiography really begins with the Renaissance and the early modern accents of an emerging and at times insistent individuality that can be heard in different ways in Jerome Cardano, Benvenuto Cellini, and Montaigne. In the entry on Cardano in the biographical-historical volume of his treatise on the theory of colors (completed shortly before he set to work on *Poetry and Truth*), he mentions all three, stating of the first two, "the biographies or confessions of both . . . have in common that their authors speak of their errors with disapproval but also a certain enjoyment, and that mixed in with their remorse there is always a sort of self-complacency about what they have achieved" (HA 14:84). Goethe's perception of the audacity inherent in modern autobiographers' secularizing of religious confession—"that which until now was only fearfully confided to the priest as a secret in the confessional [is] now presented to the whole world with a bold confidence" (84)—points forward to Rousseau, although Goethe does not mention him. Goethe also throws out the suggestion that a comparative study of "the so-called confessions of all times" would yield rich results, and he characterizes the three autobiographers he has mentioned as bespeaking a Protestant origin, one that is of course also a defining context of his own subsequent contributions to the genre.[4]

Goethe's interest in and knowledge of modern autobiography is evident as well in more immediate interventions on behalf of the genre, including his arranging in 1777 for the publication of the narrative of the youth of Jung-Stilling (Johann Heinrich Jung), the medical student friend of Goethe's Strasbourg days who wrote the best known of the German Pietist autobiographies. And he also undertook the translation of Cellini's autobiography, which appeared in his edition in 1803. His contacts with living German autobiographers came to include, beyond Jung-Stilling, the author of the most influential German confessional novel of the age (an early and powerful hybrid between autobiography and fiction), Karl Philipp Moritz, whose *Anton Reiser* he read upon its publication in 1785, and whom Goethe met and became good friends with during his stay in Rome two years later.

The prehistory of *Poetry and Truth* also includes as a significant component Goethe's interest in biographies and the biographical dimension of literature. Here it must be stressed for purposes of clarification that for Goethe and his age, what we conventionally see as the separate if related genres of biography and autobiography were not yet sorted out or categorically distinguished. Or, more accurately in Goethe's case, he reflexively thought of autobiography as a species of biography, as evident in his tendency to use the latter term for instances of the former, including *Poetry and Truth* (see his remarks quoted above about Cardano and Cellini.) Indeed, although the terms "autobiography" and "self-biography" had begun to come into use in Germany by the end of the eighteenth century, Goethe does not use the term, but relies, in addition to "biography," on the Latinized *Konfession* as well as (more usually) its German synonym, *Bekenntnisse*.[5] It was only in the later eighteenth and early nineteenth centuries that autobiography came of age and was constituted in the hands of its major practitioners as a separate literary genre, one that in the introduction to this study I correlate with the rise of Romanticism. Ironically, the uncritical merging of the genres of biography and autobiography in the eighteenth century is mirrored in the recent critical practice of reconceiving autobiography and biography as different types of "lifewriting."

Just as Goethe's active interest in autobiography is witnessed by his translation of Cellini and his finding a publisher for Jung-Stilling's memoir of his youth, his practical involvement in biography is evident in the essay he contributed in 1805 to the collection *Winckelmann and His Century*, as well as the biography he wrote several years later of the painter Philipp Hackert, with whom he had become acquainted on his Italian journey. These ventures into biography can be seen as steps toward his own autobiography, something evident in the *Annals* entry for the year 1811: "I had reason to ask myself, why I didn't venture to undertake for myself what I was doing for another? Thus even before the completion of that volume [the Hackert biography] I turned to my earliest life history" (HA 10:509). In writing the lives of others he was whetting his appetite and gaining practice for the vastly more demanding project of writing his own. The thematically organized *Winckelmann* essay in particular shows Goethe's awareness of the challenge of biography to apprehend the spirit or living form of the subject in the context of his age, as opposed to the dry accumulation of biographical facts into which, as Trunz observes (HA 9:600), biography in practice had degenerated in Germany.

In keeping with the high value Goethe put on the individual and on individuality, he thought of biography as the living cell of history. In a discarded draft passage possibly intended as a preface to *Poetry and Truth*, he asserts that biography has a great advantage over history in that it shows the living individual and how the century acted on that individual. The true task of the biographer—and thus also of the autobiographer—is to seize the meaning of the life of an important individual in the context of his world and his age: Winckelmann *and* his century.[6] Unfortunately, the historian, by seeking to discern general patterns and results, loses track of that individual element; thus even "the best [history] always has something corpse-like about it, the odor of the grave" ("Schemata and Outlines," HA 9:747). Given the low state of biography in his own time, however, Goethe seems to have dreaded the thought of someone else writing his life after his death. He was not the only writer to suffer from this fear—for instance, Count Vittorio Alfieri, born in the same year, mentions in the preface to his autobiography that one of his reasons for writing it is "that as soon as I should be no more, some bookseller, in order to enhance his gains on a new edition of my works, would prefix to it a life of the author. This life would probably be written by someone who was completely ignorant of the events which compose it, and who drew the materials from doubtful or partial sources" (Vincent 1–2). Moreover, Goethe had a well-founded fear of what in our own time has developed into the near-tabloid genre of *pathography*, a fear of "base-minded necrologists" ("Schemata and Outlines," HA 9:746), which motivated him to act as his own biographer and which he shares with the Rousseau of the *Dialogues*. In a letter of 27 May 1801 he comments sarcastically on "those necrologists" who in a show of "hypocritical justice" sort out the good and the bad of a recently deceased, important person's life and "destroy, much worse than death, a personality that can only be thought of as the living combination of such juxtaposed attributes" (*Briefe* 2:417).

"The individual is lost": Goethe's decision to write his life is also a function of a need to assert his highly evolved and richly elaborated identity in the face of his knowledge of temporality and mortality and of the pronounced awareness in his later years of the historicity of his life and his age. By late middle age he saw the world around him subject to unexpected and even cataclysmic changes. The sudden death of the ten-year-younger Friedrich Schiller in 1805 had spelled the end of an era in Goethe's life. The belated but highly productive friendship and collaboration between them, based on the fruitful tension between antithetical intellects—the more critical and philosophical Schiller played Coleridge to the Wordsworth of Goethe's more spontaneous and intuitive mind— had come to a sudden stop. And on the stage of European politics, the unprecedented pace of events involved in the sequence of the French Revolution and the Napoleonic Wars, which came literally too close for comfort with the Battle of Jena and the sack of Weimar in October 1806, made starkly clear to him that the world of his youth had passed away. The Holy Roman Empire, whose spectacular coronation rituals he had witnessed as a boy in Frankfurt, had breathed its last in the wake of Napoleon, and the shape of a new world order was as yet uncertain. What Goethe tells us in *Campaign in France* he said in September 1792, after he witnessed the allied invasion ignominiously turned back at Valmy by bad weather and the Republican troops, can stand as the crystallized sentence of his larger awareness of the momentous historical changes besetting Europe in the last decade of the eighteenth century and the first decade of the nineteenth: "From here and today a new epoch of world history is beginning, and you can say you have been there" (HA 10:235).

A final motive of Goethe's autobiography is related to his sense of a fundamentally changed world—a need to explain himself, to present himself to the public in the complex fullness of his being and his manifold interests and achievements, in order to inform or remind his contemporaries of these and possibly to win over a new generation of readers. There is the old author's need to build his own statue, to monumentalize himself at a time when the public perception of his stature did not match his own sense of his greatness. As Goethe put it with his characteristic tact in a canceled preface to part 3, "In old age one likes to speak of the past and of what has been accomplished, especially because lively young people cannot be blamed when they assert their own merit, and seek with more or less awareness to push especially that which came just before them into the distance and relegate it to obscurity" ("Schemata and Outlines," HA 9:754). Goethe wanted to dissipate the obscurity; more subtly than the *Dialogues* of Rousseau and without their defensiveness and paranoia, *Poetry and Truth* also has aspects of the public relations campaign. The famous author of the "genius" period of the 1770s, of *Götz von Berlichingen,* which had made his a household name in Germany, and of *The Sufferings of Young Werther,* which had made him a European celebrity, was in the closing decade of the century experiencing an increasing sense of isolation, of misunderstanding and even indifference by the German public. He had returned from Italy reborn in his own eyes as a writer and as an intellect, but a stranger to—or increasingly estranged from—his friends and acquaintances at Weimar. The triumphs of his youth were two decades in the past, and what he had begun to pursue with such seriousness in the 1790s, his scientific investigations and writings, found little resonance with the German public, or even sympathy and understanding from friends of his youth like the philosophical Jacobi brothers (Johann Georg and Friedrich Heinrich) and Johann Georg Schlosser, his intellectual brother-in-law. Of his visit to the Jacobi circle in Pempelfort in November 1792, which turned a cold shoulder on his new interests and productions, Goethe wrote plaintively, "one cannot think of a more isolated person than I was then, and remained for a long time" (*Campaign,* HA 10:313).[7] Göschen, the publisher of his collected works in eight volumes (1787–90) was disappointed by their meager sales and turned down Goethe's manuscript on *The Metamorphosis of Plants* (1790); Goethe later characterized the period in which his collected edition appeared as one in which "Germany no longer knew anything of me, nor wished to know anything" (HA 13:103).

Müller has zeroed in on this motif of a disappointed and troubled Goethe and has gone so far as to dismiss the traditional view of Goethe's autobiography as the shining product of an individuality supremely confident of its achievements as "fundamentally wrong" (251), and to substitute for this hagiographic view a demythologized reading of Goethe's autobiography project as based on a "disturbed relationship" with the external world and with his public. The "failure" of his works as a "central life experience" is identified as the motive force of Goethe the autobiographer, who writes out of a "deep loneliness" (266) and even "self-alienation" (274). As one critic has strikingly put it, "one has the conception of Goethe that one is capable of rising to" (Bowman 150), and if the Olympian legend of a magisterially detached Goethe and a perfectly unified autobiographical opus (Trunz is the chief exponent of this view), reflects an earlier critical ideology, Müller's attempt to limn the outlines of a developing "new Goethe-picture" (262), next to which the old Olympian Goethe image is "a superficial mystification" (266), has a certain persuasiveness and credibility. It appeals to the iconoclast in us, even as it mirrors the critical anxieties of our own fin de siècle about the self-alienation inherent in the act of self-writing of even the most canonical of writers.

GOETHE AND ROUSSEAU

A difficult question that must inevitably be addressed in a discussion of Goethe and autobiography is the issue of his relationship to Rousseau. Since Goethe is perhaps the most widely read and intertextual of modern authors, it is relevant to ask, to what extent does *Poetry and Truth* show the influence of, incorporate, or respond to *The Confessions* of the celebrated Citizen of Geneva? What is Goethe's take on and reception of the most important modern autobiography before his own? The problem is not only Goethe's essential silence when it comes to any developed and substantive response to *The Confessions,* but his reason(s) for that telling silence about the book by the man who, according to the most exhaustive contemporary evaluation of the Goethe-Rousseau relationship, "remained a vital inspirational force for Goethe during Goethe's entire lifetime"

(Hammer 1).[8] Comments on and allusions and references to Rousseau's life and works are scattered throughout Goethe's *oeuvre*, including *Poetry and Truth*, but there is no explicit or developed statement of Goethe's views, critical or otherwise, of Rousseau the autobiographer. There are only oblique remarks and general pronouncements that seem to point to a larger critique of Rousseau's confessional approach as one he wishes to avoid.

I would suggest that if one reads Goethe's silence about Rousseau's *Confessions* aright, it is not a matter of an unacknowledged anxiety of influence, but rather his tact in not directly criticizing the most influential autobiographer, whose essential weakness or limitation, as Goethe came to see it, his own approach to autobiography was intended to overcome. If the young Goethe greatly admired Rousseau the thinker and critic of repressive social institutions—even though that criticism helped to bring about a revolution that Goethe passionately rejected—and if he pitied the sufferings of the self-torturing misanthrope and modern Timon, he could not approve of the solipsistic excesses of *The Confessions,* to which his own autobiography surely presents a very conscious and calculated corrective. Rousseau's egocentric approach was to be rejected, especially, perhaps, because it represented too great a danger to Goethe, one side of whose youthful self had suffered from that morbidly sensitive subjectivity that was Rousseau's lifelong affliction. A 1787 journal entry in the *Italian Journey* may offer a clue to Goethe's sympathetic yet self-defensive sense of similarity with and ultimately saving difference from Rousseau: "Sometimes I think of Rousseau and his hypochondriacal misery, and yet I can grasp how such a beautiful organization can become distorted. If I did not take such an interest in natural things and did not see that in the apparent confusion a hundred observations can be ordered and compared, just as the surveyor can attempt a hundred measurements with a single extended line, I would frequently take myself for mad" (HA 11:211). The difference is that Goethe is not lost, as Rousseau is in part 2 of his *Confessions,* in the maze of his inner feelings and impressions; he is saved—or saves himself—by *gegenständlich* (object-oriented) thinking and by the scientific interests that had blossomed in his first decade at Weimar. But with his characteristic good nature and generosity of spirit, and the discretion that is a hallmark of *Poetry and Truth,* Goethe was not going directly to attack the self-absorption of the much-suffering man he consistently admired, sympathized with, and pitied. Nor, given his endorsement of life-writing and (auto)biographical documents of all kinds—"so long as one communicates one's self it does not matter what one's motives are"—could he condemn Rousseau's *Confessions* out of hand.

Even though Goethe does not give an account in *Poetry and Truth* of his youthful relationship to Rousseau, the evidence of his life and writings offers convincing proof that the young author shared in his age's popular cult of Rousseau, whose writings had found an especially friendly and even enthusiastic reception in Germany during the 1760s and 1770s. Indeed, the most famous philosopher of the age, Kant, gave up the strict routine of his daily walk in order to read *Emile*.[9] In 1779, the year after Rousseau's death, Goethe visited the shrine of the island of Saint Pierre in Lake Bienne and wrote his name on the wall of Rousseau's room (Hammer 35–36), and on the same trip to Switzerland he visited the picturesque spots that serve as the backdrop to the passionate love between Julie and Saint Preux. "We went to Vevey; I could not keep back the tears when I looked across to Meillerie and the Dent de Jamant and had before me all the scenes that the eternally lonely Rousseau peopled with animated beings" (letter of 23 October 1779, Hammer 36). Several years later, Goethe made his most developed and generous remarks on Rousseau the writer, including the autobiographer, in a letter to Charlotte von Stein mentioning his receipt of "the fine Geneva edition of Rousseau; the *Confessions* are included. Even the few pages at which I have looked are like shining stars; imagine several volumes like that! What a heavenful! What a gift to mankind a noble human being is!" (9 May 1782, Hammer 37).[10] Whether "the few pages" refer to *The Confessions* or to some other Rousseau work, this brief but fulsome praise clearly suggests Goethe's enthusiastic response, in his early maturity, to Rousseau.

Goethe's most developed tribute comes very late in his life, in the expanded 1831 version of his essay "History of My Botanical Studies," in which Rousseau is praised for several pages as an amateur or dilettante botanist who is a forerunner and appropriate mentor of Goethe's own botanical career. In the course of his botanical studies, Goethe "became aware of a reclusive friend of plants, who had devoted himself to this subject with seriousness and diligence. Who would not wish to follow *Jean-Jacques Rousseau*, revered in the highest sense, on his lonely excursions where, at odds with the human species, he devotes his attention to the

world of flowers and plants" (HA 13:157). This touching appreciation of
Rousseau is "the most unequivocal expression of the mature Goethe's sentiments regarding Rousseau" and comes at a time when he "sees
Rousseau's view of nature as being essentially in agreement with his own"
(Hammer 53–54). Significantly, Goethe's last and most voluble tribute to
Rousseau is based on a shared area of interest and a perceived similarity of
outlook—the natural world—where Goethe can voice without qualification his sincere admiration of the *promeneur solitaire*. For the aged author
it is a safe ground on which to light a votive candle in memory of Jean-
Jacques, without having to mention his very different ideas about the relationship between the individual and society or how this is to be
represented in autobiography.

In the European world of letters in which Goethe came of age,
Rousseau's critique of education, culture, and social institutions was
probably as well known as Freud's ideas were by the mid-twentieth century. The references to Rousseau in *Poetry and Truth* show Goethe's easy
familiarity with his writings and, what is more, assume the same familiarity on the part of his readers, so that his works and ideas can be referred to
in passing without specific explanations. For instance, when in book 5
Goethe describes his romantic relationship with Gretchen as in part a pedagogic one, he makes a witty allusion to the "new" Abelard (146)—Saint
Preux, the tutor and lover of Julie—on the assumption that it is obvious
to his readers. At another point, when in connection with his illness as a
student at Leipzig he discusses the then-current fashion of cold bathing
and "other such follies" resulting from "misunderstood recommendations
by Rousseau" (book 8, 247), he points to the well-known phenomenon of
an influential thinker's ideas becoming distorted through populariza-
tion.[11] There is not even any need to identify *Emile* as the likely source of
these "recommendations." At another level, we are made aware of
Rousseau as a contemporary cult figure and guru when Goethe, in connection with his description of Franz Michael Leuchsenring, the traveling
houseguest and impresario who reads from his boxes of "sensible" (in the
eighteenth-century sense) letters, mentions that among these are those of
Julie Bondeli, "the friend of Rousseau." "Anyone with any connection
whatever to this extraordinary man basked in the glory emanating from
him, and a silent congregation had been established far and wide in his
name" (book 13, 411).

On the whole Goethe's statements are consistent with Hammer's conclusion "that Goethe continued to revere Rousseau while he was working
on *Dichtung und Wahrheit*" (46). The Rousseau invoked by Goethe, however, is the apostle of nature and the natural, not Rousseau the disturbed
autobiographer. This is the pre-*Confessions* Citizen of Geneva he had come
to revere as a young man and who played a significant role in the lives of
some of his friends and fellow writers, like the pedagogue Johann Bernard
Basedow, whose educational philosophy was based on Rousseau's, and
the Jacobi brothers, in whose Pempelfort circle Rousseau was to remain a
guiding light. We know from Goethe's account in book 15 that his positive
and Pelagian view of human nature is more aligned with Rousseau's insistence on natural goodness than with the Pietists' stress on original sin.
This constitutes "the real point of difference" between him and the religious circle he had sought to join in his early twenties, by which he was
not accepted "as a Christian" (465).

In fact, Goethe's most developed and telling discussion in *Poetry and
Truth* of Rousseau the philosopher comes in book 14, in his carefully elaborated portrait of Friedrich Maximilian Klinger, the Storm-and-Stress
author with whom Goethe remained on good terms in later years when
he had turned against the excesses of the "genius" sensibility anatomized
in *Werther*. Unlike some of the other young writers of this dynamic but
unsettled period (the unbalanced Jakob Michael Lenz is mentioned as a
specific contrast), Klinger was no "transient meteor . . . across the horizon
of German literature" (443), but a self-made man who cultivated his talents to achieve long-term success. The career of this avowed Rousseau disciple is a living exemplification of Rousseau's republican ideal:

Rousseau's works could not fail to have exceptional appeal for
such a youth. *Emile* was virtually his Bible, and its sentiments could
the more easily captivate him since they were exerting a universal
influence over the cultivated world. Indeed, they meant even more
to him than others because he too was a child of nature, and he too
had started at the bottom. What others were asked to relinquish, he
had never possessed; circumstances they were supposed to escape
had never constrained him, and so he could be viewed as one of the
purest disciples of that nature gospel. In view of his serious striving
. . . he could very well exclaim, "Everything is good when it issues

from the hand of nature!"—But disagreeable experiences also forced
the concluding sentence on him: "Everything deteriorates under
the hand of man!" He did not have to struggle with himself, but
with the traditional world, from whose chains the citizen of Geneva
meant to free us. (444)

Again, Goethe's citation of the opening lines of *Emile* assumes his readers'
familiarity with that famous text. As is evident from this characterization
of Klinger as a Rousseau disciple, the Citizen of Geneva's appeal, though
widely diffused, was most powerful precisely for the most talented, cultivated, intelligent, and idealistic youth. At its best, it was clearly a minority
movement, one in which Goethe obviously participated, as the Klinger
portrait obliquely implies. It has a measure of self-reflexivity, as Goethe's
portraits sometimes do, for he liked to develop the character profiles of
others as a means of "mirroring" himself, that is, as a sort of indirect or
mediated self-representation.

That Rousseau had a particular appeal for talented German youth is
also apparent in the very critical review of French Enlightenment literature and culture in Goethe's account of his student days at the University
of Strasbourg at the close of book II. Rousseau is exempted from Goethe's
disenchantment with and alienation from this fashionable world, with
whose writers he had become increasingly familiar since the days of the
French occupation of Frankfurt during the Seven Years' War. Indeed,
Rousseau's attraction is enhanced by his outsider status: "Rousseau had
genuinely appealed to us. But if we consider his life and destiny, was he
not obliged to find his only reward for all his accomplishments in the privilege of living in Paris unknown and forgotten?" (361). The idea of
Rousseau as a rallying point for the aspirations of a new generation of
German writers also surfaces in a draft outline for the survey in book 7 of
eighteenth-century German literature. In it, Goethe characterizes the
striving of the young for "a simple enjoyment of nature" and their innate
abilities as frustrated and "repressed" by narrow social conventions
(including "pedantic education, asceticism, the higher classes, philistin-
ism, the need to earn a living"). In answer to the question when such conflicts appear in literature, Goethe mentions his own *Werther* and "shortly
before . . . Rousseau's prize-winning essay against culture" ("Schemata
and Outlines," HA 9:752). It is the polemical Rousseau of the first *Discourse* who attacks culture in the name of nature who is identified as a

predecessor of and presumably also an inspiration for Goethe's similarly motivated attack on the stifling social conventions that bear down on the sensitive and nature-loving soul of the passionate young Werther, that famous confessional alter ego of the young Goethe.[12]

It is a striking feature of Goethe's scattered but generally very positive comments on Rousseau in *Poetry and Truth* that he refuses to enter into or even mention the famous quarrel between Rousseau and the Encyclopedists. He must certainly have known about Rousseau's falling-out with the *philosophes* and may have had some firsthand knowledge about it as well, since he met Grimm after his flight from France in 1792 and later again in Weimar. It is hard not to assume that Goethe would have taken the opportunity to discuss Rousseau and Diderot with Grimm, the German-born aristocrat and man of letters who, in part 2 of *The Confessions,* is the demonized chief villain—a diabolic compound of malignity and self-serving fatuousness—in the "conspiracy" against Jean-Jacques. Indeed, he does not bring up the quarrel even when there would seem to be a call for it, in the critique of French literature, in which he also exempts Diderot from his condemnation, mentioning him almost in the same breath as Rousseau. Instead he links the two erstwhile friends whose complicated falling-out takes up so much of the narrative energy of part 2 of *The Confessions.* "Like Rousseau, he was another who popularized an attitude of repugnance toward life in society, and thus subtly paved the way for those world-shaking changes which seemed to threaten every existing institution with destruction" (book 11, 362). In this positive linking of the two writers Goethe also avoids any overt criticism or assigning of blame for their role in paving the way for a revolution of which he could in no way approve.

There is only one place where Goethe allows himself any overt criticism of Rousseau, and that is in his influence on art. Both Rousseau and Diderot "pointed us away from it [art] and toward nature" (362). However, in "a small but epoch-making work," "Pygmalion" (1761), Rousseau's one-act "lyrical scene" about the narcissistic sculptor who falls in love with his statue (Galatea) and whose prayer that she come to life is answered, Goethe sees a misguided attempt to reduce art to nature. The "higher form" created by the artist is "dragged down into his earthly life": "Through a most commonplace sensual action he wants to destroy the highest thing that thought and deed can produce" (363). "Much could be said about" this playlet that had enchanted the young Goethe, an implication that much more is at stake here than is stated in his brief analysis. The higher dragged down to the lower through a destructive action: could this not also be a veiled allusion—by the author who attached himself to a court, became a minister, and was ennobled—to the political impact of Rousseau's writings, and to the great leveling of the "higher life" and the hierarchical structure of prerevolutionary European society? Much could be said indeed, but Goethe will not say it, out of respect or charity for the revered writer and sage of his youth.

The reserve, discretion, and *politesse* so apparent here also account, I believe, for Goethe's refusal to engage directly the issue of Rousseau the autobiographer, the absence of any discussion of which seems at first sight almost a perverse oversight in *Poetry and Truth*. Weintraub's assertion that "Rousseau's *Confessions* . . . remained for Goethe the problematic autobiography par excellence" is—given the lack of any direct utterances here on Goethe's part—speculative but persuasive. His conclusion that "the confessional mode itself seemed dangerous to Goethe" (345) represents something of a modern critical consensus.[13] The diary entry of 18 May 1810 that Weintraub (345) cites in support of his view—"Everyone who writes confessions is in danger of becoming lamentable, because we are never supposed to confess our virtues and confess only the morbid and sinful" (HA 11:557, my translation)—represents one of those generalizing *aperçus* that seem to be targeted at the confessional mode of Rousseau and his followers without invoking either his name or his text. Goethe's skeptical statement questioning the "know thyself" injunction of the Delphic oracle as conducive to a false contemplation of the inner self may be another arrow aimed at the morbidly subjective and self-torturing introspective tendencies fostered by the Rousseauean school of autobiography, as is his even stronger indictment in a well-known aphoristic condemnation of taking the "know thyself" injunction in "an ascetic sense," which leads to "the heautognosy of our modern hypochondriacs" and their "psychological tortures" (HA 12:413).

Pray you, avoid it is the older Goethe's response not only to the confessional approach of Rousseau but, by extension, also to the young Romantic generation that found impulses for its insistently subjective exploration of the worlds within in Goethe's earlier works. Clearly Goethe's portrait of his youth in *Poetry and Truth* shows some touches of modern hypochondria and of a Rousseauean self on the psychological precipice— for example, his serious adolescent depression at the loss of his first love,

Gretchen; the illness that caused him to leave Leipzig without a degree and to languish in his father's house for a year. However, the gist of the older writer's worldview, evident throughout *Poetry and Truth* and inculcated as well in *Wilhelm Meister's Journeyman Years,* is that one escapes the self-destructive "heautognosy" of the self imprisoned in its own subjectivity by forcing oneself to look away from that self, by objective (*gegenständlich*) thinking, and by, as Weintraub summarizes the cure, "an active involvement in the world" (376).

The older Goethe's pointed remarks on the surplus of "subjectivity" as "the general disease of the present time"—"all progressive periods have an objective tendency," but "the entire present period is retrogressive, because it is a subjective one" (Eckermann 1:159, 161, 29 January 1826)— seem to take in the whole tendency initiated by Rousseau and culminating in the lachrymose excesses and the genius for a self-torturing self-preoccupation so spectacularly evident in some of the leading figures of European Romanticism. But they also appear to be self-implicating as a critique of the Werther side of the young Goethe, which is closely related, as the passage quoted earlier from *Italian Journey* acknowledges, to the "hypochondriacal misery" of Rousseau. Thus the older writer's strong if unstated reservations about *The Confessions* are presumably also reservations about his younger Werther self. Goethe must have come to see mirrored in the latter portions of Rousseau's autobiography an unbalanced self-preoccupation and a diseased imagination that he himself had had to struggle to overcome and put behind him but that throughout his life presented a dangerous proclivity to guard against.

This self-implicating aspect is perhaps the deeper significance of his rather detailed and richly ironic account, in connection with his characterization of the Werther malady in *Campaign in France,* of "a sentimental relationship of the kind that is right out of a novel" with a Werther-like young man. When Goethe visits him in November 1792, fifteen years after their first meeting, Plessing is a professor of philosophy who has survived his earlier sufferings but still shows signs of "the morbid introspectiveness of his youth [that] had never completely subsided" (*Campaign* 727). Young Plessing is presented by the older author as a case study of "the malaise that lay deep down in young souls" that *The Sufferings of Young Werther* (1774) "had by no means caused . . . but only uncovered" (717). In the late retrospect of *Campaign,* the Werther disease is seen as an expression of the German (Storm-and-Stress) literature of the 1770s, which "was

occupied more with the internal than with the external world" and whose
source was the sentimental literature of England, especially "the influence
of Laurence Sterne," to whose "feelings" the Germans "responded quite
eagerly." "There developed a kind of tender-passionate asceticism, which
was usually destined to degenerate into unpleasant self-torment, since it
was not given to us to partake of the humoristic irony of the Englishman"
(*Campaign* 717).

Goethe "had tried to free [himself] personally from this evil"—in part
by his cathartic writing of *Werther*—"and intended . . . to assist others as
well" (717). When young Plessing wrote two impassioned letters to the
famous author of *Werther* in 1776, pleading for friendship, pity, and
advice, Goethe intervened propaedeutically, not by entering into a fruitless correspondence with the man trapped in the circle of his own feelings,
but by visiting him in the guise of "a sketch artist from Gotha" (723) while
on a journey to the Harz region. In his own eyes, Goethe's rather presumptuous charade is justified by his self-chosen role "of mentor to other
young men my age in matters of the heart and spirit" (719). Young Plessing inquires about Weimar and Goethe and complains about the famous
author's refusal to answer his "long and heartfelt letter," which he proceeds to read verbatim to his visitor. "The reader was totally identical with
what he was reading, and just as this had not appealed to me earlier at a
distance, now it was no better face to face. To be sure, I could not deny
the young man a certain respect, a certain sympathy, which after all had
led me on such a curious journey: there was a seriousness of purpose here,
a lofty spirit and intent. But although he was talking about the most delicate sentiments, his reading lacked all charm, and he exhibited signs of a
totally self-encapsulating egotism" (724).

Although the literary sources of the Werther malady dramatized here
are located by Goethe in the wave of English sentiment and melancholy
that swept over Germany in the second half of the eighteenth century, the
greater spread of that subjective self-concern can also be correlated with
the impact of Rousseau's autobiographical writings in the last two decades
of the century. And indeed, with a proper allowance for the differences in
age, outlook, and literary ability between the young Plessing and the older
Rousseau, we can guess that Goethe's reaction—sympathetic yet critical—
to Plessing's reading of the letter might also have been more or less his
reaction to Rousseau reading part 2 of his *Confessions* in Paris: "a totally
self-encapsulating egotism."

Goethe's "attempt" at a "remedy" for the misery of the young man—who unfortunately does not seem to heed his disguised mentor's advice, so that Goethe takes his leave the next day without paying a second visit—is one that he turned into a lifelong therapy, including the intensive study of natural phenomena that began at Weimar:

> [T]he only way for a person to save himself and free himself from a painful, self-tormenting, and gloomy state of mind is through the contemplation of nature and genuine participation and interest in the outside world. Even the most elementary acquaintance with nature, from whatever point of view, or active involvement, whether as gardener or agriculturalist, as a hunter or a miner, draws us out of ourselves; directing our mind to real and true phenomena affords, in time, the greatest pleasure, clarity, and instruction, just as the artist who remains true to nature while seeking to develop his inner resources will certainly achieve the most. (*Campaign* 724–25)

The antidote to a narrowly circumscribed self trapped in the bell jar of its obsessive concerns (to borrow from Sylvia Plath), is attention to the greater natural world of which it is a part. This is a lesson that the Wordsworth of *The Prelude* relearned with the help of his sister, after his massive depression because of the failure of his apocalyptic hopes for the French Revolution. It is a release that the Rousseau of the *Reveries* (Second Walk) momentarily and ecstatically glimpsed in that delicious moment of coming to consciousness after he had been knocked down and out by a large dog, when he was disoriented and without identity, before his ego could resume its old distorted form. In a lesser key, it is a path pursued in the pleasures of botanizing and "herborizing" that the old Rousseau pursued after he had abdicated all concern, as he tells us so insistently in his final autobiographical text, with his reputation in the world and the nefarious machinations of his enemies and persecutors. It is no wonder, then, that the aged Goethe chose to pay his most fulsome and poignant compliment to Rousseau the amateur naturalist, not Rousseau the self-tortured confessor.

To write lamentable and morbid confessions à la Jean-Jacques, as the young Goethe had done in the fictional epistolary confession of young Werther, is for the older Goethe a temptation to be avoided. Goethe's ideal of the style of *Poetry and Truth* also seems to cut specifically against the grain of *The Confessions*, for he recommends, in a letter of 2 September

1812, a "specific lightness of treatment" so that the work "does not become too serious" (HA 11:559). The following year he asked his assistant Friedrich Wilhelm Riemer to review a recent portion of his manuscript, particularly the portraits of still-living individuals, to make sure that the desired cheerfulness (Heiterkeit) of the presentation has not been compromised: "[S]uch things require the brightest and broadest humor, because if one is out of humor, one does not feel what could annoy others" (HA 11:563, letter of 27 July 1813). The fact that such a resolute lightness of treatment "almost entirely ignores . . . the enemy in his own breast, the heavy hypochondriacal inheritance"—the Rousseau side of his personality—has been suggested by Richard Friedenthal (569).

Goethe's larger critique and apparent rejection of the confessional mode of Rousseau is also, as Niggl has shown, correlated with the generic development of German autobiography at the turn of the century, of which *Poetry and Truth* is the *summa*. The reservations about *The Confessions* that are already noticeable in Germany in the 1780s become in the following decade a turning away from Rousseau's autobiography, which, with the extremes of its "self-revelation and simultaneous self-mirroring," becomes the negative instance of a psychological self-examination to be avoided (Niggl 104). Niggl concludes that "on the whole Goethe follows the general tendency around 1800, which is, instead of [writing] psychological confessions, to move to the center the relationship of the "I" to the times and the world" (170). But in the case of Goethe, as I have tried to demonstrate in my attempt to reconstruct his view of Rousseau and his reception of his writings, his turning away from *The Confessions* in his own practice as an autobiographer has a complex and self-implicating history. His rejection of the influential confessional mode of Rousseau and his embrace of the ideal of objective and scientific thinking is both a defense against and an antidote to the powerful subjective tendencies that he had come to identify and condemn as the destructive element both in his personality and in his increasingly Romantic culture.

GOETHE AND THE "FUNDAMENTAL" TRUTH OF AUTOBIOGRAPHY

One significant element of the view that Goethe may have worked out at least in part through his clarifying consideration of Rousseau's achievement is that of the role of *fiction(s) in autobiography,* to invoke the title of

Paul John Eakin's influential book. This is an element signaled from the start by Goethe's ambiguous choice of title—*From My Life: Poetry and Truth*—which has led to a certain amount of waffling by critics trying to explain what he meant by it. But with respect to Rousseau, this much seems clear: Goethe will *not* tell everything about his life, which was the basic rhetorical stance of Rousseau in *The Confessions*, nor will his account be strictly factual, a promise Rousseau claims he will honor to the limits of his memory. Rather, he will allow for the element of *Dichtung* (fiction, poetry) and thus for a certain play of the imagination in the presentation of his life. In so doing he programmatically solves the Rousseauean dilemma of promising to tell everything and nothing but the truth, which can only arouse reader suspicion and invite a kind of legalistic expectation that autobiography as a genre is not well suited to fulfil. To burden autobiography, that sustained *metaphor of the self* (James Olney), with a too literal and thus false demand for referentiality is to misconstrue the whole autobiographical enterprise. Goethe wants from the outset to disarm the sort of critical vigilance on the part of the reader that Rousseau unwittingly invites by protesting his veracity too much. With his title, he openly acknowledges the presence of fiction and the instrumentality of the imagination that Rousseau owns up to belatedly, and with a sophistic charade of defensive argumentation, in the Fourth Revery. What Rousseau admits only apologetically and defensively, Goethe identifies with his title and endorses as part of the genre, for which he thus wins a new flexibility and imaginative freedom.

Out of his reflection on and revision of Rousseau's juridical and literal-minded insistence on the factual truth of autobiography, which in practice Rousseau constantly violated with the play of his irrepressible imagination, Goethe evolved his own concept of autobiographical truth. From the start he was willing to allow for the imaginative element inherent in the retrospective narrative of autobiography. In so doing, he anticipated "adventurous twentieth-century autobiographers," who according to Eakin "readily accept the proposition that fictions and the fiction-making process are a central constituent of the truth of any life as it is lived and of any art devoted to the presentation of that life," as well as the current critical view of autobiography "as both an art of memory and an art of the imagination" (*Fictions* 5–6). In 1810 he wrote to Bettina Brentano, "I will confess to you that I am in the process of writing my confessions; these may turn into a novel or a story, something that cannot be envisioned ahead of time" (HA II:557, 25 October 1810); several years later (HA II:563, letter of I December 1813) he characterized the work in progress as "the half-poetry of my biographical attempt."

But Goethe, while allowing for the presence of the poetic or imaginative element, obviously does not view autobiography as simply a work of confessional fiction (like his own *Werther*). He honors what Lejeune has described as the autobiographical pact between author and reader (*Pacte* 44), and he does not seek to do away with the referential demands on or expectations of the genre that most readers (other than poststructuralist critics) have traditionally brought to it. In fact, he considerably expands the referential dimension, whose centrality Eakin argues for persuasively in *Touching the World*, to include a broad representation of the historical and temporal reality in which the autobiographical subject's life is embedded. Goethe capitalizes on the referential aspect of autobiography in a way probably no autobiographer before him had, even as he loosens the bonds of referentiality from their firm moorings in the literal ground of biographical fact.

The complement of *Dichtung* that Goethe signals with his title is of course the despair of the scholarly biographer, for whom adherence to factual truth and accuracy are the sine qua non of the task. For that reason *Poetry and Truth* is at best a tricksy and ambiguous source for the Goethe biographer, who is properly tempted to regard the work with skepticism and suspicion, as Nicholas Boyle does when he characterizes it as "that most misleading of autobiographies" (101). Goethe wrote as his own biographer, but the truth he pursued was not that of the biographical scholar, whose interpretation must always be based on the available facts of the life. Whereas the autobiographer can capture aspects of his inner experience and his sense of his own unfolding identity that the biographer cannot, the latter may disclose aspects of the life of the subject that are slighted or ignored by the former. What Goethe aimed at was not mere factual accuracy that he was more than willing to take liberties with, as is (notoriously) evident in the Sesenheim sequence of his love affair with Friederike Brion, but an elusive and deeper truth—"the fundamental truth" (das Grundwahre)—that emerges only in the light of a retrospective self-interpretation.

Such an interpretative and poetic act of narrative self-(re)construction does not seek to recapture the sheer empirical welter of lived experience, which in any event would be impossible, but seeks, in the creative interplay of memory and imagination, to discover and expand on the perceived significant or decisive "facts" of a life. He told Johann Peter Eckermann in 1831 (30 March, 2:466) that "a fact of our lives does not matter insofar as it is true but insofar as it is significant," a late pronouncement that suggests his sense of both the interpretative freedom and the challenge involved in capturing the meaning of a life. What Goethe seems to mean by *significant* is a wider relevance, resonance, and applicability that emerge only in the light of retrospection. His comment in the same conversation, that *Poetry and Truth* contains "some symbols of human life" and that he titled the work as he did because "it elevates itself through higher tendencies above the regions of a low reality" (466), bespeaks his notion of the representative or archetypal character of autobiography as a symbolic reflection of the human, and of the coincidence in the genre at its best of the individual with the species. Hence Goethe's concept of the role of *Dichtung* in autobiography takes us at another level to the philosophical and anthropological view of the genre adumbrated in Rousseau's Neuchâtel Preface to his *Confessions*.

What has become something of a consensus in contemporary autobiography studies since Pascal's groundbreaking study—that autobiographers shape the past in the light of the present and that they present not so much a past self per se as their self-understanding at the moment of writing (*Design and Truth* 4–9), or as Starobinski has strikingly put it, that "no matter how doubtful the facts related, the text will at least present an 'authentic' image of the man who 'held the pen'" ("The Style of Autobiography" 287)—informs Goethe's approach to the genre. His sophisticated awareness of the possibilities, conditions, and limits of autobiography is one that contemporary studies of the genre have only caught up with. In the *Annals* entry for 1811 in which he discusses the earliest stage of his autobiography project, Goethe mentions that he chose the original title, *Poetry and Truth*, because of his conviction that "humans model the outer world in the present, and even more in their memories, according to their individual attributes" (HA 10:510).[14] His most substantive statement about the "paradoxical" title comes in a late letter (11 January 1830, HA 11:574) that deserves to be quoted at some length as compelling evidence of his larger awareness of autobiography as a retrospective self-interpretation that merges memory and imagination. Goethe states that he chose the title because of the doubt of "the public" with respect to "the truthfulness of such biographical attempts." In order to address such reader suspicions (and perhaps with a covert pointer to Rousseau), he writes:

> Motivated by a certain spirit of contradiction and without any real need to do so, I owned up to a sort of fiction, because it was my most serious endeavor to represent and express as far as possible the fundamental truth [das eigentliche Grundwahre] that, as far as I could discern, had governed my life. But if this is not possible in later years without allowing the retrospective faculty and thus also the imagination to do their work, so that we therefore always end up in a sense exercising our poetic capacities, then it is clear that we will register and emphasize more the results of how we now think of past events than the particular events as they then transpired.

The assertion in the same letter that "all that which belongs to the narrator and the narrative I have comprehended under the word 'Poetry' [Dichtung], in order to make use of the truth of which I was conscious for my purposes" (574), presents a less critically informed view of the autobiographical act, because it sets up an untenable distinction between the "truth" of autobiography on the one hand—its content—and the manner of its presentation on the other—its narrative. Hayden White's analysis of the fictional and poetic element in historical narrative, with its emplotment of past events as much a function of the narrative imagination as of what(ever) actually happened, undoes this categorical distinction, as does Saine's reminder (in response to Trunz's ready acceptance of Goethe's distinction), "that even the selection of facts and events to be narrated is an interpretive act on the part of the author" ("Introduction," *Poetry and Truth* 4).[15] In any event, the poetic or fictional dimension of Goethe's autobiography reaches considerably beyond a narrative presentation that would leave the facts or the "truth" of his life untouched—the traditional or conservative view of the work.[16] Exactly how far it reaches no one can say with any certainty, but I expect it reaches a lot farther than has traditionally been assumed, because the deeper truth (das Grundwahre) is not so much a fixed or preexisting content that the autobiographer unearths as the archeologist of his own past as it is something discovered and formulated in the imaginative re-creation of the moment of writing. Or more precisely—since Goethe dictated the work to an amanuensis—the moment of speaking.

All of which is not to say that Goethe did not aim to tell the fundamental truth of his life to the best of his ability. Although he made considerable allowance for the play of the confessional imagination (as evident in the famous Sesenheim sequence analyzed in chapter 6), he could not simply invent freely or make up his experience out of whole cloth because he obviously felt himself bound by biographical, historical, and other referential constraints to capture the reality of his life, career, and individuality. In the preparatory stages of his "project of a self-biography," he started with the goal, as he states in an *Annals* entry of 1809, of being honest about himself and others and "of approaching the truth as much as possible, insofar as memory can in any way be helpful in this regard" (HA 10:507).

However, Mnemosyne, the muse of autobiography, is hardly an objective mirror, but has a poetry of her own that links her with the imagination. What is more, Mnemosyne is opposed by the pressure of Lethe, the river of forgetfulness, which is a constant threat to the autobiographer. From the Freudian perspective of our own century, we know that the absence of memory is not always a matter of simple or passive forgetting but often an active process of the mind to repress painful recollections in conflict with our conscious sense of ourselves. The recent bitter controversy surrounding the "recovered memory" syndrome has reopened the debate about the validity of the psychoanalytic theory of repression, but Goethe's own sense of the reality of forgetting was not that of a pathological process but of a remedy for the blows dealt to us by fate. In a letter near the end of his life he metaphorizes the healing process of forgetting as the breath of life itself. "We should bear in mind that with every breath we draw, an ethereal stream permeates our whole being, so that we recall our pleasures only moderately, and our sufferings hardly at all. I have always known to value, make use of, and increase this high gift of the gods" (HA 11:575, 15 February 1830). The phenomenon of such therapeutic forgetting surfaces explicitly in *Poetry and Truth* at the end of book 11 in Goethe's brief account of his guilty parting from Friederike Brion: "These were difficult days, and the memory of them has not stayed with me" (370).

Goethe's view of the benefits of forgetting anticipate and may even have influenced Nietzsche, who expresses a similar view in *The Genealogy of Morals* (second treatise, section 1), when he compares the ability to forget to the digestive mechanism of the human organism. Nietzsche too sees in the ability to forget "a force, a form of strong health" without which there can be no human happiness or hope (43). For both the poet and the philosopher, forgetting is a necessary human survival or coping mechanism. As Harald Weinrich has reminded us, such an ability to forget painful experiences is a large part of Faust's career. In the opening scene of part 2 of the play ("A Pleasant Landscape"), after the horrors of the imprisonment, madness, and execution of Gretchen, Faust is shown endeavoring to sleep in an alpine meadow, with Ariel singing a prayer that he may be bathed "in the dews of Lethe's waters" (*Faust* 4629).

However, if such a Lethe-gift helped Faust and his author get on with their titan-like lives without fretting too much about the human wreckage left in their wakes, for Goethe the autobiographer, the balm of forgetting clearly poses a problem and a challenge for getting down to the bedrock of *das Grundwahre* of his life. And even without taking into account this special or restorative loss of memory, ordinary forgetting in the course of our passing lives is a limit that opposes itself to the will of the autobiographer the further he moves away in time from what he wishes to recall. Thus Goethe mentions in an *Annals* entry for the year 1811 that when he turned to his autobiography and his "earliest life history," he found he "had delayed too long." "I should have undertaken this work during my mother's lifetime; then I would have been closer to those scenes of childhood and would have been transported there through the high power of the gift of memory. But now I had to recreate within myself those departed spirits and laboriously and artfully bring together, like a necessary instrument of magic, many a means of remembering" (HA 10:509–10). With her good humor, earthy nature that loved to expatiate in storytelling, and unqualified worship of her genius son, Goethe's mother—whom he had seen very infrequently since his permanent move to Weimar in 1776 and who had died in 1808—would have been an eager and rich resource in reconstructing the story of his childhood.

The dedicatory poem at the beginning of *Faust* speaks of "uncertain shapes, / Which in my early years I dimly glimpsed" (schwankende Gestalten, / Die früh sich einst dem trüben Blick gezeigt) (*Faust* 1–2, HA 3:9). Even though the elusive shapes are the figures of the Faust drama that first began to germinate in his imagination in his early youth, the phrase is also apt for the autobiographer's uncertain sense of his early memories. *Schwankend* includes the meanings of wavering, oscillating, uncertain. The motif of *schwanken* in the *Faust* "dedication" effectively registers the sense of uncertainty and the mnemonic struggle Goethe must have encountered in the preparatory stages of *Poetry and Truth*. However, this initial stage of struggle and disorientation does not itself figure in the text of the autobiography, where the period of childhood is presented with the easy mastery characteristic of the work as a whole. It is, incidentally, also a struggle one does not sense in the author of *The Confessions*, who seems to have had a much keener retrospective faculty, especially regarding the period of adolescence and youth, than did Goethe.

Goethe's attempts to remedy the shortcomings and uncertainties of his memories, not only of childhood but also of later periods presented in *Poetry and Truth*, included enlisting the help of others to clarify and supplement his recollections, and an extensive amount of reading and research in order to achieve a larger historical representation of the social, political, literary, and cultural milieu of that youth. He wrote in October 1810 (HA 11:557–58), for instance, to Bettina Brentano, who had spent long hours with his mother in Frankfurt listening to her stories about his childhood, for a written version of these—one set of memories (his mother's) refracted through another (Bettina's). The recollections of others were solicited as well, including those of his brother-in-law and the earlier mentioned Klinger (HA 11:562, 564). In that sense, it is no exaggeration to speak of his autobiography as a collaborative project. And as far as his reading and research are concerned, we know from the records of the ducal library at Weimar (Alt 87–90) that he borrowed a considerable number of literary and historical works, especially those dealing with the history of Frankfurt and eighteenth-century literature. This immersion in "world and literary history" allowed him to view his life in a wider perspective. As he wrote to his publisher in 1810, "I see myself for the first time in the circumstances which influenced me and which I influenced" (HA 11:558, 16 November).

Goethe's manifold supplementing of his own memories with the recollections of others and with considerable research gives to his narrative self-portrait an epic breadth of presentation. The development of his individual self and the attempt to present *das Grundwahre* of his life are projected against a rich and complexly layered background. Goethe, who was suspicious of the "know thyself" injunction, and whose paradigm of self and world is a dialectical one—"humans know themselves only insofar as they know their world, of which they only become aware in themselves, and themselves in it" (HA 13:38)—gives us the ultimate in a mediated self-presentation, a singular and subjective self reflected in and through a multiplicity of objective contexts. But to what extent such a cosmopolitan and mediated self-presentation can ultimately succeed in capturing the fundamental truth(s) of the self is open to question, since one could argue that the intense introspection Goethe categorically dismisses might lead to depths of self-knowledge not available to his mediated and contextualized approach. Or perhaps neither path can lead to the bottom of the self: the introspective and centripetal path, if pushed too far, can end in the prison house of the solipsistic ego chasing its own tail, and the centrifugal path of the self perpetually viewed through the other can lead to its diffusion in wider and wider contexts. Self-alienation can be achieved, as it were, through both extremes.

Goethe was not immune to such skeptical considerations, but with the hard-won stylistic lightness and serenity of *Poetry and Truth,* he refused to voice his doubts. In the Winckelmann essay that is a preparatory step toward his autobiography, however, he made a summary pronouncement that denies the autobiographer access to the fundamental truth of his life and dooms him forever to a half-knowledge of himself. Commenting on the art historian's letters, Goethe writes, "he remains altogether a riddle to himself . . . but then in general one can view each person as a many-syllabled charade, of which he can only spell a few syllables, while others can easily decipher the entire word" (HA 12:123). The autobiographer is limited by looking from the inside out; Goethe tried to maintain the fiction of the biographer's stance of looking from the outside in, thus spelling the entire word of his being. It is not for nothing that the third person and the royal "we" are so prevalent in his life narrative. The Olympian pose is impressive, and for the most part convincingly and effortlessly sustained throughout his autobiography. But in the more unguarded mode of his correspondence with friends, the voice of skepticism and doubt about our ability ever to fathom ourselves and our experiences can also be heard. "Admittedly we only come to know in old age what we encountered in our youth. Once and for all, we learn and understand nothing!" (HA 11:568, 7 November 1816).

THE PROBLEMATIC IDEAL: BILDUNG WITHOUT END

The notion of individuality that informs *Poetry and Truth* is based on Goethe's root concept of *Bildung*, that untranslatable word whose meanings include formation, development, education, and cultivation. Goethe's idea of *Bildung* or individual development is complex and far-reaching; it includes an ideal of education as a cultivation of our higher faculties that is most substantively embodied in his *Wilhelm Meister* novels and that achieved fuller definition for Goethe in part through his intellectual collaboration with Schiller in the 1790s. It is an overarching and comprehensive concept of education that is at once social, ethical, and aesthetic, and as such beyond the scope of my analysis of Goethe the autobiographer. My more limited focus on *Bildung* is on a problematic ideal of *Poetry and Truth* that on the one hand is a function of the organic and genetic outlook that marks Goethe's scientific—specifically his biological—thinking, and that on the other has theological and even mystical implications as a potentially endless process or evolutionary movement from the (material and organic) lower to the (spiritual) higher. In that sense, Goethe's ideal of *Bildung* might also be characterized as a nineteenth-century secular religion.[17]

The importance of the organic and genetic conception of human development for the self-presentation of *Poetry and Truth* has been noted in different contexts and with varying degrees of emphasis by students and critics of the work.[18] That conception is evident from a draft preface for part 3, in which Goethe acknowledges that originally he had thought of modeling the first three volumes of his autobiography "according to those laws about which the metamorphosis of plants teaches us." "In the first [part] the child was to put forth tender roots in all directions and develop only a few budding leaves. In the second [part] the boy was to put forth in stages of lively green more variously formed twigs, and this animated stalk was now in the third . . . to hurry toward its bloom and represent the youth full of hope" (HA 9:754). In the end Goethe did not use the botanical analogy, presumably because it is inexact and ignores or minimizes other aspects—chiefly history and society, which play a decisive role in our lives and figure so prominently in his autobiography. Nevertheless it is clear that his scientific inquiries into morphology, which he defined as "the study of the form, formation, and transformation of organic beings"

(*On Morphology,* HA 13:124), profoundly influenced his view of individual development. Goethe first sought to formulate "the laws of the transformation . . . according to which" nature "produces one part through another, and represents the most varied shapes through the modification of a single organ" (HA 13:64), in his 1790 dissertation on *The Metamorphosis of Plants.* There he sought to trace a complex but unitary organic process that accounts for "the outer form of the plant in all its transformations, from its germination from the grain of seed to the new formation of the same [plant]" (HA 13:89). For Goethe the scientist, both plants and humans are part of a larger, lawful nature: "Each plant announces to you the eternal laws / Each flower speaks louder and louder to you," he wrote in his poem on the same topic (HA 13:109).

In his subsequent reflections and writings on morphology, he emphasizes that both humans and plants have a given organic structure that unfolds or develops ("the idea of evolution" HA 13:121) according to the laws of nature and in the context of a particular environment (soil, climate, weather). Organic beings are never at rest or complete; rather, they are in a "constant movement" that we call "development" (Bildung) (HA 13:55). Like all emanations of nature, they are subject to its "two great driving forces," which Goethe identifies as the concepts of "polarity" and "ascension" (Steigerung) ("Elucidation of the Aphoristic Essay, 'Nature,'" HA 13:48). In Goethe's late summary of his fundamentally philosophical view of nature (1828), the former (polarity) defines the material world, as we conceive it in a material sense (caught up in "perpetual attraction and repulsion"); the latter (ascension) defines that world as we conceive it in a mental or spiritual sense (caught up in "an ever-striving ascension"). "But because the material can never exist and be effective without the mental, and the mental can never do so without the material, so the material too is capable of ascension, just as the mental will not do without attraction and repulsion" (48).

The correlation of the mental and the physical with the dialectical tension of polarity and the perpetual upward or evolutionary drive that is paradigmatic of Goethe's view of nature is also suggestive of the larger terms in which he thinks of individual human development. In Goethe's dynamic and quasi-evolutionary view, nature (both as polarity and ascension) is not so much a closed system ("natural system, a contradictory expression," "Problems," HA 13:35), as it is a force or energy field that comprehends and defines both the inorganic and organic levels of being. Already as a young student, as he tells us in book II of *Poetry and Truth*, Goethe had rejected the extremes of the mechanistic and materialistic cosmology of the French Enlightenment as formulated in Paul Thiry, Baron d'Holbach's *System of Nature*. That "system" struck him as a "gloomy, atheistic semi-darkness," a "hollow and empty" universe, "so gray, so Cimerrian, so deathly" (363–64). His totalizing and vitalistic view of nature—a macrocosm that in some mysterious sense mirrors the microcosm of the individual self—is of an indwelling but ultimately unfathomable order that cannot be reduced to any specific limit, either as point of origin or end. "Nature has no system; it . . . is life and succession from an unknown center toward a not recognizable limit. Therefore the contemplation of nature is endless; one can proceed by dividing it into its smallest particulars or with respect to the whole, and pursue the track according to breadth and height" ("Problems," HA 13:35). By implication, the study of human development for Goethe also has no beginning or end, and the task of the autobiographer in tracing and seeking to comprehend his own *Bildung* is truly an "endless" one.

Some of the older Goethe's striking morphological speculations also resonate with meaning for his perception of the formative process that is human development and carry a certain autobiographical charge. His understanding of nature, cultivated over nearly five decades—indeed, as Emil Staiger reminds us (2:126), over the course of his long life Goethe devoted more time to science than to literature—is always also a mediated or objectified mode of self-understanding. I am thinking, for instance, of the assertion near the end of his essay on "The History of My Botanical Studies" that the great variability of plant forms is "not originally determined and fixed," but includes "a happy mobility and flexibility" that allows them to adapt to their given environment (HA 13:163). Even more suggestive is his reflection in 1823 that "the idea of metamorphosis" contains two antithetical forces simultaneously at work, a "vis centrifuga" that leads into the "formless," and a "vis centripeta," a capacity to persist on the part of that which has come into being and "which at bottom nothing external can affect" ("Problems," HA 13:35)—a significant cross-pull clearly visible in his own life. Finally, the very late dissertation on *The Spiral Tendency of Plants* (1831), which identifies two fundamental tendencies of all plant life—a (masculine) "vertical striving" that effects the separation of the plant from the root and its raising of itself in a straight line toward the sky, and a (feminine) "spiral" or twining and circling movement around the aspiring vertical that seeks orderly completion and closure (HA 13:131–48)—also offers clues to human *Bildung*. Indeed, these strange morphological reflections can stand as a botanical allegory for the aged Goethe's larger organic vision of the androgynous and dialectical dance of human life and the formative process of our becoming.

Goethe's thesis about the spiral tendency of plants reflects a larger teleological outlook that also defines his notion of *Bildung* in *Poetry and Truth,* a dynamic process driven by the energy inherent in our being. As Goethe put it with a maxim that sounds like an earlier version of Nietzsche's will-to-power, "the highest which we have received from God and Nature is life, the rotating movement of the monad about itself, which knows neither rest nor calm" ("Maxims and Reflections," HA 12:396). Faust's famous restless striving was of course Goethe's own. This unceasing urge was a need to form or develop himself in many different directions. Goethe identified an "ever-active, poetic developmental instinct at work within and without [as] the central point and basis of his existence." Hence also "the many false tendencies," which, however, in the long run are not "unproductive" ("Self-Description," 1797, HA 10:529). According to this generous view of *Bildung,* our very mistakes and missteps are part of this larger process of becoming the ineffable individual we have developed into and potentially have always been. The young Goethe pursued the imperatives of his own development with a certain reckless intensity, something evident in a letter written at the age of twenty-one, where he asserts (in very androcentric language) that "this desire to drive the pyramid of my being, whose basis has been assigned to and founded in me, as high as possible outweighs everything else" (September 1770, *Briefe* 1:324). Such an energetic intensification or *Steigerung* of his individuality is a given throughout his life, as we can hear in the resolution of his last letter, quoted at the beginning of this chapter. In his *Italian Journey* he revealingly characterized his way of developing and heightening his self as that of the "screw without end" ("Schraube ohne Ende," HA 11:417).

This last trope is mechanical, not organic, but effectively figures the dynamic upward movement of the Goethean concept of *Bildung.* As Weintraub has pointed out, for the author of *Poetry and Truth* "growth is not simply an unfolding" but is represented as "an upward-moving spiral"

(363–64). Humans are part of a larger nature, but they are also its crowning achievement, its most complex and impressive development. As Goethe wrote in his *Winckelmann* essay, "the final product of an ever ascending [immer steigernden] nature is the beautiful human being" (HA 12:102). If humans are located in the upper reaches of an ascending nature, Goethe's notion of his own development places him at the very apex of that symbolic pyramid. What he once stated in an aphoristic fragment is one of the most honest and most illuminating things he ever said about himself: "I have never known a more presumptuous human being than myself" ("Self-Description," HA 10:530). Perhaps the ultimate presumption of Goethe's view of *Bildung* is that a perpetually aspiring existence like his can have no end. Like the young Keats of the famous Vale of Soulmaking letter (14 February–3 May 1819), but in a different context, the aged Goethe envisions an immortality that is existentially earned and that is ultimately nothing less than his due. "The conviction of an afterlife arises for me from the concept of activity; because if I am restlessly active until my end, nature is obliged to assign me another form of being, when the present one is no longer capable of sustaining my spirit" (Eckermann 1:288, 4 February 1829).

At once biological and theological, Goethe's concept of human development breaks with religious autobiography and—like Rousseau's, yet in a very different key—moves the history of the self and the process of its formation, for its own sake and as its own end, to the center of the stage of modern autobiography. As Derek Bowman has pointed out, "the immense energy which in former . . . ages had gone into the search for God . . . is now put into tracing the growth of the author's personality" (50). Like Rousseau's, Goethe's presentation of the subject—himself—is secular and anthropological. What sets Goethe apart from Rousseau, however, is not only his conscious avoidance of a self-tormenting introspection, but, as Dmitri Satonski has concluded (110), "the developmental idea which is the foundation" of *Poetry and Truth* and which gives it a richer confessional perspective than is found in *The Confessions*.

Despite his own botanical interests, Rousseau's perception of life was not genuinely developmental in the organic and genetic sense of Goethe's *Bildung*. Nor is there in Rousseau any sense of a paradigmatic pattern of spiritual development, of the "Schraube ohne Ende"—on the contrary, in the latter portions of his autobiography Rousseau is trapped in the circle of his paranoia. Of course, one of the signal virtues of Rousseau the auto-biographer is his acuity as a psychologist. The narrative of part 1 of his *Confessions* demonstrates a new and near-psychoanalytic awareness of the importance of our early experiences and shows, as I have argued, a pattern of lost innocence—of the boy being not so much formed as deformed by society. At its best, his presentation of central episodes of his early years, like the two famous spankings, is a brilliant apologetic analysis of the complexities of his emotional life. But as Michael Sheringham has argued, Rousseau's attempt "to give expression to a historicized self" is imbedded in an eighteenth-century psychological language of largely mechanical causation, which at best he wields with remarkable ingenuity and skill to demonstrate "the way early experiences remain alive in us" (33, 39, 42). Yet if Rousseau's confessional narrative lacks the unifying power and the per-spectival richness of the concept of *Bildung* that informs *Poetry and Truth,* conversely Goethe does not bring to the analysis of his early experiences the imaginative intensity and unprecedented analytic effort that Rousseau devotes to key episodes of his childhood.

Human development is ultimately a much more complex, problem-atic, and altogether unpredictable and uncertain matter than the growth of a plant, of course, and Goethe thus wisely chose not to use the literal botanical analogy that he had originally considered as an organizing scheme for the first three parts of *Poetry and Truth.* As a consistently applied poetic analogy, it would have been too literal and reductive. Humans have consciousness and volition, and their habitat or environ-ment is altogether different, for it includes the achievements of civiliza-tion that have, as Freud reminds us in *Civilization and Its Discontents,* become second nature to us. Individual development and identity are always imbricated in, subject to, and ultimately a function of the forces, not only of family, but of politics and history as well. For Goethe there is in any event something unsteady, incommensurable, and ultimately inex-plicable in our individual developments and the outcomes of our lives. Even at the genetic level, the very "richness of childhood" deludes us, showing more promise than is fulfilled and an unpredictable growth that only makes sense in hindsight:

If children continued to grow in line with what they first indicate, we would have nothing but geniuses. But growth implies more than mere expansion: the various organic systems constituting the individual human being originate in one another, follow one another, transform themselves into each other, displace one another, and even consume one another, so that in time scarcely a trace remains of some abilities and some manifestations of strength. While a person's potentialities, overall, are bent in a definite direction, even the greatest, most experienced expert would find it difficult to predict reliably what that might be. But with hindsight one can recognize the features quite well that were pointing toward future developments. (book 2, 64)

As Goethe points out in book 9, there are psychological indicators of the direction our growth will take: "[O]ur wishes are presentiments of capacities that lie within us, harbingers of what we shall be able to accomplish," but these are subject to the pressure of circumstances. "If a particular tendency is definitely in our nature, then a part of our early wish will be fulfilled at every step of our development, in a straight line if circumstances are favorable, and if they are unfavorable, then in a roundabout way from which we constantly turn back to the right one" (286–87). And even beyond the genetic and organic determinants of individual development, there is a larger and mysterious dialectic to the outcome of our lives that Goethe formulates paradigmatically in the famous statement of book 11: "There are few biographies that can depict an individual's progress as being pure, calm, steady. Our lives, like the context in which we live, are an incomprehensible mixture of freedom and necessity. Our desires proclaim in advance what we will do under any set of circumstances. These circumstances, however, control us in their own way. The 'what' is within us, the 'how' rarely depends on us, the 'why' we dare not inquire about, and therefore we are correctly referred to the *quia* [because]" (355).

His most comprehensive statement—at once poetic, philosophical, and symbolic—of the archetypal or normative and timeless determinants of an individual life is found in the cryptic 1817 poem, "Primal Words. Orphic," which is frequently linked by Goethe scholars with his notions of individuality and *Bildung*. There he identifies the essential moments or eternal coordinates of our being by their Greek terms (HA 1:359–60): *daimon* (the self or entelechy with which we come into the world); *tyche* (the accidental, the changing circumstances that frame our lives); *eros* (the unifying force of love); *ananke* (necessity, the laws and limitations of the cosmos in which we find ourselves); and *elpis* (hope, which allows us to rise above the "wall" of such limitations).[19] In Goethe's "daemonic" view of the human entelechy, the self is fated to be itself according to the "law" by which it entered into the world and from which it "cannot escape." "And no time and no force can dismember / A specified form in its living development" (Und keine Zeit und keine Macht zerstückelt / Geprägte Form, die lebend sich entwickelt).

Goethe's secular theology of *Bildung* as the goal or chief good of our lives is also an affirmation of the productive energies of the self and of its manifold potential of agency and activity in the world. As such, this affirmation constitutes a rejection of Christian humility and turns pride based on actual accomplishments into a positive virtue. In Goethe's this-worldly and humanistic gospel of energy and striving, we are here to cultivate and exercise our natural capacities and abilities and are entitled to derive pleasure and satisfaction from so doing. Our talents are gifts of nature, to be developed and enjoyed as such. Thus the young Goethe came to see his extraordinary poetic gift, which manifested itself quite early, "altogether as nature" (book 16, 525). The desire for public recognition as a deserved reward of one's abilities and achievements is also natural and legitimate, as is evident in the letter Goethe quotes at length in book 17 from the Reformation humanist Ulrich von Hutten: "Every desire for fame is honorable, all struggle for excellence is laudable" (553).[20] In a mass culture like ours, where the ideal of excellence seems to have degenerated, exactly as Tocqueville foresaw, into the consumer philosophy of less (quality) for more (quantity), and where fame and celebrity are often as short-lived as they are undeserved, Goethe's endorsement in the name of *Bildung* of talent, effort, and achievement no doubt has a shockingly elitist ring. But then perhaps we have forgotten that genuine cultural achievements are not possible without such a thirst and "struggle for excellence."

What Weintraub has characterized as Goethe's application of "organistic, naturalistic notions to the presentation of his own formation" (365) is, however, neither consistent nor unproblematic. As noted in some of the recent discussions of *Poetry and Truth,* there is a marked shift of emphasis or even a different outlook with respect to the issue of *Bildung* in the later portions of the work. To quote from one of these, "the biological pictures disappear." The same critic adds, "I find it impressive that he was capable

of abandoning . . . his long-maintained biological conceptual scheme,
because he obviously gained the conviction that the riddle of human existence was not to be approached through it" (Stern 279). "Abandoning" is
surely too strong a word, because the difficult concept of "the daemonic"
that Goethe mentions in a diary entry of April 1813 (HA 10:650) but only
elaborates in the concluding book of part 4 (in connection with his decision to accept the invitation to Weimar), is not so much a simple replace-
ment, as Niggl argues, for "the idea of an organic metamorphosis" (162)
as a supplement to it. The concept can be seen as an alternative explanation at another level of something important that is left out of account by
the organic conception. While Niggl is probably right in his conclusion
that "this newly adumbrated dimension" is meant to apply retroactively to
the earlier portions of Goethe's autobiography (164), I suggest it does not
constitute a rejection per se of the developmental paradigm but a re-situ-
ating of it in a larger framework. Admittedly the later "daemonic" conception exists in considerable logical tension in the text with the earlier
organic one and as such presents a real interpretive crux for the larger
developmental patterning of Goethe's autobiography.[21] That tension,
however, is a precise reflection of the real-life situation that Goethe is
seeking to account for, where the reality or experience of growth as a
steady unfolding was jostled and disrupted by the political upheavals of
the French Revolution and the Napoleonic Wars.

Thus the supplementing of the notion of organic unfolding with that
of the sudden and disruptive forces of history is a mimetic move to
account for the character of his and his contemporaries' experience. As an
explanatory category, "the daemonic" is invoked in the context of a synoptic review of his religious attitudes. Religious and metaphysical in provenance, it came to him from his contemplation of nature:

He believed that he perceived something in nature . . . that manifested itself only in contradictions and therefore could not be
expressed in any concept, much less any word. It was not divine, for
it seemed irrational; not human, for it had no intelligence; not dia-
bolical, for it was beneficent; and not angelic, for it often betrayed
malice. It was like chance, for it lacked continuity, and like Providence, for it suggested context. Everything that limits us seemed
penetrable by it, and it appeared to dispose at will over the elements

necessary to our existence, to contract time and expand space. It seemed only to accept the impossible and scornfully to reject the possible. This essence, which appeared to infiltrate all the others . . . I called daemonic, after the example of the ancients and others who had perceived something similar. (597)

As the factor of the capricious and unpredictable, and of the random and disruptive occurrences that yet appear to have a hidden meaning, the dae-monic problematizes Goethe's view of a lawful universe by subsuming the very factor of discontinuity, caprice, and chance to some occult and covert order. At one level, Goethe's controversial notion of the daemonic seems to be that of a cosmic Puck wreaking havoc with the order created by humans: "While the daemonic element can manifest itself in anything cor-poreal or incorporeal . . . its primary, most amazing association is with man, constituting a power not necessarily opposed to the moral world order, but crisscrossing it to the extent that one could be called the warp and the other the woof" (598). At another level, it is a historicizing notion that offers an ex post facto explanation of Europe's upheavals during the late eighteenth and early nineteenth centuries. In its application to the political sphere, the notion is a quasi-Hegelian one of the world-historical individual and charismatic figure, with obvious reference to Napoleon. "The daemonic principle . . . is at its most fearful when it emerges pre-dominantly in some individual. In the course of my life I have been able to observe several of these . . . They are not always the most excellent men, either in mind or talents, and they seldom have kindness of heart to rec-ommend them. But they radiate an enormous strength and exercise incredible power over all creatures, even over the elements, and who can say just how far such influence does extend? All the moral powers in uni-son can do nothing against them (598).[22] Of religious provenance but transferred to the political and historical sphere, Goethe's invocation of the daemonic can also be seen as a romantic gesture of irrationalism and mystification meant to account for the convulsive upheavals in the world around him.

That the problematic account of the daemonic in the final book is not meant to cancel out or replace the biological view of development is sug-gested by the fact that Goethe wrote the draft preface for part 3, in which he summarizes his initial plan of modeling his autobiography on the meta-

morphosis of plants several months after his first reference to the daemonic in his diary entry of April 1813. He did not adhere to the schematic
analogy once he set to work on *Poetry and Truth,* but his careful elabora-
tion of that analogy in the preface shows that it still held a good deal of significance for him when he had already begun to entertain the notion of the
daemonic. Indeed, he deployed the analogy to indicate the very setbacks
to his *Bildung* that would be the substance of part 4: "[I]n the next period
. . . the blossoms fall away . . . and even where there is some [fruit], it is
insignificant, grows slowly, and its maturity is delayed. Indeed how much
fruit falls through various mischances before it is ripe, and the enjoyment
that one seemed to have in one's grasp is spoiled" (HA 9:754).

The supplementary and mimetic character (as a reflection of his own
experience) of the introduction of the daemonic near the conclusion of
Poetry and Truth is indicated as well by a letter of 1824 in which Goethe
mentions how the death of Schiller in 1805 and "the invasion of the
French" in 1806 has spelled the end of an epoch. "That manner of educat-
ing [bilden] oneself, which in the North developed and continually
increased during the period of peace, was violently interrupted; all from
childhood and youth onward were forced to educate themselves differently, just as in this tumultuous age there was no lack of mis-education
[verbilden]" (*Briefe* 4:132, 24 December 1824). The process of a slow and
regular *Bildung* that defines Goethe's retrospectively idealizing portrait of
his youth—and that had not really been interrupted even by the French
occupation of Frankfurt during his adolescence—runs up against the
French Revolution and the Napoleonic era that disrupted and altered forever all existing social conditions. Goethe's past was history, and even
though *Poetry and Truth* stops some fourteen years before the storming of
the Bastille, the older Goethe introduces into the narrative of his youth a
concept that he developed much later and that both reflects and seeks to
account for these world-shaking changes and the chaos of contemporary
history.

If the notion of the daemonic does not constitute, as I have argued, a
rejection of but essentially a late and supplementary contextualizing of the
central developmental idea of the first three parts of *Poetry and Truth,*
there is at least one significant way in which that idea is called into question and problematized in the light of Goethe's life experience and self-
understanding—through the ideal of renunciation (Entsagung) so

important to the older Goethe as a worldly wisdom, one also central to his vision of the maturity of Wilhelm Meister. As a theme in Goethe's work, renunciation already becomes important around the time of Schiller's death (in 1805).[23] Goethe introduces that ideal at the beginning of part 4 under the aegis of his renewed study of Spinoza. It is the quintessential experience of middle age, with all its painful burdens, that the older man brings to the narrative of his youth, and the realization of the necessity of resignation that derives from it as a life strategy constitutes a limit to, if not a retrenchment of, the youthful experience of *Bildung:*

> Our physical as well as social life, our manners, habits, worldly wisdom, philosophy, religion . . . all proclaim to us that we must *renounce.* Many an inward, very personal quality is not destined to be developed for outward use; we are deprived of what we require from without to supplement our existence; and on the other hand, a great deal is thrust upon us that we find alien and burdensome. We are robbed of hard-won gains, of privileges graciously granted, and before we really know what is happening we find ourselves compelled to abandon our personality, at first bit by bit, and then altogether. (book 16, 523)

There is a somber and even tragic note here in the acknowledgment that *Bildung* is actually (as opposed to potentially) not without end, and that indeed it is too often painfully truncated and even aborted. The ideal is vitiated by the burdensome realities of life, which too often fail to answer our wishes. The young Goethe had already derived a "peaceful effect" from reading Spinoza, whose life and teachings provided a therapeutic counter-pole to his restless striving and Promethean pyramid climbing. Most of us, says Goethe, perhaps too sanguinely, are "equipped" by "nature . . . with adequate strength, energy, and toughness to accomplish the task" of swallowing the bitter cup and renouncing the fond expectations of our youth. We renounce one thing for another, "replace one passion with another" (523). For the aged author of part 4, however, the attraction of Spinoza is that he is one of "only a few persons who have . . . avoided all these partial resignations by resigning themselves totally, once and for all" (523). The purity and disinterestedness of the Spinozan ethic of renunciation—or perhaps in the Freudian sense, of complete sublimation—is one that Goethe could admire and even preach, but not one he could really or consistently practice, as his life as well as the career of his most famous fictional self-incarnation, Faust, amply attest. That redemption comes for him "who ever strives without ceasing" [Wer immer strebend sich bemüht] (*Faust,* part 2, 11936, HA 3:359), is also the basso profundo of Goethe's problematic creed of self-realization and *Bildung* without end, and the Spinozan note of renunciation so poignantly sounded as the overture of part 4 of his autobiography is but a powerful contrapuntal motif in the ninth symphony of his aspiring life.

AUTOBIOGRAPHY AS THE SUPPLEMENT OF THE SUBJECT

The author of the greatest modern autobiography did not think of the work as independent, self-sustaining, and complete in itself. As pointed out earlier, Goethe considered subsequent autobiographical texts such as *Italian Journey* a continuation of what he identified in his main title as *From My Life.* On two occasions in *Poetry and Truth* he specifically notes the *supplementary* character of the work. In the famous statement of book 7, he characterizes "all [his] published works" as "fragments of one great confession, *which this little book is a bold attempt to complete*" (214, emphasis added). And when in book 12 he comes to the period of his life that furnished the raw material for the fictional confession of *Young Werther,* he states, "this book [*Poetry and Truth*]. . . was not declared to be an independent entity, but was meant to fill the gaps in an author's life, to complete many fragments, and to preserve the memory of bold enterprises now lost and forgotten" (400). The last part of the quotation refers to planned but unwritten or unfinished works (for example, narratives dealing with mythological subjects like Prometheus, the Wandering Jew, and the founder of Islam), which he sometimes discusses in greater detail than he does his published works.

Goethe's stance here is the exact opposite of that of Wordsworth, who spoke of *The Prelude* as preparation for the major work of his maturity that was yet to come (the never-completed *Recluse*). If the older sage of Weimar was looking back and commenting on the body of his earlier work, the younger poet was looking forward to the hoped-for achievements of his maturity. But at bottom, the two writers' antithetical views of the function and purpose of their autobiographies may have a common rhetorical motive—a residual decorum and reserve inherited from the century of their birth that does not allow them openly to avow or indulge at protracted length in what would seem to be the self-centered and egotistical act of writing their lives for their own sakes. Just as *The Prelude* is no mere prelude, so *Poetry and Truth* is literally no "little book." Lacking Rousseau's penchant for self-advertisement or the bold disingenuousness of Alfieri, who in the preface of his autobiography asserts, "I frankly acknowledge, that among all the different sentiments which induced me to become my own biographer, the most powerful was self-love" (1), the more tactful and discreet Goethe required, like Wordsworth, a rhetorical fig leaf for his monumental autobiographical project.

With its device of a fictional letter from a friend requesting that Goethe provide a commentary and context for the twelve-volume edition of his works (1806–08), the preface of *Poetry and Truth* provides such a convenient cover. And the letter also allows Goethe to justify and rationalize his autobiography as a completion of his published writings. In the language of the letter, "the twelve volumes as a whole" elicit the wish on the part of Goethe's friends "to sketch a portrait of the author and his talents." Yet the "identical" volumes frustrate such a desire for authorial *identity,* because "in general" Goethe's published writings "lack connection with each other. Often it is hard to believe that they were written by the same author" (15). That is, the chronological ordering of his collected works and the commentary requested by his friends—to "make us privy, in some coherent fashion, not only to those conditions of life and mind that provided the substance for them, but also to the examples that influenced you and the theoretical principles you followed" (16)—is an enabling trope on Goethe's part for the identity-establishing and confirming role of his autobiography.[24] As a supplement to and completion of the collected edition, *Poetry and Truth* will establish the larger coherence and unity behind Goethe's seemingly disparate and discontinuous writings. The author's greater self is not adequately expressed or fully represented in these disconnected fragments; his identity is not in but behind his published writings, or in the interstices between them. Hence his autobiography will provide the missing links, fill in the gaps, provide the biographical context. Paradoxically, the missing identity—the unity and coherence not apparent in his gathered texts—will be *textually* established by bridging the gaps between and thus binding together his earlier productions. Or, his earlier and fictionalized self-writing requires still more self-writing—

the monumental project of a full-scale autobiography. Perhaps the greatest piece of poetry in Goethe's autobiography is this utopian notion of a textually constituted and fully elaborated authorial identity.

The ploy of the prefatory letter thus bears witness to a new or changed conception between author and text that might be called the autobiographization of literature, in which Rousseau had been so instrumental. Koranyi has pointed out how in Goethe's later writings the "classical concept of the work" as "the locus where a specific theme is given a conclusive treatment" is replaced by the autobiographical concept of the author as "the instance from which everything emanates and toward which everything tends" (152). Clearly, for Goethe and the new century there is no intentional fallacy—that early-twentieth-century modernist tag designed as a rearguard action to once more separate author and work—because the meaning and very being of a text are grounded in the author's experience and identity. But in Goethe the autobiographization of literature is also turned into a high literary art, or what might be called the literarization of life, of which *Poetry and Truth* is the supreme instance.

Like Rousseau's, Goethe's works are thus underwritten by the subject, the ground of being from which they sprang and to which they are reflexively bound. According to the rhetoric of the prefatory letter, they will be completed and contextualized through the life narrative of that subject. Yet the programmatic anchoring of the writing(s) in the life is not the self-confining act of a narrow subjectivity, as it sometimes is in Rousseau's *Confessions,* when the reader experiences claustrophobia in the face of a narcissistic self-concern verging at times on sheer solipsism. On the contrary, Goethe seeks to make his reach as an autobiographer coeval with his world. As he informs us in the preface, in setting out to present the story of his life, he discovered that he required the larger, objective context in which that life was embedded and by which it was defined—the wider world of history and politics, the matrix in which his subjectivity is located. "While I was trying to respond to their [his friends'] very well-considered demands and endeavoring to outline seriatim the inner impulses and outer influences . . . lo! I found myself transported out of my narrow private life into the wide world" (16). In foregrounding the subject-object, microcosm-macrocosm relationship as a dialectical one, Goethe's preface posits the historical dimension as the necessary horizon of modern autobiography. Only from its encompassing perspective can we begin to comprehend the meaning of an individual life. Just as in his view of the supplementary and self-completing character of *Poetry and Truth,* so in his stress on the reciprocal exchanges between the individual and his age, the later Goethe is concerned with the larger, problematical relationship of the part (or parts) to the whole:

> For the chief goal of biography appears to be this: to present the subject in his temporal circumstances, to show how these both hinder and help him, how he uses them to construct his view of man and the world, and how he, providing he is an artist, poet, or author, mirrors them again for others. But something nearly impossible is required for this, namely, that the individual know himself and his century . . . as a force pulling him along willy-nilly, directing and developing him to such an extent the one may well say he would have been a quite different person if born ten years before or after, as far as his own cultural development and his effect on others are concerned. (17)

If the conception of autobiography articulated here is a historicizing one, Goethe's vision of the genre is also synecdochic, because in the work that follows this preface he seeks to present the relationship of the subject to his world in all its complexity and richness.

5 ✸

Family Relationships in *Poetry and Truth*

The story of the subject is also and always that of a family. Thus the first major Western autobiographer paints a portrait of his saintlike Christian mother and his worldly and pagan father that already indicates the stresses of the Freudian family romance in the Bishop of Hippo's passionate filial idealization of Monica and his consistent hostility to Patricius, in the light of his highly ideological post-conversion perspective on his early years. However, the growing psychological awareness since the later eighteenth century and the Romantic conviction that the child is the father of the man help to account for the privileging of childhood and youth in the autobiographies of the past two centuries. In attending to the formative experiences of their early years, modern chroniclers of their own lives are naturally led to consider the figures of the men and the women who fathered and mothered the child. Given the impressive portraits of parents and family drawn by twentieth-century autobiographers—Mary McCarthy (*Memories of a Catholic Girlhood*), Vladimir Nabokov (*Speak, Memory*), Jean-Paul Sartre (*The Words*), Camara Laye (*The Dark Child*), Maxine Hong Kingston (*The Woman Warrior*), to name a few—contemporary readers and critics of the genre have come to expect the depiction of the particular family constellations of the writer's early years.[1] Indeed, the period of childhood has become the focal point of such recent best-selling memoirs as Mary Karr's *The Liars' Club* and Frank McCourt's *Angela's Ashes*.

These modern and contemporary autobiographers of childhood are following in the footsteps of Rousseau, Goethe, and Wordsworth. We recall that the biological parents played no substantive role in Rousseau's case, as his mother died in bringing him into the world and his father stepped out of the picture when Rousseau was ten. Nevertheless, as we saw in chapter 2, Rousseau presents in part 1 of his *Confessions* a rich and complexly elaborated account of a mother in the person of Mme de Warens. If in "Mamma" he creates one of the most striking versions of a mother figure in the history of autobiography, Goethe, in his presentation of his early years, concentrates his narrative energy on two family relationships that are largely absent in Rousseau: those with his father and his only surviving sibling.

GOETHE AND HIS PARENTS

As the firstborn son of a wealthy father and grandson of the leading public official of the imperial free city of Frankfurt, Goethe depicts a childhood of considerable privilege and great expectations. The chief object of attention of two doting parents, young Johann Wolfgang experienced none of the emotional insecurity of the early years of Jean-Jacques, nor his sense of downward mobility after his father's flight from Geneva. If anything, Goethe was burdened with a too attentive paterfamilias, a frustrated man of leisure who in the wake of failed professional ambitions appears to have made the education of his two surviving children the chief task of his middle years. Johann Caspar Goethe, the proud son of a self-made man of peasant origins who had accumulated a fortune in the Frankfurt in which he was a parvenu, was rebuffed when, after the completion of his university studies in law, he offered his services to his native city: "[W]hen his proposal was rejected, he became angry and sullen, and swore never to accept any position. To make this impossible he procured himself the title of Imperial Councilor. . . . Thus he made himself equal with the topmost officials and could no longer start from the bottom" (book 2, 65). Goethe observes wryly in book 1 that "all fathers cherish the pious wish to see their sons achieve what they themselves have not managed to do" (36), and Johann Caspar wanted his son to follow the same academic track he had pursued and to succeed in the legal and public service career where he had failed. This is, as we shall see, the chief burden that Goethe's father placed on his son during Johann Wolfgang's early years.

In powerful contrast to Rousseau's youthful quest for an all-encompassing mother figure, what is perhaps most striking in Goethe's presentation of his childhood and youth is the essential absence of any sustained characterization of his young mother, whose colorful and dynamic personality is confirmed by the biographers but only sporadically glimpsed in Goethe's own text. We *sense* her central role as a tender and devoted parent, but we actually hear relatively little about her, because, to put a complex issue in its simplest terms, Goethe chose not to make his relationship with her a significant issue in his life narrative. Indeed, as Friedenthal points out in his sketch of her (14–19), Goethe never spoke of his mother with the praise he reserved for others, nor is she incorporated into any of his fictional works. It is certainly ironic that while he drew, as we saw in the previous chapter, on her recollections of his childhood (by way of Bettina Brentano's recording of them), the living maternal source of those memories is mostly excluded from his autobiography. The draft of a brief sketch or "aristeia" of his mother (furnished by Brentano) was in the end not incorporated into *Poetry and Truth*. And in any event, it says next to nothing about Goethe's relationship with her.

Goethe comes closest to acknowledging the importance of his mother for his life and character in his concluding comments at the conclusion of part 2 in book 10. In evaluating what he owes to each of his parents, he gives a decided preference to his mother:

From my father I had inherited a certain didactic loquacity, from my mother the gift of depicting brightly and forcefully everything produced and comprehended by the imagination: of freshening up familiar fairy tales, of inventing and narrating new ones, indeed of inventing as I went along. On account of that paternal endowment I frequently grew irksome to company, for who cares to hear someone else's opinions and sentiments, particularly those of a youth, whose judgment always seems unsound because of the gaps in his experience? On the other hand, my mother had really equipped me well to be socially entertaining. (330)

In a sense his mother was his muse, from whom he acquired that delight in fabulation that made Goethe the poet and writer he was. One might say that at one level she represents the element of "poetry" and his father that of "truth" in the title of his autobiography. What conviviality and *joie de vivre* Goethe had he also gained from her, whereas what discipline and application he brought to his work came from his father, who imparted to him as well the hypochondriacal and touchy disposition that surfaces in *Poetry and Truth* despite the older Goethe's resolute effort at a consistent cheerfulness of presentation.

In Goethe's case, the failure to portray the relationship between him and the loving mother who took such obvious pride in the accomplishments of her talented and precocious son is certainly puzzling, but it is not in any simple sense a matter of bad faith or repression—of overt hostility, at one extreme, or Oedipal mother love so powerful it cannot be represented, at the other.[2] Friedenthal, who makes much of her absence from Goethe's writings, concludes that "she remained a secret to him" (15). It may be that in the colorful vernacular of her earthy character and the worldly and proverbial wisdom of her colloquial speech and writing, as well as in the irrepressible energy of her pervasive cheerfulness and sheer good nature, he felt a presence literally too close to home, one that he needed to keep at arm's length. Striking in this regard is the fact that Goethe did not attend his mother's funeral (Friedenthal 19), and that as Boyle points out, "after he had left Frankfurt, Goethe, in thirty years, visited her only three times ever again . . . and she was never seriously invited to Weimar" (61). Boyle's astute conclusion about Goethe's relationship with his mother points to the self-protective nature of his distancing himself, which is probably also the basic reason for her low profile in *Poetry and Truth*. "Her avalanche of love and admiration doubtless founded her son's magnificent self-confidence, but it cannot have been easy to live with, and once he had entered adulthood it threatened the very autonomy it had established" (61).

Goethe's failure to give a developed portrait of his mother or his relationship with her may also be a function of the patriarchal values of his age, class, and native or "father" city (Vaterstadt), Frankfurt. The German word signals the patriarchal ethos that shaped Goethe's childhood and that in turn is not only reflected in but also governs his presentation of that childhood. The patrician hegemony of that legal and commercial

civic order is embodied in the long-standing symbolic trappings and rituals of the office of the chief magistrate, held for over two decades by
Goethe's maternal grandfather, Johannes Wolfgang Textor, the charm of
whose antiquated rituals Goethe captures with loving detail in book 1 in
his account of the Pipers' Court (31–32). That the chief magistrate's eldest
daughter was given in marriage at the tender age of seventeen to a man of
means twenty-one years her senior is also an indication of those values, as
is the related fact that during the first years of their marriage the rather
pedantic and paternalistic husband treated his young bride very much as
his pupil. "My father had a strong didactic bent, and, having no other
occupation, he was always eager to teach everyone else what he knew or
was able to do. In the first years of their marriage he had kept my mother
diligently writing, playing the piano, and singing" (24).

Goethe was born within a year of his parents' marriage, and in the few
glimpses we get of his young mother during his childhood and adolescence, she seems to figure chiefly as a conciliatory or mediating figure
buffering the inflexibility and moral rigor of his father. Her first appearance in the opening pages of the text casts her as a nurturing figure who
effectively tempers his father's stern conception of child-rearing. In a
lengthy description of their large, old Frankfurt house, Goethe mentions
that "its many corners and gloomy places [were] suited for awakening
fearful shivers in our childish hearts":

Unfortunately, the theory of child-rearing then current required the
young to be weaned without delay from all the fear of the invisible
and ominous, and to be inured to horror. Therefore we children had
to sleep by ourselves, and if, not being able to bear it, we crept out
of bed to seek the servants' company, then our father—sufficiently
disguised for us by having turned his dressing gown inside out—
would block our path and frighten us back into our beds. Anyone
can imagine what a bad effect that had. How can a person be cured
of fear by being wedged between two fearful things? My mother,
who was always cheerful and happy and liked others to be the same,
figured out a better method of instruction: she knew she could
reach her goal by offering rewards. It was the season of peaches, and
she promised us our fill of them in the morning if we overcame our
fears at night. This worked out to our mutual satisfaction. (23)

The mother does not challenge the father's pedagogic goal, but whereas he, in the spirit of a game or prank, uses fear and intimidation, she achieves the intended goal by using positive reinforcement to work with and not against the children's natural inclinations.

Some years later, during the French occupation of Frankfurt in 1759, she seeks to mediate between her resentful husband, "with his self-torturing hypochondria that grew worse every day, and the benevolent, but nevertheless very serious and punctilious military guest" who is quartered in their house (book 3, 74). During the same period of occupation, when the boy Goethe receives a free pass to the French theater from his grandfather, he succeeds in making "daily use of it, much to [his] father's displeasure, but with [his] mother's encouragement" (77). Still later, during his early adolescence, his mother comes to Goethe's assistance twice during crucial moments in his romantic relationship with Gretchen. On the first occasion, when he fails to come home one night, she protects him from the law of the father by covering for his absence. "My mother, whose mediation was always a great help to us, had glossed over my absence at morning tea by suggesting I had gone out early" (book 5, 153). On the second occasion, when the relationship with Gretchen comes to a sudden end with the arrest of some of the young people from her circle, the mother cannot protect him outright from the father's anger and the patriarchy's legal machinery, but she does what she can to temper its rigor and to prepare him for the inquisition to come. "The next morning while I was still lying in bed, my mother entered, looking disturbed and anxious. It was always easy to see by her expression when she felt upset about anything.—'Get up,' she said, 'and prepare to hear something unpleasant. It has been discovered that you are keeping very poor company and have become involved in the most dangerous and evil affairs. Your father is beside himself, and the only concession we have gotten from him is that he will let someone else investigate the matter. Stay in your room and await what is in store for you . . .'" (162). The mother's mediating function is called upon again half a decade later, when Goethe returns to his father's house after the completion of his university career. "At the very outset I put my mother into the position of constantly having to adjust events and steer them into some sort of middle ground between my father's stern sense of order and my many eccentricities" (book 12, 373).

Even if Goethe does not say so directly, it seems apparent that as the firstborn and only surviving son, Johann Wolfgang was the center of the family's attention and concern, with the only other surviving sibling, his one-year-younger sister Cornelia, playing a subordinate and supporting role and—because of her gender—leading a much more restricted life. Four other children died in infancy or childhood; the second born, Hermann Jakob, who was nearly four years younger than Goethe and died at the age of six, lived the longest. Goethe mentions this younger brother, with whom he shared the crucial years of his early childhood, only in passing: "He was of a delicate constitution, and quietly obstinate; we never enjoyed a close relationship" (book 1, 40). The perfunctory and dismissive character of this reference seems to confirm the self-centered primacy of the firstborn son. Freud throws an interesting psychoanalytic light on this relationship by interpreting Goethe's first memory (of gleefully throwing crockery out the window of the family house with the encouragement of the three bachelor brothers residing next door), as a screen memory for the boy's emotional disturbance at the birth of the younger brother. According to Freud (who was alerted to the underlying motive of the boy's destructive behavior by encountering the same memory in a patient), Goethe's "confession" is that of a symbolic or magical action "by which a child (both Goethe as well as my patient) violently expresses his wish to get rid of a disturbing intruder," that is, "the new baby must be *thrown out,* through the window" (363). Freud backs up his interpretation with the information (provided by Bettina Brentano), that Goethe showed no grief at "the death of his younger brother Jakob who was his playfellow," but expressed "annoyance at the grief of his parents and sisters . . . and when his mother asked him later if he had not been fond of his brother, he ran into his room, brought out from under the bed a heap of papers on which lessons and little stories were written, saying that he had done all this to teach his brother" (362–63). Indeed, the wish of "the elder brother . . . to play the father to the younger to show him his superiority" (363) surfaces again, as we shall see, in the adolescent student's letters from Leipzig to his sister, which mimic the pedagogic obsession of the Imperial Councilor.

Freud's probing interpretation of the first childhood memory offered in *Poetry and Truth* provides a crucial clue to Goethe's largely unarticulated relationship with his mother. Freud quotes Goethe's statement—"I was a child of fortune: destiny had preserved me for life . . . destiny removed my brother, so that I did not have to share my mother's love with him" (367)—and suggests that "he who has been the undisputed darling of his mother retains throughout life that victorious feeling, that confidence in ultimate success, which not seldom brings actual success with it" (367). The magnificent presumptuousness of Goethe's life and career can be correlated with this firstborn son's privileged relationship to his mother, and even though Goethe fails in *Poetry and Truth* to give his mother her due, Freud is surely correct when he concludes that "a saying such as 'My strength has its roots in my relation to my mother' might well have been put at the head of Goethe's autobiography" (367).

The family relationship that Goethe presents in by far the greatest detail is the rather conflicted and highly ambivalent one with his father. However one reads this complex relationship, it would be a mistake to reduce it to any simple Oedipal formula. What is clear is that the fault line that runs through the Goethe household puts the father on one side and the mother, son, and sister on the other. Goethe's most concise and paradigmatic statement of the defining tension within the family—between enjoyment on the one hand and discipline on the other—comes in an attempt in book 6 to characterize his relationship with his sister. There he speaks of

> a pressure resulting from our domestic situation, that is, a loving, well-disposed, but sober-minded father, who hid his tender heart, with incredible persistence, under an outward bearing of iron sternness, so that he might achieve his goals, which were to give his children the best bringing-up and to build, regulate, and maintain his solid house; and, on the other hand, a mother who was still almost a child herself and developed a conscious individuality only in and along with her two eldest offspring. We three took in the world with a healthy, vital gaze and demanded immediate gratification. This simmering family conflict worsened through the years. The father pursued his aims without swerving or pausing; the mother and children could not relinquish their feelings, their demands, and their wishes. (176)

Both Goethe and his sister felt their youthful happiness compromised by and chafed under the demanding pedagogic regimen of their father, who took their education in hand, doing some teaching himself but also engaging a variety of tutors.[3] At times they escaped to their maternal grandparents for temporary relief "from these didactic and pedagogical afflictions" (40–41), but on the whole the father seems to have imposed an exacting standard of discipline and achievement. To spur his children on and set an example, he even took drawing lessons with them, showing a "tireless industry" in copying every single item from a large collection "number by number" (book 4, 96). His mania for completing projects, no matter how tedious, stands in stark contrast to the natural disposition of his gifted but easily distracted and mobile son, whose literary career is marked by an extraordinary facility to produce rapidly and spontaneously, but who also left many projects incomplete and took a lifetime to finish others, such as *Faust*, whose second part was completed only shortly before his death.[4] In Goethe's portrayal, the father's insistence on perseverance and discipline appears a defensive and compensatory trait based on the perception of his own inadequacy or lack of natural ability. "He valued my native gifts all the more since he lacked them himself. He had only been able to acquire his knowledge through endless diligence, perseverance, and repetition. He frequently assured me, both in my childhood and later, and both in jest and earnest, that with abilities like mine he would have behaved quite differently from me and would not have been so slovenly about managing them" (book 1, 36).

What is thematized in Goethe's account of his father's pedagogic concern is the egotistical but not unusual parental wish to see realized in the children a more successful reincarnation of their own lives: "I was to pursue the same path, only farther and more comfortably" (36). In a patriarchal age such an expectation can bear down with considerable force on the firstborn son. Goethe was to succeed where the father had come up short; the vicarious vindication of the father's aborted career was to come through the son's entry via the legal profession into the governing patriciate of Frankfurt. No wonder the Imperial Councilor felt frustrated by the undisciplined and prodigal expression of his son's extraordinary gifts, and felt the pedant's urge to discipline and direct them that turns up even in his need to intervene in the adolescent's incomplete and irregular sketches of nature: "He asked benevolently for my attempts and then drew lines around each incomplete sketch, having in mind to force me into completeness and fullness by this method" (book 6, 174).

Lest this appear too one-dimensional a reading of the relationship, and in fairness to Goethe's father, it should be pointed out that he was no mere Philistine and household tyrant, but a man who, despite his own disappointments and inflexible character, cared deeply for his family. As is apparent from Goethe's characterization, he was also cultivated, with a large collection of paintings, prints, and books, and went out of his way to employ the Frankfurt artists of his day. Boyle has cogently argued against the traditional negative impression of Johann Caspar Goethe as unfair. His attempt to correct the conventional judgment takes into account the larger biographical picture beyond the account offered by Goethe and shows a desire to sympathize with the father's situation and viewpoint. Boyle asserts that "he doted on his son, he lived for him and in him, and that included his literary activities," for which he allowed, during Goethe's early twenties, by hiring a secretary to relieve the young law graduate from the drudgery of the legal work he had taken on in Frankfurt. He also spent "lavishly" on his son's university education, and showed "patience" with "an adolescent who must at times have been very much more than vexatious" (59–60).

My concern here, however, is not so much with who or what Goethe's father was in his own right as with his son's representation of him and their relationship in his autobiography. From that perspective, the relationship is one of conflict and resistance as well as cooperation and admiration on the son's part, with the former two elements, however, receiving much more emphasis. Again and again, *Poetry and Truth* dwells on the conflict—especially during adolescence, predictably—and leaves the admiration sparsely stated or implied. Yet it also seems apparent enough that Goethe wanted to please his father, to live up to his expectations, and—up to a point—to follow his pedagogic and professional master plan. But he wanted to do so in his own way and at his own pace. Even though he would have preferred to study at Göttingen University, which was a center for new currents of thought, he deferred to his father's wishes and studied at his alma mater, the University of Leipzig. Even though he preferred the study of language and literature and wanted to prepare himself for a university teaching post, he gave in to his father and, after the temporary setback of his ignominious departure from Leipzig without a law degree, went on to gain such a degree at the University of Strasbourg, and to start a legal career in Frankfurt. If the fateful choice of Weimar over Frankfurt is a rejection of his father's wishes at one level—to join the bourgeois governing elite of his "father city"—it is a fulfillment of them at another, and by different means. It initiated a decade of public service, but at the court of an absolute monarch and in an aristocratic milieu in which Goethe could play the starring role of chief artist in residence. Finally, even Goethe's escape from Weimar for nearly two years in his late thirties can be seen as a midlife crisis in which his artistic identity rears up and throws off the yoke of his demanding responsibilities as an administrator—a version of earlier paternal demands and expectations—but also as a recuperation of the world and values of his father. Goethe repeats in a different key his father's earlier Italian journey as a young man by immersing himself in his own way in Italian language, culture, and art. As he put it in a letter of September 1787 from Rome, incorporated into his *Italian Journey*, "thus I am living happily, because I am [immersed] in that which is my father's" (HA 11:400).

Goethe's most sustained critical portrait of his father comes in book 3, which opens with the invasion (in February 1759) and occupation of Frankfurt by the French during the Seven Years' War. With his unbending character and his inability to accept a suddenly changed domestic and political situation, the father effectively makes the worst of a bad situation. His neurotic inability to come even minimally to terms with the exigencies of foreign occupation, and especially the quartering in his house of the king's lieutenant, endangers himself and his family and reveals to his son the full extent of his lack of perspective and self-control. His estrangement from the social and civic realities of Frankfurt has already been established in book 2, where he is described as one of "the recluses, who never constitute a society of their own. They are as isolated from each other as from the rest of the community, all the more since their odd characters acquire even more rugged contours in their seclusion" (65). A bourgeois recluse is something of an oxymoron, and it is this questionable position that he seeks to assert rigidly during a time of political upheaval that pushes the role he has chosen to a disastrous limit.

One of the masterstrokes of Goethe's autobiography is to develop the deluded, ossified, and prickly unworldliness of the bourgeois father in counterpoint to the urbane manners, self-control, and noblesse oblige of the French aristocrat François de Thoranc, who in a sense becomes the symbolic head of the Goethe household and a temporary substitute father, while the real father stews in impotent and self-destructive resentment.[5]

Ironically it is the count, with all the official power of the invader on his side, who treats the family in whose house he is lodged with "the greatest courtesy" and behaves "impeccably" (73), whereas the father, who along with his family is really at the mercy of his noble lodger—the chief judicial official of the French occupying forces—cannot swallow or hide his implacable resentment. Even the count's admiration of art and his desire to employ the local artists whose paintings are hung in the Goethe mansion cannot mollify the offended householder: "But even being approached from the direction of art failed to alter my father's sentiments or soften his character. While he let happen what he could not prevent, he remained aloof and uncooperative, and regarded the extraordinary things going on around him as intolerable down to the last detail" (73). Far from appreciating Count Thoranc's good will and dignified, honorable behavior, or seeing his unwanted houseguest's rank as a good insurance policy, Goethe senior gives in to his demons. "Father's ill humor intensified, for he could not resign himself to the inevitable. How he tormented himself, our mother . . . the councilors, and all his friends, just to be rid of the count! They argued in vain that, under the circumstances, it was a real blessing to have such a man present in the house. . . . None of these arguments had any effect on him. The existing situation seemed so unbearable that sheer ill humor prevented him from seeing that something worse might follow" (75).

Goethe's critical perception of his father's behavior in this episode is paralleled by his consistent and considerable admiration of Count Thoranc. While the father stands isolated in "his self-torturing hypochondria that grew worse every day" (74), the rest of the family establishes an excellent rapport with their French guest. The mother employs an interpreter from her circle to make "the count understand the predicament she was in because of her husband's attitude," and the count responds by becoming for the duration of his stay of several years "the very model of a billeted officer" (74). She even flatters the count by trying to learn French, who responds with a "reserved gallantry," and "an excellent relationship developed between them" (74). How far that relationship developed is not something Goethe invites us to consider, but clearly the model of restrained authority and exemplary behavior on the part of the count undermines the previously unchallenged authority of the husband and father. Because of the father's intensifying "ill humor," Goethe and his sister find "it very pleasant to be freed, to a certain extent, from [their] regular lessons and strict discipline" (75). A whole new world opens up to the boy, who is exposed to French culture and rapidly learns the new language by regular attendance at the French theater in Frankfurt.

Book 3 offers altogether a vivid and detailed portrait of "the count's remarkable character" (75), which implicitly scripts the French officer as an elective or alternative parent next to the discredited and sulking father. A poignant irony of the lack of understanding between the two men is that in some ways they are remarkably similar. Both are cultivated older men with a high sense of justice, honor, and moral obligation; both have a love of art; both suffer from occasional spells of melancholy and bad humor. The chief temperamental difference between them, however, is that the German bourgeois gives in to his neurotic inclinations, while the French aristocrat masters his. The count's self-control is based on a knowledge of his character weakness that appears to be lacking in Goethe senior. "The man himself was acutely aware of his idiosyncrasies. At certain times a sort of ill humor, hypochondria, or whatever one may call this evil demon, would take hold of him, and during those hours, which sometimes stretched into days, he would retreat into his room, where he would see no one except his valet. . . . But as soon as the evil spirit passed from him, he appeared to be as mild, cheerful, and busy as before" (75). Given that Goethe himself was not immune to spells of hypochondria from adolescence on, it is probable that with the hindsight of his autobiography, he offers Thoranc as a positive example of how to manage such an affliction and intends an implicit critique of his father's contrasting weakness and lack of perspective.

The disastrous and ill-timed confrontation between Count Thoranc and Goethe's father is one of the most dramatic and powerful episodes in *Poetry and Truth,* and again the burden of guilt is placed squarely on the father's shoulders. During the Battle of Bergen (13 April 1759), Goethe's father foolishly ventures outside Frankfurt to cheer the Prussian forces in what he assumes will be their victory over the French; he returns home in disgust at their failure, "rejected [his family's] caresses and all food, and took himself off to his room" (84). The return of the count, who has earlier assuaged the mother's fears about the family's safety, forms a striking contrast to that of the father, whose place in a sense he takes. "The king's lieutenant . . . at last returned. His presence in the house was required more than ever. We jumped up to greet him, kissed his hands, and showed our delight. He seemed greatly pleased by this. 'Well!' he said, in a friendlier way than usual, 'I am also happy for your sakes, dear children!' At once he gave orders for us to be brought candy, sweet wine, the best of everything, and then he went to his room, already surrounded by people with petitions and urgent demands" (84). When the family finally succeeds in persuading the angry father to descend from his room for dinner, they unwittingly set the stage for a "calamity":

> In descending, Father had to pass directly by the count's room. Because the corridor was full of people, the count had decided to step out into it, so as to handle several matters at once, and unfortunately this happened to be the very moment when Father was coming down. The count happily approached him, greeted him, and said, "No doubt you wish to congratulate yourself and us that this dangerous affair has turned out so fortunately."—"By no means!" replied my father, inwardly seething. "I wish they had sent you to the devil, even if it had meant my going along with you."—The count paused for a moment, and then flew into a rage. "You shall pay for that!" he shouted. "You shall not insult me and our just cause like that with impunity!" (84)

It is only through the good offices of the interpreter, the friend of the Goethes who has acted as an emissary between the count and family, that the deeply offended officer is persuaded to countermand his order for the father's arrest. The interpreter's diplomatic pleading with the count, which is re-created verbatim by Goethe, involves an appeal to his noblesse oblige and self-control. The count's angry and dismissive expostulation about the moral blindness of his host, who fails to see that in the case of a Prussian victory and a French retreat his house and family would have been endangered, seems eminently justified by the context and puts Goethe's father morally in his place, exposing his essential bourgeois disingenuousness. "Do you suppose the enemy would be sitting there with his hand in his lap? He would be throwing grenades and whatever else was at hand. . . . This householder of yours, what does he want? A fireball would probably be bursting into these rooms, immediately followed by another—into these rooms with that confounded Peking wallpaper I have spared and refrained from nailing my maps on!" (86). It is telling that the interpreter's most persuasive argument for placating the count is Thoranc's intimate connection with the family: "You have no reason to thank the man of the house for any good will, but the mistress of the house has been most obliging, and the children look on you as their uncle. At one blow you will have destroyed the peace and happiness of this home forever. Yes, one may well say that a bomb falling on the house would not inflict greater damage on it" (87). The interpreter's invocation of "posthumous fame" as the count's reward for sparing Goethe's father is rejected out of hand, because Thoranc's only concern "is to do the right thing at the given moment, not to shirk [his] duty, and not to compromise [his] honor" (87). It is an avowal that crystallizes in the mind of the reader his open, manly, and honorable character.

It is part of Goethe's superb irony, however, that the very appeal to his vanity that the count rejects out of hand allows Goethe to commemorate his generosity. The very palm the aristocrat is too modest and generous to consider is graciously handed to him in Goethe's idealizing portrait, by way of the interpreter and at the expense of his ill-humored father: "'I have not sent the wife and children to kneel at your feet, because I know you hate such scenes, but let me portray this wife and these children in their gratitude to you. Let me describe how for the rest of their lives they will talk about the Battle of Bergen and your magnanimity on that day, how they will tell it to their children and children's children, and will also awaken other people's interest in you. An action like that can never be forgotten'" (87). And thanks to the efforts of Goethe the autobiographer, it won't be. A final ironic twist in this vivid reenactment is Goethe's shifting to the interpreter the element of fiction inevitably inherent in such a dramatic re-creation of the past (including extensive dialogue): "Whether the interpreter really spoke so wisely, or whether he was merely imagining the scene in the way one is apt to do after carrying something off well and successfully, is a moot question" (88).

Goethe's contrapuntal presentation of the tension between his real and very flawed German father and his elective and probably idealized French father draws to a close with their meeting in a momentary truce on the common ground of art. Both admire contemporary painting, and the count has commissioned (for his estate in the south of France) some of the leading Frankfurt artists whose works are on display in the Goethe house:

However much the count's interests corresponded to his own; however gratified my father might feel about seeing his principle concerning the employment of living masters adhered to productively by a wealthier man . . . still his antipathy to the stranger who had invaded his house was so great that none of the man's actions could win his approval. . . . In short, despite the count's own broadminded efforts, any friendship was entirely out of the question. My father only visited the studio when the count was at table, and I remember just one single time, when Seekatz had outdone himself and the whole household was drawn there by its desire to see the pictures, that my father and the count, on meeting, expressed a mutual pleasure in these artworks which they could not find in each other personally. (93)

This singular moment allows Goethe to present the two men on neutral ground; if their viewing of the same paintings cannot be a true meeting of minds, at least it permits Goethe to present both the French officer and the German householder in the same physical space, with the father's disabling hostility momentarily suspended. In his lifelong love and study of painting and the visual arts, Goethe is the true son of both men, and his narrative re-creation of the two antagonists admiring the same painter suggests both the humanizing and mediating role of art, as well as the limitations of that role in overcoming deep-seated conflicts and resentments.

Goethe's contrasting of the two men represents by far his most critical evaluation of his father, as well as the most developed version of an alternative male role model. Other such paternal role models are offered as well in Goethe's profile at the end of book 4 of "some men who exerted significant influence over my youth" (125). These older men were influential citizens and professional men endowed with certain character quirks that made them memorable, and "each [of them] influenced [Goethe] in his own way." "I was as attentive to each one as were his own children, or more so, and each of them, as if I were his beloved son, attempted to recast me in his own spiritual image so that he might approve of me even more" (128). Taking into account his acknowledgment of these older men, as well as friendships during his college days and beyond with a series of talented older male friends and mentors—Ernst Wolfgang Behrisch, Herder, Johann Kaspar Lavater, and Johann Heinrich Merck among them—it becomes apparent again how much Goethe's early years and his presentation of them in *Poetry and Truth* were shaped by the patriarchal values and outlook of his age and culture. To be sure, Susanna von Klettenberg, that beautiful Pietist soul who played an important role as spiritual advisor during his protracted period of illness after his return from the University of Leipzig, is the exception to the patriarchal rule. Unlike Rousseau, for whom Mme de Warens functions as by far the most influential formative and educational influence, Goethe almost exclusively invokes male figures as mentors, eliding or downplaying the role of women as significant formative influences and assigning or consigning them largely to the romantic sphere of his young life.[6]

To return to the relationship between Goethe and his father, the periods of cooperation and mutual good will between them are few and far between. Some of the tasks imposed on the boy and his sister by the punctilious parents are "troublesome" (100) and much resented, like those (described in book 4) of helping the father breed silkworms in the attic or clean and restore his faded engravings of Rome. But there are periods of friendly collaboration as well. For instance, during the imperial coronation ceremonies in Frankfurt, father and son immerse themselves in research about "the last two coronations" and pore over the election- and coronation-journals "all day long until late at night" (140). And some five years later, when Goethe has returned to Frankfurt after earning his law degree at Strasbourg, he spends "a large part of the day, at [his] father's request, on legal work," even though his real interest is literature. His father is happy to help the young lawyer with his legal briefs, as this allows him to "resume an activity of which he had long been deprived. . . . And so this activity became a more pleasant diversion for me, since it brought me closer to my father" (416).

These periods of happy cooperation, however, are short-lived. The legal work dwindles to nothing when Goethe's father hires a secretary to relieve him of the drudgery of the law on which he is spending less and less time.[7] And the good will between them is compromised by the father's reservations about Goethe's engagement to Lili and by his republican opposition to his son's acceptance of the Duke of Weimar's invitation to his court. Their mutual enjoyment of the coronation rituals comes to an abrupt end with the adolescent Goethe's house arrest for his involvement with Gretchen's circle, and after the boy's slow recovery from the depression occasioned by that debacle, he experiences a growing "aversion to [his] native town [Vaterstadt]" (book 6, 184). The aversion is not so much to the physical city of Frankfurt as it is to the life and values of his father and the governing patriarchy that has helped turn him into the diminished and frustrated man he is. "And just as my old walls and towers were gradually palling on me, so too the municipal organization and everything once held so sacred now appeared before me in distorted images. As grandson of the chief magistrate, I was not ignorant of the secret shortcomings of this republic" (184). Because of his unhappy father's example, he desires not only to leave his native city behind, but also his father's academic plans for him. "And did I not see that, in spite of all of his studies, efforts, journeys, and broad education, he was in the end leading a lonely life within his four walls, the very opposite of what I wanted for myself? These things together put a terrible weight on my spirits, from which I could only free myself by trying to devise a life plan quite different from the one prescribed for me. In my thoughts, I rejected the study of law" (184).

In the event, Goethe reluctantly accepts his father's choice of a university for him and, once there, almost immediately gives up his secret scheme of leaving the study of law for that of "languages, antiquities, history," with a view to preparing himself "for a university teaching position" (184, 185). In thus acceding to his father's plans, he is thrust into the elegant Enlightenment culture of the Frenchified Leipzig, the "little Paris" where his Frankfurt dialect, his quaint clothes, his manners, his writing style, and even his trump card, his poetry, are all found wanting in the narrow university circle in which he is at first quite out of his element. The young student has left his *Vaterstadt* but not the mental world of his father. One commentator has astutely pointed out how some of the "confining literary conventions of Leipzig" are correlated in Goethe's account with the intellectual and moral attitudes of his father (Barner 289). Indeed, the night display of a "pandaemonium of will o' the wisps" (186) that he witnesses on the journey to Leipzig can be seen as a symbolic indicator that he is on a false path, and his departure from Leipzig some three years later (in September 1768) without a degree, to return home "like a castaway" (252), ill and dispirited, demonstrates the dangers of acquiescing in a paternal decision so contrary to his own inclinations.

The period of convalescence back in Frankfurt is one of uneasy tension with his father punctuated by occasional flare-ups between them that in the end hasten Goethe's departure for Strasbourg to complete his legal studies. Goethe's father tries to hide "his disappointment at finding, not a robust, active son about to take his doctorate and make strides in his pre-scribed career, but a valetudinarian who seemed to be more afflicted in mind than in body" (book 8, 253). He does "not disguise his desire to see [Goethe's] cure expedited," and Goethe has "to guard against making any hypochondriacal remarks in his presence, because then he could become bitter and vehement" (253). Significantly, it is during this time of illness and estrangement from his father that he becomes open to the spiritual ministrations of the Pietist devotee from his mother's circle, Susanna von Klettenberg. She takes delight in his "natural gifts" and acquirements and seeks, from the elevated perspective of her "religious culture," to provide a steadying influence for what he describes as "my restlessness, my impa-tience, my striving, my seeking, inquiring, pondering, and wavering" (254). In the long run this influence proved short-lived, as Goethe the apostle of striving had to part ways with the quietist, otherworldly orien-tation of the Pietists, but during his slow recovery it must have provided considerable balm to his troubled spirit.

Toward the end of his stay in Frankfurt, his relationship with his father degenerates into mutual incomprehension and hostility, which, as Goethe's balanced comments imply—and without any need to invoke Freud's Oedipus complex—is in some respects not untypical of many ado-lescent males' tense relations with their fathers. Goethe is hurt by his father's impatience with the pace of his recovery and resents his frequent "cruel remarks about something that is beyond all human control as though it were simply a question of willpower" (book 9, 265). But with the hindsight of his own maturity (and perhaps too in light of the trou-bled relationship with his own son), he adds, "But he was wounded and offended by me in many ways too" (265). From the judicious outlook of his later years, there was plenty of fault to go around. As he wrote in a let-ter after completing this section of *Poetry and Truth,* "if from the side of the father as well as that of the son one iota of awareness had entered into this estimable family relationship, both sides would have been spared much. But that was not to be and does not at all appear to belong in this world" (*Briefe* 3:213–14, 3 December 1812).

Goethe's youthful provocations of his father show the adolescent son beginning to assert his own independent viewpoint at the expense of the father, and they have a comic edge. He boldly criticizes his father in his most vulnerable spot, the style of the house that he had taken so much trouble and expense to rebuild and renovate according to his own taste after the death of his mother. Goethe, who at Leipzig had spent more time on the study of art than on law, had acquired "a general notion about architecture, arrangements, and decoration of houses," which he "incautiously applied . . . to [his father's] house" (265). To add insult to injury, he criticizes in particular the placement of the open staircase that runs through the house—the same infernal staircase that had given the Imperial Councilor one of the worst moments of his life: "That alarming scene with the king's lieutenant would never have taken place . . . if our staircase had been placed, in Leipzig fashion. . . . Once I warmly praised that way of building and explained the advantages of it; I showed my father how it would be possible to shift his staircase also, whereupon he flew into an incredible rage, one that was all the more violent since shortly before I had criticized some ornate mirror frames and spurned certain Chinese wallpapers. A scene ensued which, although hushed up and smoothed over, definitely hastened my departure to beautiful Alsace" (265). The emotional flare-up of this "scene" is a repetition in a different key of the earlier explosion between the father and Count Thoranc; significantly, Goethe's aspersion on the wallpaper was also made by (or attributed to) Count Thoranc ("that confounded Peking wallpaper," 86), in his sarcastic comments to the interpreter about the Imperial Councilor's disastrous outburst on the staircase. The wallpaper link reinforces what the staircase motif suggests as well—Goethe's unconscious identification with Count Thoranc in this decisive disagreement between father and son. The subtext of this masterfully concise, vivid, and ironic account is the nineteen-year-old's rejection of his father, expressed through criticism of his house; and the father's outburst betrays his deeper understanding of the nature of his son's provocative criticism of his taste in home decoration. This episode also shows the student-son's frustrated need for independence and self-assertion.

It is understandable that after Goethe's return from Strasbourg with a law degree in hand—even if it is only a licentiate; the university authorities did not accept his Latin doctoral dissertation—his father treats him with new consideration and respect. True, as Goethe acknowledges, at

Strasbourg, what with his excursions into the beautiful Alsatian countryside, his love affair with Friederike Brion, and his impassioned writing of
lyric poetry, he had "considered this central business to be a matter of secondary importance" (book 11, 350). The university degree is a rite of passage that establishes Goethe's identity as an adult even as it fulfils his
father's pedagogic script, as does Goethe's admittedly less than enthusiastic entry into the legal profession of his native city.

Goethe senior had always taken pride in and encouraged his gifted
son's literary abilities, so long as these were subordinated to the primary
pedagogic scheme. When as a boy Goethe surprised his father with a
bound copy of his poetic efforts, "he was greatly pleased and encouraged
me to prepare a quarto like this every year. He said this with all the more
conviction since I had accomplished the whole thing in my so-called
'leisure hours'" (book 4, 115). The change that seems to have occurred in
the father's attitude to these literary efforts after Goethe's return from
Strasbourg is his growing recognition and acceptance of the fact that the
young man's talents and the success they will lead to are in the field of literature rather than law. One sign of this is his eventual willingness to
relieve his son from the burden of legal work, and to see him spend progressively less time on law and more on literature. Already during the
early phase of Goethe's post-Strasbourg Frankfurt years, when his father
helps him with legal briefs, the father, "being perfectly satisfied with my
conduct in this matter, was glad to indulge me in whatever else I was
doing, with the ardent expectation that I would soon reap fame as an
author" (book 13, 416).

Once Goethe has fulfilled this expectation with his first major success,
the historical play *Götz von Berlichingen,* his father does not object to
Goethe absenting himself from the felicity of the law, and the "little
chancery" that operates under his direction runs very smoothly without
his now famous son: "Since it is a well-known fact that an absent person is
never missed, they granted me my pastimes and tried to establish themselves more and more firmly on ground where I was not destined to
thrive" (book 19, 592). Indeed, the father has now so completely accepted
his son's literary identity that he becomes personally involved in the completion of his poetic projects. "Fortunately, my father's sentiments and
wishes coincided with my inclinations. He had such a high opinion of my
poetic talent and too so much personal pleasure in the favor my first

works had won that he would often talk to me about my new projects and those I would undertake in the future" (592). The need for vicarious living through his son is still there, as is the paternal and pedagogic urge to force him to a disciplined productivity and completion that we saw earlier with respect to the adolescent's unfinished sketches. When, after the triumph of his historical drama, Goethe casts about for another subject and seizes on another heroic historical figure, Count Egmont, Goethe's father "could not contain his desire to see this play, which was already complete in my mind, on paper, in print, and admired." "I made considerable progress, for I was being spurred on day and night (I do not exaggerate) by my father, who knew my slothful work habits and thought he should be able to see a play so easily conceived also easily completed" (593). Indeed, the otherwise staid father was so pleased with his son's literary celebrity that he was willing to entertain the sometimes unruly friends, fellow authors, and admirers—like those young wayward brothers, the Counts von Stolberg—who were drawn to Goethe as to a magnet during the Storm-and-Stress "genius" decade of the 1770s.[8]

After this substantial accommodation and reconciliation between Goethe and his ever demanding parent, the "daemonic" conclusion of *Poetry and Truth*—with its fateful choice of Weimar and companionship-cum-service to an absolute monarch over republican Frankfurt, marriage, domesticity, and an independent literary career—shows a final clash of wills and parting of the ways between the two. Yet even this parting is not entirely neat or clear cut, because Goethe almost accepts his father's compromise of a journey to Italy, which would have been a repetition of the Goethe senior's postgraduate grand tour, of which he had written an account in Italian. With a dramatic gesture, the octogenarian Goethe attributes the choice *he* ultimately made as a young man, for Weimar and against Frankfurt, to a "daemonic" concatenation of circumstances. There is a certain irony in the fact that he does so with the help of a famous quotation from the play (*Egmont*) that his father had hounded him to complete—a quotation that invokes the trope of the charioteer as a figure of fate who literally and metaphorically will carry him away from his *Vaterstadt,* his fiancée, and his family. "As though whipped on by invisible spirits, the sun-steeds of time run off with the flimsy chariot of our destiny, and nothing is left for us to do except grasp the reins with courage and composure and divert the wheels, now right, now left, from a stone here, or a sudden drop there. Who knows what the destination is? The driver scarcely remembers from whence he has come" (book 20, 605). The spectacular rhetoric of this impressive poetic finale is supposed to put his decision beyond debate, but it can also be seen as the Goethean mystification of an existential choice—of one way of life and career over another—that may not have been quite as daemonically inevitable as it sounds here at the fateful close of his *Poetry and Truth*.

GOETHE AND HIS SISTER

When Goethe's sister died several weeks after the birth of her second child in June 1777, some four months short of her twenty-seventh birthday, a part of Goethe died with her. As he wrote to his mother several months later, "with [the death of] my sister so strong a root that held me to the earth has been hacked off, that the branches above which derived nourishment from it will also have to die off" (*Briefe* 1:240, 16 November 1877). If Goethe's portrait of his father, distanced and balanced in the objectifying lens of later years, is, as Bowman has observed, "by far the most detailed" (28), his portrait of his sister is clearly the most problematic in *Poetry and Truth*, the one that gave him the most difficulty. At one level Goethe's problem is inherent in the genre; his professed aim is a life narrative with a consistently light and cheerful touch, yet Cornelia's story is essentially a tragic one. Indeed, the depths of her tragedy are such that they threaten to explode the frame of his autobiography. At another level the problem is a profoundly personal one of Goethe's inability to fathom his sister's complex personality or come to terms with her fate, partly because of his still unresolved feelings. As in Rousseau's characterization of Mme de Warens but in a different key, there is in Goethe's attempt to find the sum of his sister a sense of frustration that he cannot get to the bottom of her character or their relationship. His struggle with this problem ends in silence, or in a textual void, as he can only ask the reader to read between the lines.

References to Cornelia are woven throughout Goethe's narrative of childhood and youth and appear naturally and frequently in connection with the father's pedagogic regime, which builds between the two siblings a natural solidarity and helps to account for the intensity of the bond they develop. From the start the sister is more burdened by that regime than is the brother. Because she is a girl, Cornelia is given less freedom than he is, and after his departure for the university she is the exclusive object of her father's almost unremitting pedagogical pressure. In addition to the references that occur with some regularity throughout the text, there are two major sections, in books 6 and 18, devoted to the characterization of Cornelia. The writing of the second one is separated by nearly two decades from the writing of the first and repeats the gist of the earlier sketch, so that one wonders whether Goethe later forgot that he had written an earlier account, or whether he was dissatisfied with the first attempt and wanted another go at it. The essence of both portraits of his sister as defined by a central discrepancy or incommensurability is reproduced in summary and in somewhat cruder form in Eckermann's version of Goethe's comments on his Cornelia portrait in *Poetry and Truth:* "This chapter . . . will be read with interest by many educated ladies, for there will be many like my sister in this respect, that, with superior mental and moral endowments, they do not experience at the same time the good fortune of a beautiful body" (2:463, 28 March 1831). Goethe then offers his interpretation of Cornelia, which has become the standard one:[9]

> She was a remarkable being . . . she stood morally very high, and did not have a trace of sensuality about her. The thought of resigning herself to a man was repulsive to her, and one can imagine that from this peculiarity arose many unpleasant hours in marriage. Women who have a similar aversion, or do not love their husbands, will feel what this is meant to say. Thus I could never think of my sister as married; she would have been much more in her proper place as an abbess in a convent. And because she was not happy in marriage even though she was married to one of the best of men, she passionately advised against my intended connection with Lili [Anna Elisabeth Schönemann]. (2:464)

My sister, the spiritual woman undone by marriage: that is the view Goethe wants to convey to the reader. A strong intellect, a beautiful soul full of delicate feeling, a sensitive and sympathetic friend to both women and men, a mentor and advisor to the young women in her circle, yet a woman who can be willful, hard, and cold when her wishes are thwarted, as they are by her father—but not a wife, because she is an asexual woman keenly aware of her lack of physical beauty, who because of the rigid conventions of her age and class is forced into and violated by the bonds of matrimony. This interpretation may be justified by the biographical record, but that it is also partial and self-serving has been argued by Christoph Michel, who analyzes Goethe's presentation of Cornelia in *Poetry and Truth* in the light of independent biographical evidence, including her letters. Michel attempts to reconstruct Cornelia's view of herself in order to show how it differs in significant ways from her brother's perception of her, including the crucial matter of Goethe's insistence on her unhappiness in marriage, which Michel asserts is not an accurate reflection of her situation. According to Michel, what Goethe failed to see at the time and what is reflected in his autobiography is that Cornelia, in responding to the wooing of Schlosser, the cultivated lawyer, "had begun to lead her own life," and that indeed she was a happy bride, as is evident from her assertion in a letter of 13 December 1773 , "all my hopes, all my desires are not only fulfilled—but far—far exceeded" (63). From this letter and other indications it appears that Cornelia was indeed initially very happy with her new life. But Michel's reading of Cornelia's situation is seriously skewed because the letter cited above comes just six weeks after her wedding; what his picture of the happily married Cornelia ignores is precisely what is developed at considerable length in the chief source Michel relies on, Georg Witkowski's elegant and powerful biography of Cornelia.

In his two concluding chapters on Cornelia's marriage, illness, and death, Witkowski demonstrates that Cornelia's new life took a downward turn even before the birth of her first daughter in October 1774, which left her bedridden and depressed for nearly two years (142–43). Physically isolated in the rural setting of Emmendingen and largely cut off from her family and friends in Frankfurt, Cornelia came to realize the deeper incompatibility between herself and the husband whose proposal she had accepted because he had impressed her with his intellectual seriousness and his promise as a writer and administrator. Ill at ease in her new domestic role and environment, and unable to join in the religious enthusiasm of Schlosser and his friends or to share the gusto with which her enterprising husband threw himself into his time-consuming new administrative post, she came in the end to view her marriage as a prison from which she yearned for release "at any price, even the highest" (Witkowski 149). With his robust self-centeredness and his condescending and dismissive view of women (evident in his writings), Schlosser failed to understand or appreciate the complex nature of his wife (152, 176). It is consistent with his character that after the first shock of grief at a death he apparently failed to anticipate, despite Cornelia's long bouts of illness since their marriage, he rapidly recovered his balance and within several months of her funeral was again engaged to be married. That he had come to realize that at some point he had lost his wife's love is evident in a thinly veiled marriage parable he wrote and in an even more telling sentence written in a letter to his brother, "she is nauseated by my love" (153–54). After the first trial of childbearing, which had nearly done her in, Cornelia clearly was not ready for a second pregnancy, which did in fact liberate her from the prison of her marriage, but at the highest price.

Whatever the greater biographical truth about Cornelia's self-perception, sexuality, and marriage, it is clear even without recurring to evidence above and beyond Goethe's account that the Cornelia portrait in *Poetry and Truth* is both self-serving and idealizing. The text itself shows Goethe's need to perceive and circumscribe her principally in her role as his soul sister and to assert his primacy in her emotional life. His emphasis on her unhappiness in marriage ("although she was married to one of the best men") is a function of that partial perception—and this is true even if we accept the conventional view that she was miserable. Simply put, whatever the real situation and wishes of Cornelia, Goethe is unable or refuses to see her in the role of a willing wife, because this would run counter to his insistence that he was the most important man in her life. Also, by unsexing or neutering his sister, he keeps the deep-rooted and passionate sibling attachment between them from running up against the incest taboo.

Goethe presents the intensity of that bond as a defining feature of their relationship, as he does the consistent tendency of "this beloved, enigmatic person" to make him the focal point of her life. The fissure that runs through the Goethe household, with the mother and children on one side and the father on the other, drives brother and sister together and bonds them in a larger psychic identity:

In their early years, this brother and sister had their play and study, their growth and cultural development, so completely in common that they could have taken themselves for twins. And this communion, this mutual trust, did not diminish with the increase in their physical and mental powers. Hand in hand, these siblings shared and survived youth's amazed interest in the awakening of its sensual desires and spiritual needs, the latter masked in sensual forms and the former in spiritual ones; also all the reflections about these matters, which tend more to obscure than to enlighten, as a fog, when lifting, covers a valley instead of brightening it; and the many errors and aberrations that spring from all this. But the clarification of their strange condition was hampered by the wholesome dread they felt of their close relationship, which kept them forcibly apart, the more they tried to approach each other in the search for knowledge. (book 6, 176)

Goethe's characterization is remarkable for its blend of frankness and discreet obfuscation. Bound together in their oppression under the father's pedagogic regime, which, as Michel points out (44), offers Cornelia the unusual privilege of receiving the same education as Wolfgang, brother and sister share the sexual awakening and confusions of adolescence. But her restricted freedom versus his permission to range abroad—Cornelia "was never permitted to leave the house as long as I" (176)—makes her need for him greater than his for her: "Thus her need to converse with me was intensified by her pining to accompany me to distant places" (176). From the start, then, the patriarchal pressures of the age force her into a dependence on both father and brother, in Goethe's case an emotional dependence that he accepts and makes the defining feature of his portrait of Cornelia.

Already during childhood Cornelia feels the pedagogic pressure more intensely than her brother does, because for her it also includes the area of female accomplishments valued by her age, such as music. When a friend of the father persuades him to purchase a piano and have the children take lessons, Goethe acknowledges that while he "scarcely touched it . . . it caused [his] sister that much more torment, because in due honor of the new instrument, she had to spend still more time at daily practice. Alternately standing next to her through this were my father, as supervisor, and . . . the encouraging family friend" (book 4, 99). Encouragement indeed! The reality of the gender inequality of her age comes starkly into play when her brother leaves home for the university at the age of sixteen.

After his departure for Leipzig, fifteen-year-old Cornelia, the resentful victim of his paternal tyranny, has "to bear the whole brunt of [her father's] didactic dilettantism." "She had to study and work on French, Italian, and English alternately, and was also required to practice piano for a great part of the day. Writing could not be neglected either, and I had certainly noticed beforehand that he was supervising her correspondence with me and was having his teachings communicated to me through her pen" (book 8, 252). No wonder Cornelia's self-chosen motto as a young woman was "liberty."[10] Even the correspondence with her brother, which serves as an imaginative outlet from the prison that is home, cannot escape the oppressive shadow of the father, and what is worse, her brother too assumes a pedagogic attitude toward her. As Goethe acknowledges in book 8, when after his return from Leipzig he reread the letters he had written to her, "I was much amused to see how much I had at once relayed to my sister whatever Gellert [one of his literature professors] had taught or recommended in his lectures, without realizing that fact that in both life and reading, what is suitable for a young man may not be appropriate for a young woman. The two of us made fun of this mimicry" (261). The last sentence permits a glimpse of Cornelia's good humor and generosity toward her brother, yet Goethe's account of his "mimicry" does not show any awareness that in imitating his professors he was in fact also parroting his father's didacticism.

The few surviving letters to Cornelia from this period, which are partly written in French, show Goethe's amazement and admiration at the intellectual development evident in her correspondence, as well as his playful yet presumptuous attempt to force her back into a more conventional feminine role. Thus in May 1767, in response to a sophisticated fictional sketch that Cornelia had written in French, he exclaims (in French), "I am amazed by your letter, by your manner of thinking. I no longer see the little girl, Cornelia, my sister, my pupil; I see a mature spirit . . . an author from whom I can learn in turn. O my sister, no more of these letters in the future, or I shall be silent."[11] Dumbfounded by her intellect (apparently exercised in criticism of some samples of his creative writing), he praises her "sentiments," and counsels, "follow your simple heart and your extraordinary integrity; your naivety will win out over the study of the world, knowledge, and the criticism of your brother" (*Briefe* 1:41, 11 May 1767). In the same year he writes another absurdly hectoring epistle in which he seeks more explicitly to pressure his sister into the conventional role of an accomplished female of her culture and class. He finds that her "ideas about most subjects" are "confused," praises her "fine sentiments" but finds even these "too easily felt and too little considered." With its condescending injunction that she read less and write more letters (to him), the male adolescent's self-centered and paternalistic attitude is transparent:

> Further I notice that various readings have notably spoiled your taste in various matters . . . for that reason I would like to request that you read as little as possible for the year that we will still be apart; and to write much, except nothing but letters, and if possible, genuine letters to me; to continue cultivating your languages, as well as to study housekeeping and cookery; also to help pass the time to continue practicing on the piano; for these are all things that a girl who wants to be my pupil must necessarily possess. . . . Furthermore I desire that you perfect yourself in dancing, practice the usual card games, and learn the art of tasteful makeup. (*Briefe* 1:49, 12–14 October 1767)

The didactic element that was crucial in Goethe's romantic relationship with Gretchen (which occurred before his departure for Leipzig), is now heightened in the vision of Cornelia as his pupil and in his expectations of her relationship to him after his return from the academy. This element gives an erotic tinge to his fraternal and paternal need for control, as does his pressuring Cornelia to cultivate the conventional adornments of an eligible young woman. These immature Leipzig letters show a relationship of easy intimacy between the siblings, but not one of equality.

After his return from Leipzig, Goethe notes a change in Cornelia's attitude toward their father, a deepened resentment of his oppressive strictures, which she now obeys with barely repressed hostility: "[I]n a way that seemed dreadful to me, she had adopted a very hard attitude toward our father, and could not forgive him for having held her back from or spoiled so many an innocent pleasure during these three years; and she absolutely refused to recognize any of his good and excellent qualities. She did everything that he ordered or directed, but in the most ungracious way imaginable. She did it according to regulations, but not a jot more or less" (book 8, 253). In her relationship to her brother, however, the old intimacy is reestablished—"my sister at once attached herself to me" (252)—and intensified. "[S]ince my sister was as much in need of love as any other human being, she now bestowed all her affections completely on me. Her attention to my care and entertainment consumed all of her time" (253). Her attempt to pull him out of his illness and depression is a continuation of her earlier role, when she sought to console him during the Gretchen crisis. In the earlier account of their adolescent relationship, in book 6, Goethe's explanation of his sister's social predicament pushes up against the limits of the incest taboo in its acknowledgment of their emotional codependency. Because of a "lack of beauty" that "was somewhat repellent," as well as a "dignified" demeanor that puts off young men, she is the only one in her circle of female friends without a male partner:

> She felt this keenly, did not conceal it from me, and turned her affection to me all the more strongly. It was certainly an odd situation. Just as confidants can take such a heartfelt interest in a love affair one has revealed to them that they become actual participants, nay, develop into rivals, and finally appropriate one's affections for themselves, so it was between us siblings. While my relationship with Gretchen was being torn asunder, my sister consoled me with all the earnestness based on her secret satisfaction that she was rid of a rival. And thus I too could not help feeling, with a quiet touch of malice, that she would have to admit I was the only one who truly loved her, understood her, and revered her. (177–78)

Three years later, the specter of possession and jealousy that haunts this description of their early adolescent attachment appears to be gone, as the now emotionally more mature younger sister takes the lead in consolidating her nurturing bond with her ill brother. One manifestation of their renewed intimacy is the coded language in which Cornelia takes the initiative: "Soon we evolved a private language between the two of us, so that we could talk in front of other people without being understood, and she was frequently impudent enough to use this argot in our parents' presence" (253).

Cornelia's experience of her brother the university student is one of departure and return, and thus of an intermittent soul-communion and emotional attachment. In *Poetry and Truth,* Goethe shows no awareness that she has a life of her own in his absence, but on his return to Frankfurt after the completion of his legal studies at Strasbourg—"healthier and happier than the first time" (book 12, 373)—we see her growing maturity and self-assurance. "My sister had gathered a circle of clever and amiable young women around herself. Without being domineering, she dominated them all, for her intelligence took much in at a glance and good will smoothed out many things; moreover she was in the position of playing the confidante rather than the rival" (373–74). At this point, Goethe also mentions Georg Schlosser's helpful advice about the legal career he is about to enter. What he does not mention, however, is the likelihood of an already developing relationship between his sister and his friend. Goethe informs us at the close of book 12 that he learned of that relationship from Schlosser himself only later in Wetzlar, where he had gone to take up a position at the imperial supreme court. Goethe is amazingly frank about his chagrin at being thus surprised:

> Schlosser revealed to me that he had entered first into a friendly, then a more intimate relationship with my sister, and that he was looking for an immediate position, so that he could marry her. This declaration rather took me aback . . . and now I first noticed that I was really jealous with regard to my sister, and it was harder to conceal this feeling from myself since our relationship had grown even closer after my return from Strassburg. How much time we had spent in exchanging information about the little romances, the love affairs and lovers' quarrels which had occurred in the meantime! And had not another new world in the imaginative sphere opened to me, into which I had to introduce her also? My own little works and a broad expanse of world literature had to be gradually presented to her. (407)

Again the pedagogic element is crucial, as is the sharing of his personal and literary life; he used to show her his poetry, the letters he wrote and the responses he received. But once he left Frankfurt his heart was captured by Lotte (Charlotte Buff), and the intimacy with Cornelia suffered accordingly. "All this lively movement had come to a standstill since my departure from Frankfurt. . . . In a word, she felt herself alone, perhaps neglected, and so was all the readier to listen to the sincere wooing of an honorable man who, serious and reserved, reliable and estimable, had shown her a warm affection of which he was normally very chary. I had no choice but to resign myself and grant my friend his good fortune, although I was self-confident enough to tell myself secretly that without the brother's absence the friend would not have prospered to this extent" (book 13, 408). The "honorable man" is damned in the faint praise Werther bestows upon Albert; the jealous brother has not been bested by a man who won his sister on the strength of his own merits but only because of the absence of the brother, who is clearly more important to his sister than her default fiancé—a presumption that is equally condescending to Cornelia. Michel speculates persuasively that the attraction between Schlosser and Cornelia in all likelihood predates Goethe's journey to Wetzlar, and that even if Goethe remained the main figure of her inner life, he was not the only one, for "in the meantime Cornelia had begun to live her own life" (62–63). He attributes Goethe's categorically negative view of Cornelia's marriage—evident in his account, in book 18, of his visit to his sister's new home in Emmendingen, in which he describes her as intensely unhappy because of her social isolation—to "his innermost conviction . . . that Cornelia should have remained his sister and only his sister" (64).

The self-interested character of Goethe's view of Cornelia as a spiritual woman constitutionally unsuited for marriage appears to be a signal failure of the objective thinking that Goethe makes a criterion of faithful autobiography, and of the balance he so impressively brings to the portraits of others, including even the father with whom he was less than enchanted. In some respects, his overall presentation of her seems to be motivated by a frustrated masculine will to power. The Faustian side of Goethe wishes to subordinate his sister as an extension of himself, as his female twin or Shelleyan "antitype." The presentation of Cornelia as Goethe's soul sister, and the spiritualized female as the male's reflection and complement, also takes us into the realm of the Romantic view of love and, more specifically, the trope of an incestuous sibling attachment and the ideal of a passionately shared imaginative response to the world— as we see it for instance in Byron (*Manfred*) and Shelley (*Epipsychidion*), and in real life in the relationship between William and Dorothy Wordsworth (also a year younger than her brother).[12] It has not escaped notice (see Boyle 294, Michel 62) that Goethe transferred the sister archetype to some of his romantic involvements, most notably the strange relationship with Charlotte von Stein during his first decade at Weimar, to whom he wrote a poem that contains the lines, "Oh, in ancient times you were / My sister or my wife" (du warst in abgelebten Zeiten / Meine Schwester oder meine Frau) (HA 1:123). What might be called the sister complex also appears in some of his fictional works, most spectacularly so in the sibling incest that is the clue to the mystery of Mignon's parentage in *Wilhelm Meister's Apprenticeship.*

Given these perhaps not fully acknowledged emotional undercurrents of Goethe's relationship with Cornelia, it is not surprising that the task of a definitive summing up of her character and being eluded and—at least so he seems to have felt—ultimately defeated Goethe, despite the two major attempts at a larger portrait in books 6 and 18.[13] There was a fundamental discrepancy or contradiction in "this beloved, enigmatic person" (176) for which he could not quite find the formula. As he put it in book 8, "my sister was and remained an indefinable nature, the strangest mixture of sternness and softness, of stubbornness and tractability" (252). In the attempted summing up of book 6, Goethe mentions that he had "conceived of the idea of a poetic whole . . . to depict her individuality" in the imaginative form "of the novels of Richardson." "Only by means of the most precise detail and infinite particulars, all vividly characteristic of her whole self and indicative of the mysterious depths from which they emerged, only by this means would I at all have succeeded in giving some idea of this remarkable individual, for a spring can only be imagined as flowing" (176–77). A favorite of Cornelia's developed literary taste, the Richardsonian psychological novel of sentiment, with its epistolary *writing to the moment,* might capture her elusive individuality, but Goethe will have to make do with conjuring "the shade of that blessed spirit for just a moment" with the perplexed profile portrait conjured in the "magic mirror" (177) of his autobiography.[14]

One of the decisive features of both attempts to define Cornelia is her physical appearance. Curiously, as Bowman notes, she is the only family member of which "he gives a physical description" (31). In the cruder profile of the conversation cited by Eckermann, her lack of physical beauty is stressed, but in *Poetry and Truth* her body is actually described in positive terms ("she was tall, well and delicately formed," book 6, 177; "her lovely figure was an advantage," book 18, 562). Even though her eyes are striking—"[though they] were not the loveliest I ever saw, they were the deepest, making me wonder what lay behind them" (177)—it is the incongruity of her face that is stressed: "[S]he was . . . really disfigured, to the point where her face could sometimes actually look ugly, by the fashion of those times, which not only bared her forehead but also enlarged it to the utmost. . . . Although her forehead was feminine and smoothly curved, she had a pair of heavy black eyebrows and prominent eyes, and the resulting contrast, if it did not repel a stranger at first sight, certainly did not attract him" (177).[15] But for her brother, who shared the high forehead with her, Cornelia was "a magnet" that always drew him "homeward again" (book 6, 175). She had other admirers as well—a young Englishman for whom she developed passionate feelings and whose sudden departure for England was a real blow to her, and of course the serious Schlosser, not to mention some earlier proposals of marriage that Goethe mentions were dismissed out of hand.

In the physiognomic categories of the eighteenth century that the friend of Goethe's youth, the theologian Lavater, had done so much to popularize, Cornelia's "high and strongly arched forehead" is, as Goethe puts it in the second portrait, "excellent evidence of her moral and intellectual qualities" (562). Thus, ironically, a defect of facial symmetry by the aesthetic standards of the age is actually an indication of mental superiority, something that is decisively emphasized in the second portrait. "[S]he had . . . superior cultivation of mind, excellent knowledge, as well as talents, mastery of several languages, and a skilled pen, so that, had she only been well favored on the outside, she would have been counted among the most sought-after women of her time" (563). While it may be tempting to castigate Goethe for making Cornelia's physical appearance so decisive an element of his account of her, his foregrounding of her facial asymmetry reveals clearly enough the tragic discrepancy of Cornelia's dilemma in a patriarchal culture. Despite her extraordinary talents, abilities, and acquirements, she lacked the one attribute of physical attractiveness that could have made her an unqualified success.

Goethe is certainly no feminist, but he is on the threshold of an awareness that he achieved an extraordinary success and influence in the world of literature and culture, while she, though also possessed of great talents, died tragically young and unhappy, with no significant opportunity to realize and have the world recognize her unusual abilities.[16] As I have argued, his unsexing of her and his refusal to see her as another man's wife, coupled with his insistence on scripting her principally in the role of

soul sister, is self-serving and bespeaks a masculine will to power. This idealizing unsexing of her turns their relationship into an incestuous idyll
even as it subordinates her to his needs, making her the Dorothy to his
William. "[H]er nature harbored not the slightest sensuality. She had
grown up beside me and wished to continue spending her life in this sibling harmony. After my return from the university we had remained inseparable, with such heartfelt intimacy that we had our thoughts, feelings,
and whims in common, our impression of everything that happened"
(563). But Goethe's portrait is nothing if not unambiguous, for he also
casts her in his imagination in the romanticized role of intellectual, moral,
and spiritual leader and female master in a world that has in fact denied
her the expression of such talents. Because "she exercised an altogether
irresistible influence over feminine souls," Goethe confesses, "I liked to
imagine her, when I sometimes engaged in fancies about her destiny, not
as a wife, but as an abbess, the mother superior of a noble convent" (563).

Cornelia Goethe—an intellectually and morally superior young
woman too good for this world, trapped in marriage, done in by childbearing. Perhaps this human root that held him to the earth of childhood,
his other half, was at bottom as talented as he was, and could have
achieved a success similar to his. But she was a daughter caged at home
under her father's *Bildungs*-tyranny and then isolated in a less than happy
marriage and betrayed into childbearing. He, on the other hand, the adolescent male and then young man and famous author of *Götz* and *Werther,*
had flown the coop and left her behind, writing her only very infrequently
and visiting her only once in the years after her marriage. While she felt
cut off from her Frankfurt friends and social circle in rural Emmendingen,
ill and depressed, he was living a life of masculine independence and
agency as the companion of the young Duke of Weimar, and steering well
clear of marriage. Her chosen device, *la liberté fait mon bonheur,* had the
illustration of a bird flying out of a birdcage (Michel 60). But unlike her
brother, Cornelia's only escape lay in death. Perhaps in Goethe's sadly perplexed tribute, there is an unarticulated element of survivor guilt on the
part of the old and world-famous brother looking back on the childhood
he shared with the sister who died so accomplished, young, and
unknown.

No wonder, given his feelings about her marriage, Goethe's only visit
to her new home—the last time he ever saw her—was marked by reluc-

tance and mixed feelings. There are some things that cannot be said simply or explicitly about a deep and complex relationship, one viewed in the hindsight of a lifetime that is perhaps being superimposed on the earlier experience being narrated. "[A] perceptive reader who can read between these lines and see what has not been written but only hinted at will begin to understand the solemnity of my feelings as I entered Emmendingen at that time" (564). *What has not been written* but only implied is perhaps what matters most in Goethe's portrait. He knew he could not capture the living source of his sister's elusive spirit, but his perplexed yet decisively etched portrait says as much as he could of his sense of her and their strange relationship.

Goethe finishes the second portrait without any description of his actual visit to Emmendingen, but reports that to his chagrin his sister urged him in the strongest terms to break his engagement with Lili Schönemann. Her reasons for this suggest no selfish desire to keep him always in the role of her brother, but point instead to a mature young woman who can give eminently sensible advice for difficult life questions. She had the insight to point out to her brother that his worldly and elegant fiancée would not fit into the stultifying bourgeois confines of the Goethe household, with a taciturn and didactic father and a mother set in her ways. "Although she approved of her [Lili] highly, she thought it cruel to tear a young woman of this type away from an existence that was lively and active, if not really brilliant, and to bring her into our house" (564). Her sound, frank advice shows that even if she ultimately had not found happiness in marriage, she loved her brother enough and understood sufficiently the character and situation of his worldly fiancée to risk hurting his feelings by letting him know that this match would make his bride, and thus him as well, unhappy. From her own tragic experience, she knew whereof she spoke.

6 ❧

Romantic Love in *Poetry and Truth*

In addition to the richly elaborated portraits of his father and sister, Goethe devotes a considerable amount of his autobiography to his relationships with others, both friends and lovers. Goethe had a genius for friendship, and *Poetry and Truth* is a veritable portrait gallery of close relationships with a host of different men, some older than Goethe and cast in the role of mentors. It would require an extended discussion to do justice to young Goethe's many friendships, which are a function of his open nature and his mobile and impressionable personality and which stand in contrast to some of Rousseau's early friendships (for example, those with Bacle and Venture de Villeneuve), which reinforced his most questionable tendencies.

My purpose in this final chapter, however, is to examine Goethe's confessional presentation of his early *amours*. Romantic love played a major role in Goethe's life well into his later years and is very much a part of the popular legend of that life, from the passion for the eighteen-year-old Charlotte Buff in the summer of 1772 that became the basis of the confessional fiction of *Werther,* to his last great infatuation, at the age of seventy-two, with the seventeen-year-old Ulrike von Levetzow, whose rejection of his marriage proposal occasioned the overflow of powerful feelings in the lyrical "Trilogy of Suffering" (1824).[1] The surviving letters from Goethe's adolescence already make frequent reference to "Mädgen" ("girls"), and in *Poetry and Truth* he gives the romantic sphere of his young life more than its proper acknowledgment. However, he eschews the religious and the secular confessional modes respectively of Saint Augustine and Rousseau, both of whom dwell quite explicitly on the adolescent experience of sexuality. Goethe does not present his sexual history in the way Rousseau does, with the narrative of the first spanking, or in the way Augustine does in book 2 of his *Confessions,* where he recounts his succumbing "entirely to lust" at the age of sixteen (44).

Goethe refuses to make the neat Augustinian distinction between "the clear light of true love" and "the murk of lust" (43), a dichotomy replicated by Rousseau's sundering of romantic love and sexuality.[2] Goethe's account of romantic love, especially the famous Sesenheim sequence, is as poeticized as it is discreet; it suggests the merging of the sensual and the spiritual in a highly stylized portrayal whose inexplicitness never answers, or invites us to ask, the pointed question, "Did they or didn't they?" If there is also a burden of confession in Goethe's portrayal of love, it is certainly not Augustine's guilt about lust or Rousseau's shame about his masochistic desires, but a guilt about (his) masculine unreliability and willfulness in an unequal gender relationship in which men have the upper hand. Goethe's portrayal reflects the inequality in love in a patriarchal world epitomized in the farewell letter of Byron's disgraced Donna Julia to her teenage lover: "Man's love is of man's life a thing apart, / 'Tis woman's whole existence" (*Don Juan,* Canto 1, stanza 194).

"THE NEW PARIS"

If, unlike Augustine and Rousseau, Goethe does not directly address the issue of his budding sexuality, he does allude to it with the richly symbolic "The New Paris: A Boyhood Fairy Tale," which he incorporates in book 2 as a sample of the storytelling gift with which he entertained other boys. An intricately layered intertextual *Märchen,* "The New Paris" is hardly the product of the boy's imagination but that of the older author who uses elements of Greek and Eastern mythology to suggest, through the traditional motifs of the secret garden and the battle of the sexes, the awakening and transgressive consequences of masculine desire. The tale opens with the boy's dream that Mercury hands him three apples that he is "to give to the three handsomest young men in town, and then each of them will find, to match his prize, the very best wife that he could wish to have" (50). The red, green, and yellow apples change into doll-sized women with dresses of corresponding colors who escape from his grasping fingers.[3] After their departure, he sees "the loveliest girl imaginable dancing around on [his] fingertips" (50). The suggestion of autoerotic fantasy is followed by the impulsive assertion of the masculine will to possess. As the new Paris attempts to seize this charming figurine, he feels "a blow on [his] head" and falls down unconscious—an action that parallels Faust's attempted seizure of Helen's conjured form at the emperor's court in *Faust* (part 2, act 1).

He meets up again with the girl, whose name is Alerte, at the center of a secret garden he subsequently discovers. As he enters the pleasure garden (after changing into "Oriental-looking clothes," 53), the birds call him both Paris and Narcissus—an appropriate mythological indicator of the self-involved character of adolescent eros—and with the help of the mysterious gatekeeper who has admitted him he is eventually able to enter the inner garden guarded by a circular fence and canal. The sexual symbolism of the fence ("countless numbers of pikes and halberds whose strangely decorated points were linked to form a complete circle"), is further enhanced when the lances and spears are lowered to form "a splendid bridge" that allows his crossing of the canal into "the most colorful garden" (52, 53). At the center of this inner garden is "an exquisite summer house" whose gatekeeper turns out to be "the dainty girl who, in my dream, had danced on my fingers" (54). He is welcomed into the house by three ladies dressed in red, green, and yellow whom he recognizes as "the sylphs of [his] dream" (55). They have been playing string instruments and seat him next to Alerte, enjoining him to listen, "if you are a lover of music." The romantic suggestion of the music is carried further when Alerte first plays and dances to the mandolin, and he eagerly joins her in "a sort of little ballet." In addition to this metaphoric food of love, he also consumes "with great appetite" the enticing "fruits which were either foreign or out of season" that she serves him—"oranges, figs, peaches, and grapes" (55).

But as in the biblical Eden, so in this Eastern "paradise" of sensual delights there is a also a fall in store. Alerte's suggestion that they play on the golden bridge with two sets of toy armies leads to a battle of the sexes: "The girl gloried in having the queen of the Amazons to lead her female army, while I found myself in possession of Achilles and a very stately troop of Greek cavalry" (56). In the heat of their miniature Homeric battle, the two antagonists get carried beyond the bounds of play and he angrily smashes some of her "female centaurs," leading her to cry out "that [he] had caused her an irreparable loss, one much greater than could be put into words" (56). This implicit complaint about the loss of virginity through male violence only fuels the boy's sadistic and aggressive impulses: "I was angry enough to delight in doing something to hurt her, and I threw my remaining pellets among her troops with blind force" (56). The childish conflict comes to a predictable conclusion: "It was my angry intention to annihilate her whole army; but she suddenly jumped at me and gave me such a box on the ear that my head rang. I had always heard it said that a girl's slap must be repaid with a rough kiss; therefore I took her by the ears and kissed her repeatedly. She, however, uttered such a piercing scream that I myself was startled and let her go" (57).

I have briefly summarized the central symbolic sequence of "The New Paris" in order to indicate how Goethe clothes in a charming symbolic fable the same issue—the awakening of sexuality—that Rousseau presents more explicitly in the narrative of the first spanking. On the pretext of having actually told this story as a boy, Goethe's suggestive *Märchen,* which artfully hints at the budding erotic feelings of early adolescence, shifts his autobiography entirely to the "poetry" or *Dichtung* side and gains a new imaginative freedom for the genre. While for more conservative critics Goethe's figurative transposition of his own experience into a fairy tale would constitute a transgression of its referential boundaries, for others like Müller *Poetry and Truth* represents the successful transformation of autobiography from a practical prose form into a fully realized work of art (242).

ROMANTIC MYSTIFICATIONS:
THE HISTORY OF LOVE AND THE LOVE OF HISTORY

A similar poeticizing process, but in a very different key, is at work in Goethe's account of his relationship at the age of fifteen with Gretchen, which is presented in book 5 in the dramatic context of the election and coronation of the young Joseph II as king of the Romans in Frankfurt in the spring of 1764. Given the fictionalizing bent of *Poetry and Truth* and the lack of any independent information about Gretchen, biographers have been skeptical about what Goethe tells us of his relationship with her.[4] The possibility that she may be the poetic condensation of several of his adolescent infatuations is supported by the fact that Goethe's original conception was to use the love story of the novel *Manon Lescaut* (by Abbé Antoine-François Prévost) as an intertextual mirror or literary frame for presenting his own version of first love. A surviving draft summary of the relationship between the faithless Manon and her devoted lover des Grieux, intended as an epilogue to Goethe's narrative, concludes with the acknowledgment that the novel had an impact on his own experience of romantic love. At the time, Goethe responded only to the subject matter of the story and did not appreciate "the inestimable art with which it is executed." "I imagined that I could be as loving and as faithful as the knight, and because I considered Gretchen infinitely better than Manon had proved herself to be, I believed that everything that could be done for her would be very well applied" (HA 9:751).

As in the case of the young Rousseau's novel reading with his father, here too the romance of early reading appears to play into and shape the actual experience of life. Goethe's imaginative immersion in the fictional world of *Manon* makes his own experience of romantic love "richer, more enjoyable, even ecstatic," and after the relationship with Gretchen is abruptly "destroyed," his grief and suffering is that much more intense (751). His poetic re-creation of first love, however, not only deals with the subject matter of that experience but also embodies the artistic mastery the boy had failed to notice on his reading of the famous love story. The high artfulness of Goethe's presentation of romantic love, here and even more so in the Sesenheim narrative, has been repeatedly noted by the commentators, including Goethe's use of the novella form in his arrangement of the Gretchen story.[5]

At one level, the narrative captures the magic and wonder that is first love. The somewhat older and more mature Gretchen, a girl "of incredible beauty," leaves young Goethe with "the first durable impression that a person of the feminine sex had ever made on" him (book 5, 132). He even goes to church in order to be near her: "[T]hus throughout the long Protestant service I could gaze at her to my heart's content" (133). Like the

Catholic James Joyce of "Araby," the Protestant Goethe effectively captures a universal aspect of young love. "The first amorous inclinations of unspoiled youth assume a thoroughly spiritual character. Nature seems to use the difference in sex to make us become aware of the good and the beautiful through our senses" (135). The chief of these senses—the erotic modality par excellence—is sight, and Goethe, who in book 6 informs us that "the eye was above all others the organ with which I apprehended the world" (173), consistently appeals throughout book 5 to that sense. The innocent intimacy that develops between Gretchen and Wolfgang takes the form of their spending much time together, but with only fleeting moments of timid yet tender physical contact. One of the great charms of first love, after all, is that very little counts for very much. From the start, Gretchen assumes control of the physical element in their relationship. Although they are "together almost every day," she does not allow him to touch her, "but sometimes she would sit down beside me, especially while I was reading aloud or writing, and then she would lay her arm familiarly on my shoulder and look into my book or on my sheet of paper" (137–38).

This scenario suggests that the romantic relationship is also a pedagogic one in which the younger male assumes the role of tutor. As we saw in the previous chapter, the student Goethe was to assume such a pedagogic stance in his letters from Leipzig to his sister. Indeed, the adolescent Goethe's teaching of Gretchen is the first instance of a romantic pattern that persisted well into his old age, when he liked to strike such an attitude with younger women. A signal instance of this romantic-pedagogic constellation involves the beautiful young Milanese woman in the *Italian Journey* to whom Goethe gives an impromptu English lesson after she has expressed her frustration at missing the opportunity (because of the restricted education of Italian women) to learn foreign languages.[6] Like the young Milanese more than two decades later, Gretchen too resents the gender restrictions that deprive her of an education. She repays with "unflagging attention" Goethe's historical lectures about the imperial coronation ceremonies: "[S]he thanked me and said she envied (to use her expression) those who were versed in the affairs of this world and knew how various things happened and what they meant. She wished to be a boy, and acknowledged in a very friendly way that she was already indebted to me for many pieces of information. 'If I were a boy,' she said, 'we would go to universities together and really learn something'" (145).

Goethe registers an awareness of female frustrations with the gender inequalities of the era even as he summarizes the romantic dynamic of the student-teacher relationship with pointed references to the medieval philosopher Peter Abelard and his famous eighteenth-century fictional reincarnation, Rousseau's Saint Preux, the tutor and lover of Julie, the new Héloïse:

> If a young couple is at all harmoniously constituted by nature, nothing can be more conducive to a lovely union than the girl's desire to learn and the young man's inclination to teach. The relationship that ensues is as solid as it is pleasant. She sees in him the creator of her intellectual existence, and he in her a creation owing its perfection not to nature, chance, or a unilateral wish, but to their bilateral will. This interaction is so sweet that we must not be surprised if such a meeting of two personalities has generated the most overwhelming passions and as much happiness as unhappiness, ever since there have been Abelards, old and new. (146)

The fantasy of masculine mastery inherent in this erotic-pedagogic scenario is counterbalanced, however, by the greater maturity and practical wisdom of the older girl-student. Even though she comes from a lower social class, she more than holds her own when she lectures him on the foolishness and potentially serious consequences of his having allowed himself to be drawn into a scheme of writing forged love letters. And because she is realistic about her marital prospects and knows that class differences will prevent a union with the son of a leading patrician family, she does not respond to the intoxicated boy's flattering description of "the spouse [he] wished to have," who "turned out to be Gretchen's perfect double" (137).

That Gretchen is not only older and more realistic in her outlook but also more experienced, worldly, and less innocent than he takes her to be is suggested by the motif of masking or disguise, which at one level adds to the charm of the relationship. On a visit to a milliner's shop, Goethe notices the milliner's assistant, "a female person sitting in the window who looked very young and pretty in her little lace cap and very well shaped in her silk mantilla." As he looks at her again, he is struck by "her incredible similarity to Gretchen." "[I]ndeed [I] became convinced that it was Gretchen herself! My last doubts were removed when she winked an eye at me and made a sign that I was not to reveal our acquaintanceship" (139). The element of intrigue and secrecy introduced here is part of a larger pattern of Goethe's involvement with the Gretchen circle that takes a traumatic turn at the end of the book with the sudden arrest of Gretchen's friends and Goethe's interrogation about his involvement with them. It is also, we should remember, a relationship that he had kept secret from his family. This element of secrecy carries over into their final encounter, which culminates in their first and only kiss. During their night promenade through a Frankfurt lit up for the coronation festivities, Goethe, "to keep from being recognized," had "disguised [him]self a little, and Gretchen approved" (161).

The world of secrecy, intrigue, and disguise into which the romantic boy is drawn, innocently enough, in his relationship with the older girl, and which blows up in his face at the close of book 5, is already intimated in its aphoristic opening: "There is a bait for every bird, and there is also an individual way to lead, and mislead, a human being" (131). Book 5 shows Goethe's ability to layer his presentation with multiple levels of ironic significance, and to set up an intricate interdependency of mutually implicating contexts unrivaled in autobiography until our century, in that modernist masterpiece of poetic self-refraction, Nabokov's *Speak, Memory.* The most artful touch in book 5 is the way the narrative of the Gretchen relationship is structurally and thematically interrelated with that of the spectacular coronation ceremonies. The references to *bait* and to being *misled* in the opening sentence in fact allude—and can be applied as interpretive keys—to both narratives. The crucial link between them is the organizing theme of book 5, the psychological phenomenon of "mystification" introduced in its opening pages (131–32). In both the Gretchen and the coronation sequences, such "mystifications" are a function of the sense of sight that mislead the romantic boy as well as the impressionable public. Both private or romantic history (Gretchen) and public spectacle (coronation) are subsumed under the same concept, which is presented as the adolescent's history of first love as well as his love of history as spectacle.

Unlike the case of Rousseau's *Confessions,* history and the historical—as sequence and action, as well as perspective, frame, mode of understanding—are ever present realities in *Poetry and Truth,* and figure in a variety of contexts and guises, from the account of the occupation of Frankfurt during the Seven Years' War in book 4 to the panoramic history of eighteenth-century literature in book 7. But nowhere is Goethe's presentation of an individual life in the context of his age handled with such deftness and dramatic sweep as in book 5. His narrative here is not only intricate and complex because of his contrapuntal account of first love and coronation ritual, but also because his presentation of personal and public events is at once romanticizing *and* demystifying. Both the lovely Gretchen and the magnificent ceremonies of imperial election and investiture delight and dazzle the adolescent boy, but by the time the book is over, both seem to be revealed as false shows in which there is in fact much *less* than first met his eager eye.

At the beginning of this book, the adolescent Goethe becomes involved in a romantic prank or "mystification" (131) at the expense of a young man in his circle of friends, when he forges a series of love letters that supposedly pass between the young man and a girl he is made to believe is infatuated with him. It is in associating with these young people "of the lower class" (131) that Goethe meets and falls in love with Gretchen. In writing in her company the epistle in which the young woman supposedly responds to the young man, Goethe promptly imagines that Gretchen is writing to him: "Thus, while thinking to gull another person, I humbugged [*mystifizierte,* or mystified] myself" (133). However, this narrative of first love is contained within and framed by the larger public narrative of the coronation sequence. By the end of the fifth book, this greater historical sequence is implicated in ironic hindsight as another type of romantic *mystification.* Like the fraudulent letter that Goethe penned but imagined was coming to him from Gretchen, the coronation spectacle that has so enchanted him and that he takes in with such a greedy eye stands revealed as a kind of public forgery. The implied and ironic parallel between the intertwined narratives of first love and coronation ritual is that in both cases the gorgeous surface of romantic mystification (the young Goethe intoxicated by Gretchen's beauty and by the splendor of the public ceremonies) is undermined by less than romantic realities. In hindsight at least, Goethe has learned to take a hard or disenchanted look at the enchanting surface of both personal and public history.

Gretchen's sexual mores are not impugned, but she is revealed as the older girl who played a game with the younger boy. After their sudden and forced separation, he is mortified to discover (at the beginning of book 6) that she is reported to have said, "I saw him often and gladly, but I always regarded him as a child, and my affection for him was altogether sisterly" (170). It is of course possible that under the pressure of interrogation by the authorities, Gretchen lied to protect him and herself, although the young Goethe believes what she says and his chagrin at the revelation helps to bring him out of his depression. On the whole, Gretchen is guilty at best of playing a disingenuous role in their relationship and at worst of cruel artifice—as implied in the scene in the milliner's shop. But the circle of questionable acquaintances Goethe continues to associate with because of his relationship with Gretchen in the end unwittingly draws the prodigal grandson of Frankfurt's chief magistrate into a nether world of criminal intrigue and fraud. The arrest of several members of this lower-class group, including a job candidate whom Goethe had been manipulated into recommending to his grandfather for a trusted clerical position in the city administration, is what exposes and brings to an abrupt end his relationship with Gretchen. (Their misdemeanors are not specified by Goethe, although the context implies that they forged documents and papers—a motif that makes for a telling thematic link with the forged love letters.)

In the wake of his house arrest, the enforced separation from Gretchen, and his having to answer for the disreputable company he has been keeping, the devastated youth succumbs to a fit of self-torturing imagination reminiscent of Rousseau: "The only satisfaction I felt now was in ruminating on my misery and letting it multiply a thousandfold in my imagination. All my inventive gifts and knowledge of poetry and rhetoric concentrated themselves on this morbid spot and by their vigor threatened to inflict an incurable disease on my body and soul" (166). If his physical illness and near-suicidal state are resolved only by the subsequent discovery that Gretchen had been toying with him all along, the larger presentation of Goethe's first love is that of an extravagant and consistent self-mystification. Only in the distanced reflection of book 7 does Goethe point to the underlying questionable (social and historical) realities to which his eyes have so rudely been opened as a consequence of his first infatuation. "In connection with the Gretchen affair and its aftermath I had gotten a precocious look into the extraordinary labyrinth that underlies town society. Religion, mores, law, status, circumstances, custom—all these hold sway only on the surface of municipal life" (216).

Goethe's richly detailed coronation narrative, like the linked story of first love, can also be subsumed under his key concept of "mystification" in the manner in which the gorgeous but antiquated "surface" of this grand historic spectacle is compromised and undermined by contemporary political realities. As in the love story, so in the coronation narrative *writing* also plays a significant role in the demystification of romantic (self-) delusion, with the activity of writing (love letters, a coronation diary) described in the text serving the cause of "mystification" and the text of book 5 itself helping to undo the boy's (double) self-delusion in the very process of a vivid and careful narrative re-creation. Not only does Goethe consult with his father accounts of earlier imperial coronations, but at his father's behest he also compiles a detailed eyewitness report or coronation diary. He derives pleasure from this scribal activity even as he gains an appreciation of the political character of history beneath the ceremonial surface of medieval pageantry. Thus he is pleased that "such symbolical ceremonies made the German empire, which was almost buried under a heap of parchment, papers, and books, seem alive again for a moment," but he is disconcerted to note that during the electoral negotiations, "several forces counterbalanced each other in their opposition here, being in agreement only in respect to their intention of limiting the new regent even more than the old one" (143).

Goethe's cinematic narrative of the imperial displays in Frankfurt approaches the climax of the coronation ceremony in an accelerating rhythm of vivid description in which *seeing* and *writing* are connected as ecstatic activities, doubly romantic in the sense that everything he witnesses will be transformed into a historical narrative (written) for his father and (oral) for Gretchen: "During these days I was in a constant whirl. At home there was writing and copying to do, and to see everything was both our wish and our duty. . . . I had promised Gretchen a faithful, detailed explanation of the latest happenings and of what was to be expected on the coronation day" (152). That "great day" seems to live up fully to the boy's aroused expectations; when the father, Francis I ("the emperor in romantic clothing"), and the son to be crowned, Joseph, proceed to the cathedral, "the eye simply no longer sufficed! One wished for a magic formula that would capture this vision for just a moment; but the splendor passed by inexorably" (155). In its romanticizing of history, the coronation narrative is also a mystification of political power: "There is infinite charm in a ceremony that combines politics and religion. We behold the earthly majesty. surrounded by all the symbols of its power" (156).

Yet both narratives—first love, royal investiture—end in anticlimax and disappointment. The morning after celebrating the public festivities in the company of Gretchen, Goethe suffers house arrest, never to see her again. And the coronation spectacle too ends on an absurdly discordant note. Coming from the ceremony, the young king of the Romans hardly makes a favorable impression. His appearance is comically incongruous because the symbolic vestments don't fit the youth—the young king has, as it were, the wrong clothes, a discrepancy of which, to his credit, he betrays an ironic awareness. While his father in "his emperor's dynastic robes . . . seemed to be quite at ease in this costume . . . the young king, on the other hand, dragged himself along in these vast garments and Charlemagne's jewels as though in a masquerade costume, and he himself could not repress a smile when he occasionally glanced at his father" (157).[7] The larger discrepancy between the romantic trappings of the venerable office and its actual political standing is suggested by Goethe's final glimpse of the empty place settings at the coronation dinner, which takes on the aura of a ghostly charade "because of the splendid preparations made for so many invisible guests." Because so many delegates have absented themselves from the banquet due to political differences, the sad sight of "the large empty table in the center" of this "spectral appearance" (160) is a telling real-world indication of the true standing of the moribund Holy Roman Empire. Written several years after that empire had in fact officially expired, Goethe's account scripts the coronation sequence as an empty masquerade, dazzling on the surface but hollow at the core.

After a veritable orgy of seeing and beholding in which Goethe and his friends eagerly participate, there is a void at the center that even the spectacular illumination of the city during the festive night cannot fill. Thus the coronation narrative is not only an extremely vivid rendering of history of which earlier autobiographers, including Rousseau, are largely oblivious; it is also a subtly ironic critique of the mystification(s) of history, one that gives full credit and bears powerful witness to the appeal of such romantic mystifications for the adolescent Goethe's curious mind and eager eye. And by the ironic logic of implication of the "mystification" theme common to both the coronation and the Gretchen narratives, his romantic obsession with the girl whose beauty, like the imperial proceedings in Frankfurt, was such a feast for his eyes, is also demystified and deflated in hindsight.

Even Goethe's professed cheerfulness of autobiographical presentation cannot disguise or mitigate the crisis of his sudden separation from Gretchen. His mother's and sister's ministrations are fruitless, as is a complete amnesty offered by his father after the boy has been cleared of any serious wrongdoing by the authorities. He isolates himself in his room and "obstinately" refuses his father's offer that they view together "the imperial insignia, which were just now on display for the curious. I declared that I could take no more interest in the world or the Holy Roman Empire until I was informed how that sorry affair, which would have no further consequences for me, had turned out for my poor acquaintances" (165). The news that his friends have gotten off "with a gentle rebuke" and "that Gretchen had left town and returned to her home" does not cheer him either, but stimulates his imagination to further self-torture: "[O]nly now did my distress really begin, and I had ample time to torment myself by imagining the oddest romance, made up of sad events and leading inevitably to a tragic catastrophe" (166).

However fictionalized the Gretchen episode may be, Goethe's account of his intense grief and gradual recovery, which is the substance of the first part of book 6, rings true to life. His attempts at "activity" as therapy for his "debilitating ideas"(171)—including the study of philosophy under the guidance of a guardian-tutor who has been engaged to keep an eye on him—are partly successful. But a new morbid or hypochondriacal tendency manifests itself when he ventures back out into the streets of Frankfurt, and he is afflicted by the exacerbated self-consciousness that in the end drove Rousseau to paranoia. "I had lost the bliss of being able to walk around unselfconsciously, blameless and unrecognized, not suspecting that there was any observer in the largest crowd. Now the morbid conceit began to torment me that I was attracting people's attention and their gaze was fixed on my behavior, determining, investigating, censuring it" (172). To avoid the hostile gaze of the *other,* Goethe escapes with his guardian "into the woods" to hide "a poor, wounded heart" (172). This youthful retreat to nature as a healing force aligns Goethe with fundamental themes of European Romanticism—with Rousseau at Charmettes in *The Confessions* and in his boat on Lake Bienne in the Fifth Revery, and with Wordsworth in the Lake District in *The Prelude.*[8] Equally Romantic is his praise of natural religion (a "divine worship . . . which issues purely from a dialogue in our bosom with nature!" 173), and the sublime ("those vague, wide-ranging [feelings] characteristic of youth and primitive peoples," 173).

GOETHE'S ANTI-PYGMALION: NATURE, ART, AND INTERTEXTUALITY IN THE SESENHEIM CONFESSION

The two romantic interludes Goethe briefly discusses between Gretchen and Friederike Brion can be seen as thematic stepping stones toward the issue of male guilt that is foregrounded in his relationship with Brion. At Leipzig his love for an innkeeper's daughter, "Annette" (Anna Katharina Schönkopf), turns into a destructive jealousy and is marked by an ungovernable urge to vent his "bad humor" and frustration on her. He finds some compensation for his well-deserved loss of her, however, in the "curative powers" of his "poetic talent" (book 7, 215); already during his adolescence the lifelong pattern of writing as a balm for the pain of love begins to emerge. Later, in the Lucinde episode at the close of book 9, the theme of the destructive character of men's love is invoked with the legendary motif of the cursed kiss that symbolically sets the stage for the Sesenheim narrative adumbrated in the next book. Goethe's imbroglio with the daughters of the French dancing master in Strasbourg—he is attracted to the younger, but the older, Lucinde, is taken with him—ends with the latter passionately forcing jealous kisses on him. "Misfortune on top of misfortune, forever and ever, to her who kisses these lips for the first time after me!" (294). Thus before we even meet Friederike, Goethe dramatically anticipates his relationship with her with the premonitory note that casts her as the victim of his romantic attentions.

Goethe distributes the presentation of his Sesenheim romance over books 10 and 11, offering it in the larger context of his account of his student days, his journeys, and his intellectual development—including the instrumental influence of his friendship with Herder—during his stay at Strasbourg (April 1770–August 1771). The symbolic focal points of this decisive phase of his life are the gothic spire of the Strasbourg cathedral rising into the skies and the "altogether paradisiacal region" (309), the Alsatian landscape that he explores on horseback and that in the Sesenheim idyll is painted, as Edgar Bracht has shown (273–74), in distinctly

Arcadian colors. It is part of the complex layering of Goethe's Sesenheim narrative, however, that its idyllic character is framed by a somber motif of male guilt presented by way of sinister foreshadowing as well as a poignant narrative coda.

Goethe introduces his Sesenheim love with a veiled poetic allusion in book 10. On a journey through the coal country of the Saar, he sits in a solitary vigil on the side of a mountain under "the vault of the burning stars." The distant sound of hunting horns is "like the fragrance of balsam" and awakens in Goethe "the image of a lovely creature that had been relegated to the background by the motley impressions of these days of travel" (313). This renascent image motivates Goethe to an early morning departure that will take him to his "beloved Sesenheim" and "a young woman to whom [he] was deeply attached" (315). This lyrical and allusive opening, in which Friederike is not mentioned by name, contrasts starkly with the troubled moralizing and confessional reflection of "gloomy remorse" in book 12 that concludes his narrative of his relationship with her. There he acknowledges that her answer to his letter of farewell (written after his return to Frankfurt upon completion of his law studies), "broke [his] heart." "Only now did I understand the loss she had suffered, but I saw no way to make it good or even moderate it. She was ever in my mind; I always felt how much I missed her, and the worst of it was, I was responsible for my own unhappiness. Gretchen had been taken from me, and Annette had forsaken me, *but here for the first time I was guilty.* I had deeply wounded the loveliest heart" (385, emphasis added).

In its picturesque stylizing of the Alsatian landscape and the rustic dwelling and simple manners of the Brion family, Goethe's Sesenheim narrative is akin to Rousseau's rural idyll of Charmettes (book 6 of *The Confessions*), but the confessional burden of his love having nearly destroyed an innocent young woman also makes it his ribbon of Marion.[9] At still another level, Sesenheim is Goethe's anti-Pygmalion. As noted in chapter 4, Goethe in book 11 criticizes Rousseau's "lyrical scene" (of the sculptor embracing the statue in whom he has embodied his ideal of female perfection, after his prayer to have her come to life has been answered by Venus), because "it alternates between nature and art and misguidedly tries to reduce the latter to the former" (363). Goethe's Sesenheim is a celebration of nature and the natural, but one that consciously and consistently elevates these to the level of art. It is one of the supreme instances in *Poetry and Truth* of the aesthetic heightening and poeticizing of experience. Goethe told Eckermann that "the story of Sesenheim" resembled his *Elective Affinities* in that it "contains no line that was not experienced, but no line, exactly *how* it was experienced" (1:368, 17 February 1830). Goethe, as it were, capitalizes on the fictionalizing penchant that Rousseau in his poetic portrait of Charmettes gave in to covertly. However, Goethe chose not Rousseau's *Confessions* for his intertextual mirror, but a popular if ultimately minor eighteenth-century sentimental novel. The oft-noted novelistic tendencies of Goethe's narrative are in fact thematized in the developed parallel between the Brion family and that of Oliver Goldsmith's *Vicar of Wakefield*.

What to the biographer is the relatively simple issue of the autobiographer "flagrantly" casting "an idyllic glow over the story of his love of Friederike" (Boyle 100), is to the student of autobiography the much more complex issue of life consciously transposed into art. That Goethe chooses to interrupt the account of his journey to his beloved's "rustic abode" (315) with a substantial characterization of Herder's reading aloud of the novel and his own enthusiastic response to it shows how deliberate and controlled is his poeticizing or "literarizing," through the intertextual mirror of the English novel, of his own experience. Goethe's need to experience life through art is explicit in his discussion of the work that he claims "did much to kindle [his] affection [for Sesenheim] and to enhance the satisfaction it afforded [him]" (315). In Goethe's account, he first went to Sesenheim after listening to Herder's reading, so that in effect his journey was a surprising transit from "this fictitious world into a similar real one" (318). In actuality, his experience of Sesenheim came well before his encounter with the novel via Herder's reading; thus in the retrospective mirror of his autobiography Goethe reverses the stated chronological sequence (novel to life) by textually transposing his lived experience into art.[10] Even if in real life his reading of *The Vicar of Wakefield* did not color his experience of Sesenheim, in his autobiographical recollection he allowed his later response to the novel to play into his earlier experience; that is, he allowed literature to reorder life and imagination to reshape memory.

By deliberately incorporating the English novel as a kind of fictional template for his own experience, Goethe consciously put himself into opposition to Rousseau's "Pygmalion," which he saw as an indiscriminate attempt to turn art back into nature. For the late Goethe, art and nature cannot be an identity or a seamless whole, and even the art that celebrates the simplicity and naturalness of the rural life and manners of Sesenheim has to employ artificial means to create the illusion of the natural. As Goethe put it, in the context of how Rousseau and Diderot pointed his generation away from art to nature, "the supreme task of every kind of art is to use semblance to give the illusion of a higher reality. But it is erroneous to strive for a semblance so real that it amounts to mere everyday reality" (book ii, 362). The highly contrived Wakefield-Sesenheim parallel, like the earlier contrapuntal interplay of the Gretchen and coronation narratives, represents the anti-Pygmalion Goethe's heightening or intensification of a lived experience that is never allowed to sink to the level of "mere everyday reality." To insist too much or too literally on nature and the natural—which is the gist of Rousseau's influential philosophy and writing—is to destroy the very basis of art, which is illusion and artifice. Goethe's Sesenheim is lived experience consciously rearranged through the lens of art; but in this poeticizing of his relationship with Friederike and her family, Goethe makes sure not to reproduce, nor to confuse the illusion of art with, the pedestrian everyday reality that is the biographer's burden. That the Sesenheim narrative is fiction is a commonplace of Goethe criticism, but one that must be qualified with an awareness of how the poetry of this legendary episode is both grounded in and an imaginative transformation and novelistic rendering of Goethe's actual experience.[11]

That Goethe chose for his intertextual mirror a sentimental, moralistic fiction whose plot is as improbably melodramatic as its characters are conventional may put off the contemporary reader—especially given Goethe's praise of Goldsmith's novel as "among the best ever written" (316) in a century that in England produced Fielding, Richardson, Sterne, and Smollet. Like Werther's enthusiasm for the bard Ossian, whose overblown excerpts in Goethe's novel are today all but unreadable, Goethe's praise of *The Vicar of Wakefield* reflects the popular literary culture of his youth, for Goldsmith's novel, which was translated into German within a year of its publication (1766), proved to be even more popular in Germany than in England. What the mature author of *Poetry and Truth* sees in the novel is clearly different from the enthusiastic and uncritical reception, nearly half a century earlier, of the young listener who irritated Herder by allowing his emotions to be "overwhelmed by the subject matter," rather than paying attention to its "form and substance" (317). Herder "viewed the work only as an artistic product," and in a sense Goethe also wants us to view his Sesenheim story in that aesthetic light and not just for its subject matter.

Specifically, what the older Goethe sees in Goldsmith's Christian fable, offered "without a trace of sanctimoniousness or pedantry," is a "pervasive irony" that makes "this little work strike us as not only wise but amiable" (316). To a much higher degree and in a much more sophisticated manner, Goethe's style as an autobiographer is pervaded at one level by the irony of an amiable wisdom that he praises in the English writer. In seeking to account for the powerful impact of *The Vicar of Wakefield* he experienced as a young man, he describes as well the ironic ideal of his own autobiography: "The work under discussion had made a great and lasting impression on me, which I could not explain to myself. But I felt that I was actually in agreement with the ironic frame of mind that rises above things, above fortune and misfortune, good and evil, life and death, and thus comes into possession of a genuinely poetic world. To be sure, I was not really conscious of this until later" (318). In a somewhat cryptic diary entry of May 1810, Goethe contrasts "the ironic view of life in the higher sense, through which biography raises itself above life" with "the superstitious view, by which it [biography] again draws back toward life" (HA 11:557). Goethe adds that the former approach appeals to our reason and understanding, the latter to our senses and imagination, with the result that a balance of the two will produce "a satisfying totality." Clearly his Sesenheim narrative employs both approaches in tandem to achieve its powerful poetic effects, from the elevated synoptic overview of his later years (from which he surveys his romance with Friederike as he once surveyed the landscape surrounding Strasbourg from the tower of the cathedral)—the ironic view, to the re-creation of the naive charm and the sensual delights of young love—the superstitious view.

The moral dilemma of male guilt at the heart of the Sesenheim narrative is that the young Goethe loved being in love but was unwilling or unable to make a lasting commitment. As Boyle has concluded, "Goethe shied away from marriage to Friederike because the fixity of such a commitment was incompatible with the only poetry that he could write, a poetry of continuing desire" (108). That desire finds a literary vehicle in Goethe's powerful lyrical outpouring in the Strasbourg period (which introduced a new style into German poetry), including his famous literary ballad, "Rose upon the Heath" ("Heidenröslein").[12] Probably written early in the summer of 1771 at the height of his passion for Friederike, the symbolic action of the poem is a covert confession that turns on the same issue of male erotic waywardness, violation of female innocence, and subsequent remorse that is also the moral gist of the Sesenheim narrative. The pressure of desire is also evident in the passionate letters that Goethe wrote from Sesenheim to an older friend in Strasbourg in June 1771. These reveal an "animula vagula" that turns, as he puts it, like a weathervane on a church tower, and for whom even the fulfillment of desire leaves something to desire: "[T]he world is as beautiful as I have not seen it for a long time. The most pleasant region, people who love me, a circle of friends! 'Are not all the dreams of your childhood fulfilled?' I ask myself sometimes, when my eye feasts itself on the horizon of my happiness; are these not the enchanted gardens for which you yearned?—They are, they are! I feel it, dear friend, and I feel that one is not one hair's breadth happier when one obtains what one has desired" (*Briefe* 1:122, 19 June 1771).

Normally, such a passionate and openly avowed love between two young people as that between Goethe and Friederike would lead to engagement and marriage. Marriage is the central issue in Goldsmith's novel, for what precipitates the series of disasters that land the amiable and unworldly Dr. Primrose in prison is his grasping wife's scheme to find advantageous matches for her two beautiful daughters. But unlike the sinister young Squire Thornhill, who ruins the reputation of the older daughter—a disaster in which both parents are complicit because they have been warned of Thornhill's reputation as a seducer—the young Goethe is no heartless rake and villainous deceiver, just a thoughtless young man who is carried away by his libido: "[H]ow can a beguiling emotion give us advance knowledge of where it may lead us?" (book 11, 369). In some respects the Sesenheim history is also a coming-of-age story, for the young Goethe, in his guilt over abandoning Friederike, learns a lesson about male responsibility in the courtship ethic of his culture. "A girl who has encouraged a man . . . can renounce him without nearly as much embarrassment as a youth who has gone equally far in his declarations to a young woman. He always cuts a dismal figure, for as someone developing into manhood he is certainly expected to have a fairly clear notion of what he is doing, and pronounced irresponsibility is most unbecoming to him" (369).

However, the real-life consequences of Goethe's heedless romance are actually much more serious than those of the nefarious fictional schemer, for Squire Thornhill's machinations, detected and undone by the providential benevolence of his rich uncle (disguised throughout the novel as the poor Burchell), result only in the *deus ex machina* contrivance of a happy ending. Goethe suggests the destructive impact of his romantic irresponsibility with a dramatic trope: "Such a thoughtlessly nurtured youthful affection can be compared to a bombshell hurled at night, which ascends in a gently gleaming line, mingles with the stars, nay, seems to linger with them for a while, but then, descending, describes the same arc, only in reverse, and finally brings ruin on the place where it ends it course" (369). These of course are the summarizing and self-inculpating moral reflections in book 11 of Goethe's distanced and ironic perspective on his final parting from Friederike. The presentation of his developing romance with her that precedes this somber judgment is a vivid and richly textured account that blends elements of nature and art in its romantic portrait of "young people" whose "first loves can promise no permanent result" (344). If in Goethe's critique Rousseau willfully confuses art and nature, Goethe's Sesenheim portrait offers a canny, playful, and ironic concatenation of the two.

From the start, Goethe presents his youthful perception of Sesenheim as influenced by aesthetic categories of representation. The young student who had cultivated in himself the habit of seeing "nature" through the eyes of different painters (book 8, 241) also sees the parsonage in such painterly terms the first time he lays eyes on it: "[I]t had precisely the quality called picturesqueness and all the magical appeal that I found in Dutch art" (book 10, 319). In the same Strasbourg period, when he turned against the hegemonic influence of French literature and took an active interest in the literary manifestations of folk culture, he discovered in the Alsatian border territory between France and Germany a pure and picturesque emanation of that culture. In their rural dress, the simplicity and artlessness of their manners, and their romantically dilapidated parsonage, the Brions represent a bourgeois idyll of German pastoral life. The poetry of Goethe's picturesque portrait is focused on Friederike, who is fully at home in "the little world in which she moved" (322). With her blond pigtails, blue eyes, turned up nose, and straw hat, her slim figure and her lightness of step, she seems almost an emanation of the landscape that frames her "charm and loveliness" (320). Yet there is also a touch of the liminal about her; she is a threshold between the inside of the family dwelling and the surrounding landscape, situated "on the borderline between country and city girl" (320).[13] In her own world she is completely natural, a pure embodiment of Rousseau's ideal of transparency. Of his first moonlight stroll with her, Goethe writes, "it seemed to me as though I were looking into her heart, which I could only deem very pure because she was revealing it to me with such naive volubility" (322).

For Goethe, however, Friederike, like her family, can be seen as natural and happy only in the limited perfection of her rural setting. The Brions' little world cannot be successfully translated into a larger or more cosmopolitan context, as is evident in their trip to Strasbourg to visit some relatives—a trip that scholars suspect is a fiction Goethe created to suggest both their discomfort when out of their element and his own inability to imagine taking Friederike as his wife. Like insects in amber, the Sesenheim family is trapped in the idyllic frame of Goethe's perception of them: "[A]ccustomed to see [them] only amidst rural scenery . . . now I saw them for the first time in spacious, but nevertheless confining, town rooms, in relation to wallpaper, mirrors, tall-case clocks, and porcelain figurines" (348).[14] Actually, unlike her older sister, Friederike acquits herself rather well in this "fashionable society," although "she did not fit in well either" in her "German" dress (349–50). Goethe's malaise is dispelled only by the Brions' departure: "When I finally saw them drive away, it was as though a stone fell from my heart" (350).

Ironically, the very flexibility or variability of role that Goethe denies the Brions he spectacularly and presumptuously claims for himself in his unsettling entry into their provincial world. Here he capitalizes on the element of costuming and disguise of which he had become aware earlier, in the recognition of Gretchen in her fashionable costume as the milliner's assistant. In fact, his introduction to Sesenheim is an extended prank or "mystification" concocted in conjunction with his fellow student, Friedrich Leopold Weyland, the relative of the Brions who brings him to their parsonage. Book 10 makes much of this masquerade and of the multiple impersonations the young Goethe claims he engaged in. Indeed, before proceeding to the humorous narrative of the charade with which he disconcerts and entertains the Sesenheim family, he writes a mannered paragraph to justify his eccentric behavior. Goethe puts an apologetic frame around the coming episodes by adverting to the appealing adventures of incognito princes and deities: "It is quite in keeping with their natures, when Jupiter takes pleasure in his incognito with Philemon and Baucis, or Henry IV with his peasants . . . and this is attractive to us. But when an insignificant, unrenowned young person takes it into his head to get some amusement out of being incognito, some people might interpret this as unpardonable arrogance" (318). Goethe, characteristically distancing himself from his youthful indiscretions by writing in the third person, pleads "the sake of our own entertainment" as "an excuse for the young man's conceitedness."

Purely as a prank, Goethe enters the Sesenheim household disguised as a poor theology student. Immediately charmed by the family and enchanted with Friederike, he begins to "play [his] role in moderation, half ashamed to deceive such good people" (320). When he awakens early the next morning after a moonlight stroll with Friederike that has already established an intimacy between them, he is mortified by the reflection in "a little mirror" of the shabby and "abominable wardrobe [he] had so mischievously selected for [him]self" (323). He rides off in a bad humor, asking his friend Weyland to make an excuse for his precipitous departure. In the nearby village he sees the son of a prosperous innkeeper in a smart outfit and talks him into exchanging clothes with him "for something comical [he] was planning to do in Sesenheim" (324). The element of disguised identity is present in the intertextual mirror of *The Vicar of Wakefield*'s Burchell, but Goethe's clothing swap is more in the spirit of Shakespearean romantic comedy, with which he was of course familiar. Indeed, it was at Strasbourg that Shakespeare became Goethe's new literary deity, after he turned "on the French border" against French literature and culture (book II, 364).[15]

As in Shakespeare's romantic comedies, at Sesenheim too disguise and mistaken identity lead to comic confusion that in the end serves the purposes of romantic love. Upon his return to the parsonage, the disguised Goethe succeeds in passing for George. The mother however, sees through his disguise when she invites him in for some refreshments and looks into his face: "'I was looking for George,' she said after a pause, 'and whom do I find! Is it you, young sir? How many disguises do you really have?'—'In earnest, only one,' I replied. 'For a joke, as many as you please'" (326). She willingly enters into the spirit of his masquerade and sends him out of the way while she prepares things to keep the joke going. Outside he finds a secluded area in a wood with the inscription "Friederike's Rest" on a tree trunk, and the older man looking back adds the ironic confessional reflection, "it did not occur to me that I might have come to disturb her rest" (326). When Friederike arrives and in a shock of recognition and fright discovers that the apparent George is really the student visitor of the day before, the successful prank leads to further intimacy between them once she has recovered from her fright. Friederike has already heard from her relative Weyland the story of Goethe's first disguise, and Goethe now explains his second impersonation, "to be sure with all modesty, but still so passionately that it could have passed for a declaration of love in narrative form. I celebrated the pleasure of finding her again by kissing her hand, which she then left lying in mine" (327).

The masquerade is kept going when Friederike joins in to fool her older sister, who arrives with Weyland and is dumbfounded to discover Friederike holding hands with the putative George. Several others are successfully duped as well, including the father and then the brother at the midday meal, which is capped by the entrance of the real George, who "made the whole scene still livelier" (329). In keeping with the role-playing mode of his successful mystification, Goethe has made this whole sequence of multiple impersonation a theatrical interlude the upshot of which is the romantic bonding of the incipient couple.

Goethe concludes book 10 (and part 2) by foregrounding the issue of storytelling and fictional narrative that is implicitly a key concern throughout the Sesenheim sequence as a poeticized history of young love. The creative impersonation that has endeared him to the Brion family ends with Goethe as storyteller: "I recited a fairy tale which I later wrote down under the title, 'The New Melusina.' It corresponds to 'The New Paris' much as the young man does to the boy, and I would insert it here if I were not afraid that its strange play of fancy would detract from the simple rustic reality now agreeably surrounding us" (330). The invocation of a *simple rustic reality* is supremely ironic, since that is in fact the illusion created by a highly literarized and intertextual narrative. The stated parallel with the earlier fairy tale of sexual awakening implies that the oral tale (not incorporated into the text) is also a confessional fable, one whose burden of meaning appears to be, as Müller suggests (305), the incompatibility of the two young lovers. The gist of the 'The New Melusina,' written down much later and inserted into *Wilhelm Meister's Journeyman Years,* is the problematic and ultimately impossible love of an irresponsible young man for a beautiful and wealthy young woman who turns out to be the daughter of a fairy-king. Goethe's characterization of his success "in garnering the reward desired by the inventor and narrator of such productions" (330) adds weight to his foregrounding of narrativity, because his comments on his telling of the fairy tale can also be seen as an analogue to his deft performance as the narrator of the Sesenheim story. Finally, Goethe's logocentric privileging of speech over writing, in his comment on the skeptical reaction of future readers to the printed version of his fairy tale, must also be taken as an ironic conceit: "Someone at a future time may read this fairy tale in print and doubt whether it could have produced such an effect; but let him then consider that a human being is really only required to be effective in the present. Writing is a misuse of language, and solitary silent reading is a sad surrogate for discourse" (330). Goethe, the most prolific of writers, is dictating his autobiography as a written text for readers, not listeners. Yet he seeks to create the illusion of voice, of the primacy and immediacy of living speech, just as his intricately layered narrative of young love seeks to create the illusion of rustic simplicity and unmediated experience.[16]

In addition to his narrative performance of a fairy tale of his own making, Goethe mentions that he also read to the Brions two other works, so that literature not only furnishes telling parallels for his Sesenheim sequence but enters directly into his relations with the family. The first of these is in fact Goldsmith's novel, which he eventually reads aloud at the request of his friend Weyland: "I was able to compose myself and read as cheerfully and unselfconsciously as I possibly could. The faces of my listeners also brightened at once, and they did not seem to be at all displeased at being compelled to make comparisons again. If they had found comic counterparts for Raymond and Melusina, here they saw themselves in a mirror that was by no means disfiguring. They did not expressly admit, but did not deny either, that they were in the company of persons of kindred spirit and feeling" (book 11, 344). In this sentimentalizing account, the Brions behold a flattering reflection of themselves in the English vicar's family; if they had taken in the material read to them in a different spirit, they might have found as well some unflattering applications to themselves. Like Dr. Primrose and his wife, who help to bring about their elder daughter's downfall by allowing the Lovelace-like young squire access to her, the Brion parents are not entirely innocent in the coming heartbreak of their daughter. Of the budding love between himself and Friederike, Goethe writes, "it was allowed to happen and continue without any real question about what the result was to be" (345). Had the parents been more inclined to question Goethe's intentions, they might have looked into the textual mirror for a possible parallel to the charming stranger before them and the consequences of his obvious attachment to their attractive daughter.

Goethe observes that in Sesenheim he read aloud frequently at the request of the family, but the only other text he mentions is one he offered at the bidding of Friederike for the benefit of her Strasbourg relatives on the family's visit to the city: "[I]n one evening I read the whole of *Hamlet* without interruption, penetrating into the sense of the play with all the force at my command and expressing myself with the liveliness and passion peculiar to youth. I received great applause" (349).[17] Friederike does "not deny herself the small pride of having shone [*sic*] to advantage in me and through me," and Goethe's command performance of his favorite Shakespeare play serves to further cement their relationship. While Goethe's mention of his reading does not invite us to draw any textual parallels between the play and his romantic relationship, I would suggest that at least one exists in the tragedy of Ophelia and the presumptuous Hamlet's role in her downfall, which can stand as a remote textual reflection or symbol of Goethe's sense of guilt about Friederike.

At the conclusion of Rousseau's "lyrical scene" of romantic narcissism, the difference between the sculptor and his statue merges into a sensuous identity, as the beautiful Galatea, brought to life by Venus, touches herself, exclaiming, "me," and then touches Pygmalion: "[S]he places one hand on him; he trembles, takes this hand, places it on his heart, and covers it with ardent kisses." The play ends with a reciprocal mirroring, as Galatea sighs, "ah, still me," and her creator replies, "it is you, you alone: I have given you all my being; and I shall live only in and through you" (*Oeuvres* 2:1230–31). Goethe's highly textualized portrait of romantic love rejects such a complete merging of identities, but it does create an aesthetic mirror in which the pair's love is reflected in idealized form. Unlike that of her sophisticated and widely read lover, Friederike's cultural development is limited. Before Goethe's reading aloud of *The Vicar of Wakefield*, an acquaintance asks Friederike about several novels that she has not read: "I had *Wakefield* on the tip of my tongue, but did not dare to offer her the book, since the similarity of conditions was too striking and significant.—'I love to read novels,' she said. 'One finds such nice people in them, whom one would like to resemble'"(340). Friederike and her student-lover come from different social and intellectual worlds, and their identities can never become one, but, like Werther and Lotte, they both look to literature for ideal models of human conduct.

But Goethe, unlike the obsessive young reader of *The Confessions,* who fuels his autoerotic fantasies with novels, does not confuse or conflate literature with life. In connection with the account of his reading aloud of Goldsmith's novel, Goethe observes that "as they progress in their cultural development, all people of good quality sense that they have a double role to play in the world, a real and an ideal one." This double awareness, which is "the basis of every noble impulse," is stimulated by literature. "Surely the youthful propensity for comparing oneself with characters in novels must be numbered among the most pardonable attempts to progress to something higher" (344–45). Unlike Rousseau, who with the alter ego of the totalitarian tutor of *Emile* strictly circumscribes the youth's reading, Goethe will not keep the poets—in this case, the novelists—out of his republic, for they foster an awareness of the ideal by providing productive models of human aspiration. Or at least they can lift us temporarily out of the sphere of humdrum life: "How often the litany is repeated about the injuriousness of novels! And is it really a calamity when a well-behaved young girl or a proper young man identifies with personages who have a better or a worse lot in life? Is everyday life of such great value, or do daily needs so utterly consume a person, that he must reject all the claims of beauty?" (345).

This defense of popular fiction is in a sense also a backhanded defense of Goethe's intertextual novelization of his own experience. However, Goethe's highly literarized Sesenheim idyll does not elide the real-life issue of moral responsibility and guilt prefigured through the motif of the cursed kiss. Since the Lucinde episode, Goethe informs us, he "had been superstitious enough to guard against kissing any girl, for fear of injuring her in some mysterious spiritual way" (338). The male fear of injuring the female is linked thematically to the battle of the sexes in "The New Paris," in which Alerte complains of the unspecified but suggestive "irreparable loss" (book 2, 56) the boy's actions had caused her when he destroyed her miniature centaurs. Goethe in fact claims that this fear made him go to great pains to avoid kissing Friederike in the little social games played among the young people in the Sesenheim circle, which to "a great extent [were] based on forfeits" to be redeemed by a kiss (338). Only after ingenious efforts on his part to "introduce and conduct games without forfeits" (339) and to resist the efforts of others to force him into kissing her does he give in to the temptation. On a "day of rash merriment that knew no bounds" he overcomes his scruples: "She seemed lovelier to me than ever; all my hypochondriacal, superstitious crochets vanished, and when the opportunity arose to give my tenderly beloved a hearty kiss, I did not pass it up, and even less did I deny myself the repetition of this joy" (342). During a quiet interlude on this overheated day of wine and merriment, Goethe and Friederike in the privacy of a "quiet clearing" acknowledge "that [they] loved each other deeply" (342).

But almost immediately his guilty conscience asserts itself in the form of a nightmarish episode of negative or self-torturing imagination. After several hours of feverish sleep, he suffers an anxiety attack in the form of the demon of remorse and "care" (*Sorge*) that also bedevils Faust's career:

> [M]y imagination painted me the most vivid pictures: I saw Lucinde as she angrily retreated from me after her vehement kiss, as she spoke that curse with glowing cheeks and sparkling eyes. . . . I saw Friederike standing opposite her, petrified at the sight, pale and feeling the effects of a curse she knew nothing of. I found myself in the middle, able neither to deny the spiritual effects of that adventure nor to avoid that kiss with its prophecy of misfortune. Friederike's delicate health seemed to hasten the threatened disaster, and now her love for me appeared quite fatal. (343)

These night fears of a youth "excited by love and passion, wine and dance" who finds himself "in seemingly boundless despair" are dispelled soon enough by the coming of day. Yet the vivid rendering of this nightmare years later is powerful and haunting and symbolically sets the stage for the dismal end of the relationship. The cursed kiss motif amplified to horrendous proportions by the night vision soon enough finds its real-life correlation in the serious illness that Friederike suffers as a consequence of his departure, an illness that presents a symmetrical reversal of the abrupt end to his earlier relationship with Gretchen, when the young Goethe was the one who fell ill at the shock of a forced separation. The proverbial shoe is now on the other foot, and it almost seems that Friederike has to pay for the suffering inflicted by the loss of Gretchen.

Goethe may have repressed the painful memory of the difficult final encounter with Friederike, but the account of his leave-taking is poignant enough in its stark simplicity: "When, from horseback, I gave her my hand for the last time, there were tears standing in her eyes, and I felt very bad" (370). The Sesenheim idyll has turned tragic, but Goethe refuses to give his narrative a tragic ending, like that of Gretchen's story in *Faust*, part 1. Instead of such a dismal closure, Goethe offers a hopeful opening into a distant future. As he is leaving Sesenheim, he has a psychic experience in the form of a premonition of his surprise visit nearly a decade later, now a famous author and Weimar minister, to Sesenheim:

> As I rode along . . . I was seized by the strangest premonition, namely, I saw myself, not with the eyes of the body, but those of the spirit, coming toward myself on horseback on the same path, and, to be sure, in clothing I had never worn: it was bluish gray with some gold trimming. As soon as I shook myself awake from this dream, the figure vanished. Yet it is curious that eight years later I found myself on the same path, coming to visit Friederike once more and dressed in the clothes I had dreamed about, which I was wearing not by choice but by coincidence. However the case may be with such things generally, at these moments of farewell the vision gave me some comfort. (370)

Comfort, because it alleviates the trauma of departure from the symbolically linked charms of Alsace and Friederike. With this promising glimpse of the future, in which Goethe encounters himself as his own double heading back to Sesenheim as he is leaving it, he can shake off the tragic pressure of the present and recover his "composure to a fair degree on a peaceful and diverting journey" (371) from Alsace back to Frankfurt. From his first appearance at Sesenheim in the guise of a poor theology student in threadbare clothes, to his ghostly premonition of his final visit to the Brions in his court gentleman's costume, Goethe's Sesenheim narrative is an ingenious theatrical charade with youthful innocence and sincerity at its confessional core.

After the heartrending leave-taking from Friederike, the two pages describing his visit to the Hall of Ancient Sculpture in Mannheim may strike the reader as heartless and artificial. It is true that he seems to have recovered his balance very quickly after the nightmare of a guilty separation, but I suggest that he is no mere aesthete diverting himself with the cold pastoral of a visit to the hall of antiquities. Those pages devoted to the "forest of statues" (371) that he beholds at Mannheim (reproductions of famous late classical works, including the Laokoon group), represent yet another means of aesthetically shaping or poeticizing his Sesenheim experience, this time not through literature but through the plastic arts. The significance of these pages lies not only in their obvious function as a prelude to the fully elaborated classical experience of the Italian journey, for Goethe's response to these statues is analogous to his confused and unresolved feelings about Friederike and Sesenheim. In his delighted visual feasting on the statues, he is unable to move from "enjoyable contemplation to accurate comprehension" (371). Like his love for Friederike, his enjoyment of these works of art is a powerful but confused experience that will become clarified and productive only at a later and more mature point in his life. Indeed, Goethe's summarizing statement about the long-range impact of these statues can be read at one level as a displaced version of his feelings about the traumatic parting from Friederike: "But hardly had the door of this splendid hall closed behind me when I felt the urge to return to my own self again, indeed I tried to banish those figures as being burdensome to my imagination; and only by a very roundabout way was I to be led back into their sphere" (372).

The roundabout and belated way is, in a sense, the confessional acknowledgment of guilt in his autobiography. But the burden of guilt was also immediate, for Goethe could not simply banish the figure of Friederike from his imagination. She appears in a variety of guises in his post-Sesenheim writings, the most famous being Gretchen in *Faust*. After his return to Frankfurt there is a "period of gloomy remorse" for "having deeply wounded the loveliest heart" (385). "But a person wants to live," explains Goethe, and so he gains the epithet of "the Wanderer" because he seeks relief by roaming the region around Frankfurt: "[T]he only way I could soothe my spirit was to be out under an open sky, in valleys, on heights, in fields and woods" (385). In addition to the Romantic release of the landscape, Goethe also turns to the proven therapy of creative writing for relief from his "grief over Friederike." "I continued my old poetic confessions, hoping to receive inner absolution in return for this self-tormenting penance" (386). The provisional and veiled confession of the fictional works he produced then is finalized by the Sesenheim narrative in *Poetry and Truth*. Like the Catholic Rousseau who claims he wrote *The Confessions* in part to purge himself of the guilt of his slander of the innocent servant girl Marion, Goethe seeks final "absolution" in his autobiography for his guilt at having wounded an innocent heart half a century earlier.[18] However, the guilt and confession of both men are self-centered and largely self-serving to the extent that neither one shows any real concern for the woman he hurt in terms of her situation at the time of writing his autobiography. Just as Rousseau appears never to have bothered to find out what actually happened to Marion, so Goethe (after his final visit to Friederike eight years later), seems to have had little or no interest in the remainder of Friederike's life.[19]

Some of Goethe's Strasbourg acquaintances at the time passed harsh judgment on Goethe's abandonment of Friederike. The poet Lenz, in his own courting of her the year after Goethe's departure, "concluded that Goethe had sacrificed her to his genius," and Weyland, the friend who had brought Goethe to Sesenheim, saw Goethe's treatment of Friederike as a betrayal "and refused to have anything more to do with Goethe afterwards" (Boyle 108, 102). Contemporary biographers continue to pass similar judgments. Friedenthal explicitly endorses Lenz's accusation and sees her as Goethe's victim, a suffering human being and not simply a fictional construct: the curse of Lucinde was fulfilled much more terribly than Goethe's novelistic treatment allows us to suspect (114–15). The more generous Boyle reluctantly concludes that "the episode, it must be said, reflects little credit on Goethe" (102). In the light of Goethe's self-presentation in *Poetry and Truth*, these moralizing judgments lack the force of new revelation, since they cannot be any more severe than the sentence Goethe passes on himself, and the open avowal of the pangs of conscience and the agony of remorse that are the confessional upshot of the aesthetically exponentiated Sesenheim narrative of young love.

Guilt, of course, was a passing mood for the young Goethe, who, like his Faust, was able quickly enough to move on to new life and experiences. His conscience went hand in hand with his presumptuousness, as is evident in his letter of September 1779 about his side trip to Sesenheim on his journey to Switzerland. To drop in out of the blue on the young woman who almost died from the shock of his abandoning her eight years earlier (as he acknowledges in the letter), takes a special kind of chutzpa. Like his earlier introduction into the family, this final surprise visit is also theatrical; and if Goethe was looking for reassurance that his former victim and her family were all right and had forgiven him, he more than found it. By Goethe's account, the self-control and generosity of the woman who was thus surprised by a ghost from her past is more than apparent: "[S]he gently passed over telling me what still remained of her illness of that time, and behaved so sweetly and with such heartfelt friendship from the first moment when I unexpectedly came face to face with her and our noses touched that I felt very comfortable." They again converse under a full moon, but she does not seek to reawaken his old passion. Her family's reception is equally open and generous. We cannot know what impact the visit actually had on Friederike or her family, but it clearly served his emotional need for a reconciliation with his unfinished past. "I stayed the night and took my leave the next morning at sunrise, sent off by friendly faces, so that I now can think again with satisfaction of that little corner of the world, and can live in inner peace with the spirits of these reconciled ones" (*Briefe* 1:272–73). Reassured that all is well in their little corner, the Weimar minister can get on with his life in the big world.

In the wake of the publication of Goethe's autobiography, Sesenheim became a nineteenth-century literary shrine, and Goethe's love for Friederike entered German folklore. In 1822 a university professor visited the solitary parsonage (where neither Friederike nor her family were residing any longer), and wrote a report revealingly entitled "Pilgrimage to Sesenheim" that he sent to Goethe and later published in 1840. By way of a very distanced reply, Goethe wrote the famous and cryptic "Repeated Reflections" (1823), in which he used an elaborate analogy from optics to suggest the complex sequence of mirroring consisting of the actual love experience of his youth, its afterlife in his imagination and its transformation into a text, its literary impact and reception, which motivated readers to visit Sesenheim, and, finally, the reassembly in the pilgrim-visitor's mind of all these pieces of past and reported experience into a renewed image of the amiable Friederike. "Now if one considers that repeated reflections of morals and manners [wiederholte sittliche Spiegelungen] not only keep the past alive, but even intensify it to a higher life, then one will think of those entoptic phenomena, which in a similar fashion do not at all fade from mirror to mirror, but indeed really catch fire" (HA 12:323). The mature Goethe's generalizing view of his own experience, in which the passionate Friederike relationship becomes merely symbolic of a larger pattern, can also stand as a trope for the complex process of autobiography, which begins with one individual's personal experience, proceeds to its transformation and inevitable alteration into a text—usually decades later, and by way of many other (inter)texts—and ends at best with a reflective and at times miraculously intensified reception in the minds of its attentive readers.

UN(DER)REPRESENTED LOVE: LOTTE AND LILI

Less than a year after his guilty parting from Friederike, Goethe was in love again. At Wetzlar, the seat of the imperial supreme court where he had gone ostensibly to broaden his knowledge of the law but where he spent most of his time on literary and other pursuits, he met the eighteen-year-old Charlotte Sophie Henriette Buff. He initially got to know her pretty much in the way Werther first met Lotte, as they rode together with others in a carriage on the way to a country ball that lasted into the early hours of the morning. He was charmed by this vivacious young woman who after her mother's death had assumed the responsibility of running the household for her father and raising her younger siblings; and he discovered only after his feelings were already engaged that she was the fiancée of a serious and accomplished young man several years his senior who had a promising career ahead of him as a civil servant. The rest, of course, is literary history, for the love triangle of Johann Georg Kestner, Goethe, and "Lotten" (Charlotte Buff) that gave rise to the explosive confessional fiction of *The Sufferings of Young Werther* was immortalized in the first German best-seller to make its author a European celebrity. A generation wept over it, including even Mary Shelley's monster; Napoleon took it with him on his campaigns and called its author to an audience to discuss it with him when his conquering army brought the emperor to the vicinity of Weimar.

For better or worse, *Werther* was the book by which Goethe was largely known to the public for the remainder of his long life. It was his calling card as well as the albatross around his neck. As he makes clear in book 13 in his account of the "immense" and explosive impact of his "little book," which "appeared just at the right time" (433), the celebrity it brought him was burdensome and distracting from the start and made him painfully aware of the "vast gulf [that] separates authors and their public" (436). *Werther* is the most intense and acute version of Goethe's lifelong practice of confessional writing as therapy, of the processing of life into art, and of his "having transformed reality into poetry" (432). He claims he produced the epistolary sensation in several weeks "rather unconsciously, like a somnambulist," and "without having written down in advance any scheme for the whole work" (431). When he wrote about this period of his life in *Poetry and Truth,* however, his love of Lotte had been in the public domain for generations; to try and consciously re-create in old age the love story that had already jelled in the fictionalized confession of the famous "little book" of his youth would have been tedious if not impossible. His autobiography is meant "to fill the gaps in an author's life," not to tell twice-told tales: "[W]hat is already done . . . cannot, and should not, be repeated" (400).

Thus Goethe wisely chose not to make his relationship with Lotte the subject of extended autobiographical treatment as he did with Gretchen and with Friederike; instead he offers a highly stylized summary. He also chooses a very different key, for the calm, distanced, and idealizing account of the romantic threesome of "the bridegroom," his fiancée, and "the new arrival" forms a sharp contrast with the extended passionate epistolary outbursts of the tearful young Werther:

> The new arrival, quite free of any ties, felt unconcerned in the presence of a girl who, since she was already spoken for, would not interpret his most agreeable services as wooing, and thus could take the more delight in them. . . . Idle and dreamy because the present did not satisfy him, he found what was lacking in this female friend. . . . She was glad to have him as a companion, and soon he could not do without being near her . . . and so they were soon inseparable companions on the fields and meadows, in the vegetable and flower gardens. . . . The bridegroom [my modification for "fiancé"], for his part, was also present, if his duties permitted. All three had grown accustomed to each other without meaning to, and did not know how it had come about that they were indispensable to each

other. So, right through the splendid summer, they lived a genuine German idyll, for which the fertile land provided the prose, and pure affection the poetry. (book 12, 401)

The young Goethe's rather unstable emotional state at the time, as witnessed by his letters and chronicled by his biographers, is actually somewhere between the extremes of Werther's suicidal passion and the older writer's idyllic glossing of a harmonious threesome. Like the portrait of his love for Friederike painted in epic breadth, this romantic miniature is also replete with explicit literary resonances—Goldsmith's (rural-descriptive) poem *The Deserted Village* and Rousseau's *New Héloïse,* including a well-placed poetic quotation from the novel whose love triangle (Julie–Saint-Preux–Wolmar) is relevant to the young German poet's situation. "And so one ordinary day followed another, and all seemed to be festival days. . . . I will be understood by anyone who remembers what was predicted for the happy-unhappy lover of the new Héloïse: 'And, sitting at the feet of his beloved, he will card hemp, and he will wish to continue carding hemp, today, tomorrow, and the next day, indeed for the whole of his life'" (401–2). That Rousseau's famous epistolary novel influenced *Werther* must be obvious to any reader of both works, and Goethe's strategically placed quotation is presumably also an elegant way of acknowledging as much. In addition to Goethe's telling reference, we also have Kestner's statement at the time that the young Goethe "has a high opinion of Rousseau but is not a blind worshipper of him."[20] This characterization strikes just the right balance, because if Goethe's *Werther* is indebted to Rousseau's *New Héloïse,* his novel is clearly not an imitation of it but very much the tragically heightened version of his own love experience at Wetzlar.

Because she was engaged to someone else, Goethe's dalliance with Charlotte Buff never threatened him with the specter of marriage. After the troubled parting from Friederike, his attraction to a betrothed woman added up to a safe love. Goethe-cum-Werther could, as it were, enjoy the romantic music while Lotte's fiancé, Kestner-cum-Albert, had to pay the marital piper. If only young Werther could have known what the wise old autobiographer knew, he would have been the happiest of men in his condition of unfulfilled desire, like Keats's young lovers in the perpetual freeze-frame of their erotic pursuit/flight on the Grecian Urn: "If, as is said, we find our greatest happiness in longing [Sehnsucht], and if true longing is directed solely to the unattainable, then everything coincided to make this young man . . . the happiest of mortals" (403). However, Goethe's intention in his post-university years in Frankfurt to keep himself free of any serious romantic entanglements (book 17, 545) evaporated in the face of the charms of the worldly and self-assured banker's daughter, sixteen-year-old "Lili" Schönemann. His passionate and tortured relationship with her brought him to the brink of a marital commitment that he could avoid only through physical flight—the first time by his impromptu journey to Switzerland, and the second time by his acceptance of the invitation to Weimar that put an end to the young poet's halfhearted and ambivalent attempts at an *embourgeoisement* of which his marriage would have been the capstone. Instead of committing to a professional career and married life in Frankfurt, he opted for a totally different path.

Two years before his death, Goethe told Eckermann that Lili was the first and also the last woman whom he "deeply and truly loved," and that he "had never been so close to his proper happiness as at the time of his love for Lili" (2:674, 5 March 1830). Given his earlier and later *crises de coeur,* this sounds odd and hyperbolic, but it is in keeping with the consensus of the critics and biographers that, in the words of Boyle, "Lili presented him for the first time with the fully real possibility of marriage and for that reason the crisis in which he rejected her was the most serious, and most decisive, of his life" (199).[21] One of the reasons why Goethe deferred so long in writing the fourth and final part of *Poetry and Truth* was his reluctance to tackle the Lili relationship, charged for him with so many painful and unresolved feelings. Accounting for that relationship and its ultimate failure is a challenge he meets in the end with only partial success; indeed, the reader who knows nothing about Goethe and Lili other than his version is hard put—without a preternatural talent for reading between the lines—to comprehend what exactly went wrong and why Goethe bolted from the engagement almost immediately after entering into it.

The weakness in Goethe's account is his failure to present the relationship in an adequately embodied dramatic narrative, something he did so effectively in the Gretchen and Friederike sequences. The failure of representation is not complete, for there are several short dramatic scenes, especially the framing episodes of his first encounter with her and his last (covert) glimpse of her. But too often the material in between, distributed over several books, relies more on *telling* than *showing*. Goethe's impatience in part 4 is evident in his need to summarize rather than present his relationship with Lili, and in his willingness to fall back on sample poems of his youth (inserted into his autobiography) to convey his feelings at the time. For instance, at the beginning of book 17, he eschews "a recounting of the pleasure excursions that ended in displeasure," and after a perfunctory inventory of causes of this displeasure, he adds rather lamely, "all these troubles which if related in greater detail in some novel would certainly find sympathetic readers . . . must be dispensed with here. However, so as to give some degree of immediacy and youthful empathy to this objective portrayal, let a couple of poems be inserted which, although well known, may be especially effective at this point" (535–36). The novelistic strategy of poeticizing his experience, so pronounced in the first three parts of *Poetry and Truth,* is largely abandoned in the final part, where the attempt at a summarizing "objective portrayal" seems thin by comparison. Perhaps Goethe had held off too long writing about Lili and, unlike his love for Friederike, this love of his youth was too remote in time to be brought vividly to life by way of a repeated reflection. His failure effectively to *represent* the Lili relationship can be seen as part of the larger problem of his very late style, a disproportion between the narrative and the reflective elements, with the result that the former are overborne by the latter in a near hypertrophy of sententious wisdom and generalizing aperçus—some of which admittedly have a gnomic brilliance and resonate powerfully in the attentive mind.[22]

What Goethe's struggle to account for the aborted engagement to Lili does reveal with almost paradigmatic clarity is the difference between love and marriage in the patrician milieu of Frankfurt in which their relationship is set. It is evident from their first meeting that the attraction between Goethe and Lili is immediate and mutual, but even if we discount Goethe's near phobia about marriage, the social and familial differences that stand in the way of a harmonious union between them are also considerable.[23] Indeed, as Robert Gould has observed, "from the way the older Goethe describes the situation it appears that the only thing they had in common was their love" (78). The immediate attraction between them as well as the societal constraints that complicate it are implicit in the elegant scene of their first meeting. The famous author of *Werther* and son of the Lutheran titular councilor is taken one evening by a friend "to attend a small concert . . . in the house of an eminent Calvinist merchant," where he observes the only daughter of the family play the piano "with notable skill and grace." Although her demeanor and performance are natural, he and she are in a world of polished manners; after a polite exchange of pleasantries, the salon setting prevents "any further approach this evening." But their eyes have already silently done the work that their tongues could not. "I could see that she was observing me closely and that I was really on display, but I did not mind at all, since I too had been given something charming to behold. We continued to gaze at each other, and I shall not deny that I began to feel an attraction of the gentlest kind" (529). Goethe repeats the visit, and soon enough they are "ruled by an irresistible desire" and cannot do without seeing each other (535).

As the only daughter of a wealthy and cosmopolitan banking family of partly French Huguenot extraction, Lili "had grown up amid every social advantage and worldly pleasure" (535). When Goethe met her, her father had been deceased for more than a decade, and the family, which included her four brothers, was presided over by her mother. The potential husband of such a privileged young woman was expected to be a man of substantial means and position, and the famous young writer who was just starting his legal career in Frankfurt did not seem to come up to the material mark. What Goethe did not know at the time is that despite the appearance of great wealth and a lavish style of entertaining, the fortunes of the family were already in a decline that resulted some years later in scandal and bankruptcy.[24] The mother and brothers wanted a more substantial match for Lili, and Goethe's father in turn found his prospective daughter-in-law, whom he sarcastically called the "grand lady" in private conversations with his wife, "by no means to his taste" (book 19, 592). Even after a third party gained the reluctant consent of both families to the engagement of Wolfgang and Lili, the "parents had not succeeded in starting and developing any mutual relationship: no family connection, different religious customs, different manners!" (book 17, 548).

A binding commitment to Lili meant establishing a successful legal career in Frankfurt, and Goethe informs us that at first he trod this professional path with some assiduity, spending less time seeing Lili in the suburban-rural setting of her uncle's estate and his social circle in Offenbach and more time in Frankfurt on legal briefs. His love of Lili and the resulting engagement pushed Goethe, as Gould puts it, toward "integration into the social and commercial fabric of society" and forced him "into activities in the practical business world in which he had no real interest" (78–79). The poetry that is romantic love pressures him into the grind of business that is bourgeois marriage. Although Goethe does not say so explicitly, his impromptu accompaniment of those free-spirited aristocrats, the Stolberg brothers, on their journey to Switzerland without saying farewell to Lili is an act of artistic rebellion. His "genius journey" with these young Storm-and-Stress poets is the beginning of the end of his attempt at "integrating into a way of life which was totally unsuitable for him" (Gould 79). Actions here speak louder than words (as Lili realizes in his absence, book 19, 589), and his flight from his engagement is a choice he made, even if he did not consciously reason it out or formulate it as such at the time. In the rationalizing hindsight of his autobiography, he seeks auxiliary support for his impulsive choice and subsequent final break with Lili in the advice of his sister, who "urgently recommended to [him], indeed ordered [him] to part from Lili" because this lively and elegant young woman would be cramped and unhappy in the Goethe household (book 18, 564).

However, on the very divide between Switzerland and Italy, the summit of the Gotthard, the bond with Lili reasserts itself and draws him back to Frankfurt when his traveling companion suggests that they descend from these alpine heights into Milan. Goethe resists "the spur of the moment" suggestion of a metaphoric "leap downward" (book 19, 577) into Italy that the more impulsive young Rousseau would have embraced with open arms. Goethe is symbolically held back by the ribbon with which Lili had hung the present of "a little golden heart" around his neck. Once he is back in Frankfurt, however, the impossibility of their union reasserts itself. In his absence, Lili has been persuaded that the break with him is necessary, although she too has her fantasy of escape: it is reported to him that out of love for him she was ready to go with him to America, "in those days . . . the Eldorado of those who found their present situation confining" (book 19, 590). Their painful impasse is resolved by Goethe's opting for "flight a second time" (book 20, 599), now under the auspices of the "daemonic" note that is the invitation to Weimar. If the first flight from Lili was also in effect a farewell to his abortive professional career in the free city of Frankfurt, this second and final escape lifts him entirely out

of the confines of the bourgeois sphere that a marriage to Lili would necessarily have entailed. The move to Weimar is a felicitous and dramatic
ascent into the gilded cage of court patronage, but (as I argued in the previous chapter in my analysis of Goethe's relationship with his father), not
one as inevitably fated as Goethe makes it out to be.

Goethe's final glimpse of Lili is an ironic inversion of his first meeting
with her. Because the coach that is to take him to Weimar has failed to
appear after he has already said his goodbyes, he has been living for days
in a ghostly netherworld, arrested on the threshold between his past and
his future, neither here nor there. In order to avoid the awkwardness of an
explanation and a second round of goodbyes, Goethe "had pretended to
be absent" on the morning of his supposed departure for Weimar, leaving
the house only at night. Here the incognito and disguise motif that we
saw in the Gretchen and Friederike narratives makes its final appearance,
but now in a somber setting in which Goethe appears as the ghost or
revenant in the world of his moribund past. "Enveloped in a great cloak I
skulked around the town, past the houses of my friends and acquaintances, and did not fail to step up to Lili's window as well" (book 20, 601).
The first time he saw her, she was playing the piano; now again she is at
the same instrument, singing the lyrics he had earlier composed for her
and that signal the leitmotif of their love: "Irresistibly, alas, you draw me!"
But the voyeuristic night stalker, the outsider looking into the setting of
his past life, is frustrated, because he can only *hear,* not *see* her:

> It could not but seem to me that she sang it with more expression
> than ever, and I could understand it distinctly, word for word. I had
> pressed my ear as close as the outward-curving grillwork would per-
> mit. After she had sung it to the end, I saw by the shadow falling on
> the shade that she had gotten up. She walked back and forth, but I
> sought in vain to catch the outline of her lovely person through the
> heavy texture. Only my firm resolve to go away, not to become bur-
> densome to her by my presence, really to renounce her, and the
> thought of the strange stir my reappearance would create, could
> persuade me to leave her dear proximity. (601)

And so at one level, the Lili episode ends theatrically, in the poignant
repetition of his own words in her voice. But at another level it is elegiac—it has the taste of death—as well as anticlimactic, for it fades out in

the unresolved blur of *the shadow falling on the shade*. Is it straining too far to discern here a parabolic figure for the autobiographer in the last years of his life as the ghost in the house of his past, in textual pursuit of shadows? As the young Wordsworth wrote in an uncharacteristically pessimistic moment in his autobiography, we see but darkly even when we look behind us (*Prelude* 3, 491–92).

Epilogue

We may see but darkly even when we look behind us, but autobiography does give a local habitation and a name to what Shakespeare's Prospero in a haunting phrase calls the dark backward and abysm of time (*Tempest* act I, scene 2). It offers, as Nabokov indicates with the earlier title of his autobiography, *Speak, Memory,* "conclusive evidence of [our] having existed" (11). In the famous Fifth Walk of his *Reveries,* Rousseau recalls how in his boat on Lake Bienne he achieved—despite the fact that everything on earth is in a constant state of flux and that even in our most pleasurable moments we hardly desire to make those moments last forever—the simple and naked "sentiment of existence" (*Oeuvres* 1:1047). That sentiment may in some sense be timeless, but he who experienced it and wrote about it is subject to time, for Rousseau's *Reveries* are stopped by his death. The unfinished Tenth Walk commemorates the adolescent Rousseau's meeting, precisely fifty years earlier on Palm Sunday 1728, with Mme de Warens, the woman who shaped the rest of his life. In this final revery, charged with emotions and regrets almost impossible to express, Rousseau returns to the memories of his stay at Charmettes with her whom he had written about in his *Confessions.* On the threshold of death, he takes up residence once more in the location of his earlier happiness, finding there conclusive evidence of having been fully alive and at home with himself.

Charmettes is an extended Wordsworthian "spot of time"—in Rousseau's final idyllic retrospect, "the space where during four or five years I enjoyed a century of life and a full and pure happiness" (*Oeuvres* 1:1099). The space of Charmettes that the older Rousseau enters in his unfinished Tenth Walk is the supplement of his imagination, his final castle in Spain. It is also in a sense the space of Romantic autobiography, a genre that I have argued merges the truth and the poetry of a life and that emerged with Rousseau in the later eighteenth century, to achieve a prominent presence by the beginning of the nineteenth. Romantic autobiography is posited on a post-Cartesian, post-Lockean sense of the subject and personal identity and is associated with the emergence of a more subjective and increasingly individualized awareness of human experience. Autobiography is a distinctive Romantic genre as well as a mode of self-knowledge. If not all Romantic writing is autobiography, much of it is certainly confessional and autobiographical. Like Goethe, in a sense all the other European Romantics wrote fragments of a great confession. In the light of this fact I must agree with Anne K. Mellor's call (in her discussion of Dorothy Wordsworth's journals), for an expansion of "the generic range of 'autobiography' to include *all* writing that inscribes subjectivity, to diaries, journals, memoirs and letters" (157).

The definition of the neologism "autobiography" that is by now some two centuries old is still a work in progress; critics and theorists have not been able to fix its meaning or assign its limits. During the decade that I have worked on this book, that meaning has become more expansive, partly in the direction indicated by Mellor. My working assumption has been the older consensus, formulated by Lejeune, that autobiography is a retrospective narrative of the self, and I have taken the leading and normative figures of Romantic autobiography to be Rousseau, Wordsworth, and Goethe. My identifying these three as the foundational figures is not meant to imply an exclusive or closed canon, because that canon includes other major works of Romantic autobiography by writers of a later generation—Stendhal's (pseudonymous) *Life of Henry Brulard*, De Quincey's *Confessions of an English Opium Eater*, Chateaubriand's monumental *Memoirs from Beyond the Tomb*, George Sand's *History of My Life*.

Rousseau, Goethe, and Wordsworth accomplished the definitive self-inscription of a highly developed individuality in a genre revitalized to capitalize on the full display of that individuality, particularly during the period of childhood and youth. If my introductory chapter provides an overview of Romantic autobiography by way of these three figures who exemplify in different ways the rise into literary prominence of Romantic subjectivity, the rest of the book has focused on Rousseau and Goethe as the paradigmatic instances in the nineteenth century—both antithetical yet complementary in their attitudes to subjectivity and imagination—of the new genre, and chiefly on their leading autobiographical works, *The Confessions* and *Poetry and Truth* respectively. Wordsworth's *Prelude*, unlike these foundational texts, had to wait until the next century to come into its own. But all three works demonstrate that the emergence of Romantic autobiography, beginning with the polemical opening of Rousseau's *Confessions*, is correlated with a new and heightened subjectivity that defines European culture in the period roughly between 1750 and 1850. That this subjectivity finds perhaps its most imaginative and richly self-reflexive expression in the exploration of childhood and youth is one of the signal achievements of Romanticism, whose literary offspring—witness those best-selling contemporary memoirs of childhood—we remain more than two centuries later.

NOTES

Unless otherwise indicated, citations of Rousseau's *Confessions* are of the Penguin edition (trans. Cohen), and citations of Goethe's *Poetry and Truth* are of the Princeton edition (trans. Heitner). Translations of quotations from Rousseau and Goethe, and from works of criticism in German and French not listed in English translation in the bibliography, are my own.

INTRODUCTION

1. For a discussion of the emergence of Romantic subjectivity, see also my two articles on the subject.
2. See Voisine for an overview of how "the autobiographical expression" ("Confession religieuse" 337) in the later eighteenth and the early nineteenth centuries operates through a variety of genres.
3. All citations of *The Prelude* are of the 1805 version.
4. Niggl (103–4) cites several instances of "Autobiographie" (and the related "Selbstbiographie") in Germany in the 1790s, before the appearance of the word in England at the beginning of the nineteenth century. The most recent and accurate history of the term is that of Folkenflik ("Introduction" 1–3), who traces the word in its adjectival form in English ("autobiographical") back to 1786.
5. In his opening chapter, Coe briefly reviews the significance of Rousseau, Wordsworth, and Goethe in the emergence of "the autobiography of childhood and adolescence" as "an independent genre" (xv, 1). Despite the promise of its title, Williams's *Rousseau and Romantic Autobiography* offers no generic discussion of or reflection on Romantic autobiography, or of Rousseau's relationship to it. See also Fleishman's analysis of "Romantic Figures" (93–108), which concludes that Romantic autobiographers rely largely on recycled "figures of autobiographical tradition," which they deploy, however, with a new "aesthetic freedom" (95–96). However, Fleishman's premise that "the Victorian age was the greatest age of English autobiography" (before the subsequent expansion of the lexicon of self-writing by twentieth-century writers, 108), leads him to downplay what he

dismissively characterizes as "the easy assumption that places the flowering of modern autobiography in the Romantic period" (106).

6. Hammer compares the two as writers of "Memories and Memoirs" (81–106); Weintraub concludes his richly informed "historical essay of the gradual emergence of individuality in autobiographic writings" (xi) with major sections on Rousseau and Goethe; Spengemann analyzes Rousseau's and Wordsworth's autobiographies as instances of "philosophical autobiography" (as opposed to "historical" or "poetic" autobiography, in what strikes this reader as an arbitrary and unconvincingly ahistorical classificatory scheme); Buckley offers brief overviews of *The Confessions* and *The Prelude* as major instances of the topic signaled in his subtitle; Egan considers both Rousseau and Wordsworth in terms of the archetypal narrative patterns she discerns in autobiography.

7. The Herder quotations are cited in Niggl, to whose developed discussion of Herder and autobiography (47–51, 53–55, 101–2) I am indebted.

8. For feminist cautions against essentializing gender differences, see Smith, 14–15, and Lionnet, whose key concept of "*métissage*" is meant to counter "all essentialist glorifications of unitary origins, be they racial, sexual, geographic, or cultural" (9).

I. ROUSSEAU AND AUTOBIOGRAPHY

1. For recent discussions of the confessional content and context of Rousseau's letters and their significance for his larger confessional project, see Kavanagh, 22–50, and Jackson, 142–73.

2. The illumination of Vincennes is not discussed in Kavanagh's and Jackson's chapters on the letters to Malesherbes, nor does it enter into de Man's influential (rhetorical and tropological) reading of Rousseau, not even in his chapter on the text that was the immediate fruit of that illumination, the *Second Discourse.* For de Man, "the self is not a privileged metaphor for Rousseau," an assertion that "obviously has consequences for the way in which his autobiographical texts . . . have to be read" (187). If de Man's unprivileging of the Rousseauean self seems to fly in the face of most readers' actual experience of reading Rousseau's autobiographies, it is not surprising to find in a radical skeptic for whom "what Rousseau calls 'truth' designates, neither the adequation of language to reality, nor the essence of things shining through the opacity of words, but rather the suspicion that human specificity may be grounded in linguistic deceit" (156). For a concise critical overview of the American deconstructive reading of the Romantic subject, see Pfau, according to whom "'rhetorical readings' tend to consider the subject a delusory 'figure' which, in the course of the text's own performance, cannot but disseminate into the differential structure of this very texture" (509).

3. Starobinski has noted the "social significance" of Rousseau's confessional project as "a manifesto from a member of the third estate." "A former lackey, he openly proclaims the superiority of the servant over the master" (185).

4. For an excellent overview of Rousseau's anthropological project in *The Confessions,* see Lejeune's analysis (*Pacte* 104–41) of the myth of the four ages of man in book 1 of *The Confessions.*

5. For instances of critics who see the connection between Rousseau the autobiographer and the philosopher, see Hartle's study of *The Confessions* as a complexly orchestrated "reply to St. Augustine"; Lejeune's analysis of the first book of *The Confessions* in terms of the relationship between Rousseau's autobiographical nar-

rative and the schemes of personal and cultural development in *Emile* and the *Discourse on Inequality* (*Pacte* 144–54); and Kavanagh's exposition of "how Rousseau's autobiographical, literary, and philosophical texts reveal a number of constants" (80).

6. In his study of the social and ethical thought of Rousseau, Ferrara traces the origin of the modern "theme of authenticity" back to Rousseau, and posits "the notion of authenticity" as a "coherent idea" underlying Rousseau's works (24–25).

2. DANGEROUS SUPPLEMENTS

1. Even before his flight from Geneva, Isaac Rousseau had already dipped into his two sons' inheritance when he sold the house left to them by their mother's estate (Cranston, *Early Life* 23).

2. The earlier second letter to Malesherbes also grounds Rousseau's estrangement from real life in "the heroic and romantic taste" ["ce goût héroïque et romanesque"] fostered by his early reading (*Oeuvres* 1:1134).

3. When Rousseau launched his proscription of masturbation in *Emile*, he had not yet read Tissot's treatise, although he later met and corresponded with him (Lejeune, "Supplément" 1020).

4. The premise that clearly informs Rousseau's attack on "the dangerous supplement" is that the legitimate purpose of the sex drive is intercourse for the purpose of procreation. Lejeune concludes that on "the moral plane" it is not certain whether "Rousseau ever thought that this vice was truly a crime," because "in the sexual morality of Rousseau the capital 'sin' is copulation—that is what Rousseau is most afraid of" ("Supplément" 1022). I am not sure about Lejeune's claim here, because it seems to me that "the dangerous supplement," which according to him Rousseau mentions so rarely and guardedly in *The Confessions,* is for Rousseau indeed a greater source of shame, guilt, and embarrassment than actual sexual intercourse could ever be. He may have feared copulation—as evident for instance in the famous episode with the young Venetian courtesan (Giulietta) in book 7—but he was much more troubled and guilt-ridden by his own onanism.

5. See Lejeune, "La punition des enfants" (*Pacte* 53–84), for a subtle analysis of Rousseau's narrative of the first spanking as a "sometimes explicit, sometimes veiled . . . demand for love" (53). Lejeune makes this episode the foundation of his larger interpretation of *The Confessions.*

6. The phrase ("Goton tic tac Rousseau") is part of three lines omitted without explanation in the Cohen translation (36). The Pléiade edition gives the standard meaning of people coming to blows for "*tic tac*" (*Oeuvres* 1:1247). In his commentary on the phrase in his edition of *Les Confessions,* Voisine (29) points out the double entendre of what the girls say, because *tic tac* was apparently also a metaphor for romantic feelings (the beatings of the heart). Thus, the girls may only have intended to tease Rousseau and Goton about being infatuated, but for Rousseau and the informed reader, the *tic tac* is also a covert signifier of the desired spanking(s).

7. I have altered Cohen's nonliteral translation ("that dangerous means of cheating Nature"), because it elides Rousseau's famous phrase ("the dangerous supplement").

8. See Lejeune ("Supplément" 1011–13) and Derrida (*Of Grammatology* 141–64). Typically, Derrida reads Rousseau's confession strictly as a text and brackets its referen-

tial dimension, although he does take into account the larger biographical setting of the central passage.

9. In a guarded manuscript variant of book 12, Rousseau acknowledges that he "could never quite cure himself" of "the vice" (*Oeuvres* 1:1569).

10. Lejeune's analysis posits Rousseau's literal innocence but his guilty intention. He believes Rousseau's assertion that he did not break the comb but is struck by the fact "in order to establish his innocence he employs exactly the same narrative techniques and the same strategies of discourse as he does to make his defense when he is guilty" ("Peigne cassé" 3). For Lejeune, Rousseau *recognized* himself in this 'crime' . . . which was exactly the kind of action he kept himself from doing, because he wanted to do it." The nightmarish aspect of the episode is "to be wrongfully accused of what one avoided doing because one wanted to do it" (29).

11. Schwartz has noted the young Jean-Jacques's "peculiarly dualistic and bisexual character" (107–8).

12. In the state of nature, "males and females united fortuitously, according to chance encounters, opportunity, and desire" (*Discourse on Inequality, Political Writings* 22).

13. Rousseau's sentimental wish was literally fulfilled—not without some controversy in the local press—on the bicentennial of his first meeting with Mme de Warens, when a golden memorial railing was installed in Annecy to commemorate the sacred spot (*Oeuvres* 1:1256).

14. For an excellent though different reading of the importance of the sign in the Mme Basile episode, see Starobinski (253–54, 255–56).

15. See Hopkins for an illuminating comparative analysis of the significance of the episodes of Augustine's pear stealing, Rousseau's theft of the ribbon, and Wordsworth's stolen boat in "the myth each author has constructed of his life" (307).

16. For Lejeune, "the history of Marion is only secondarily the history of a crime. In its origin, it is the history of a confession *manqué:* a confession *of love*" (*Pacte* 55). Indeed, for Lejeune it serves the same psychic need as the episode of the first spanking.

17. Starobinski has drawn an explicit parallel between Rousseau's exhibitionism and the pleasure he derives from his writings "in a representative image that fascinates his female audience" (175).

18. For an overview of this Romantic complex, see my "Romantic Idealization of Incest."

19. Apparently the trip to Paris of Mme de Warens was a secret diplomatic mission of some sort, although its purpose is still very much a matter of scholarly conjecture. See Guéhenno 46, and Cranston, *Early Life* 85–87.

20. In a note concerning the psychoanalytic interpretation of Rousseau's "autoeroticism," Starobinski mentions "latent homosexuality" as one factor (394).

21. Guéhenno (56) notes a strange and possibly sly confusion about facts throughout book 5; if anything, Cranston understates the narrative situation with his circumspect observation that "Rousseau's record of his life with Mme de Warens is not entirely reliable, even on matters of fact" (*Early Life* 103).

22. Cranston (*Early Life* 69–77) and Guéhenno (36–38) offer vivid accounts of Mme de Warens's flight and conversion.

23. For a summary of the controversy about the facts of Rousseau's stay at Charmettes, see *Oeuvres* 1:1341–43. The suspicious reading of Rousseau is exempli-

fied by Guéhenno, who concludes in his chapter on "The False Idyll of Charmettes" that "the disposition of the material" throughout book 6 is a profound distortion of reality, but one "so delicate that it remains altogether invisible to the unsuspecting reader" (81). Cranston, on the other hand, who in any event is always more willing to take Rousseau at his word, asserts that "more recent research has vindicated Rousseau's testimony" about the dates of his stay at Charmettes with Mme de Warens, and concludes that "there is no reason to doubt that Rousseau spent the summer and autumn of 1736 with her at Les Charmettes as he says in *The Confessions*" (*Early Life* 119).

3. AUTOBIOGRAPHY AS RESURRECTION

1. Rousseau's *Dialogues* were published in 1990 by the University Press of New England as the first volume of a planned edition of *The Collected Writings of Rousseau*.

2. See Williams 149–69, 205–14; and the articles by Kelly and Masters, O'Dea, and Jones.

3. According to McDonald, Rousseau "posits a model of reading" that is "undermined through the practice of his own writing" (724); in Kamuf's de Manian figural analysis, the inefficacy of the *Dialogues*, "whose dialectic cannot overcome the difference that drives it" (86), lies in the text's failure to deliver the "true" image of Rousseau ("the phantasm of transparent vision") that is the author's impossible goal.

4. The celebrity and the persecution are both amply documented in Cranston's *The Noble Savage*.

5. Rousseau expresses the paradox of his misperception by the public with the euphony of an untranslatable formula: "On voit ce qu'on croit et non pas ce qu'on voit" (*Oeuvres* 1:742).

6. The prevalence of the dialogue form in the eighteenth century does not mean, however, that it can be defined according to common motifs, strategies, or themes. As Berland has observed, "18th-century texts called dialogues by their authors often have little in common" (93).

7. Jones's view of the *Dialogues* as enacting "a hermeneutic quest" is an apt characterization. According to Jones, "the search for the real 'Jean-Jacques' becomes an inquiry into the very nature of autobiographical truth itself" (322).

8. By the time Rousseau writes his *Reveries*, he has abandoned the overt rhetoric of vindication and the project of reestablishing his reputation among his contemporaries. He has resigned the desperate "hope which made [him] write [his] *Dialogues*" ("First Walk," *Oeuvres* 1:998). He claims to have given up his battle with public opinion, and to embrace willingly his status as a reviled outsider and solitary: "Everything is over for me on earth. . . . There is no longer anything for me to hope for or fear in this world, and here I am tranquil at the bottom of the abyss . . . impassible as God himself" (999).

9. For an incisive analysis of "the different levels of discourse" in Rousseau's self-presentation in the *Dialogues*, see Williams on "Frames and Framing" (155–63).

10. For a concise exposition of "the place of Rousseau's system within the *Dialogues*," see Kelly and Masters, 247–52.

11. Rousseau's use of multiple personae has led some critics to consider the *Dialogues* more fictional than autobiographical. For instance, Lorgnet focuses on the fictional or "imaginary" dimension of Rousseau's "illocutionary" rhetoric (36–37,

40–41); O'Dea stresses that the work is one "constantly insisting on its own fictionality," with the names of the interlocutors "seeming to demand that the work be read referentially, autobiographically, but thwarting every attempt to answer that demand and undermining every appeal to fact" (147); and O'Neal observes that the *Dialogues* show "Rousseau's increasing predilection for a more fictional mode of writing about the self" (118). However, because Rousseau's subjective mode of being is expressed through two discursive (and admittedly fictional) personae with reference to the public controversy surrounding Rousseau and his writings, as well as to the vexed issue of his reputation in the future, I cannot accept O'Dea's strategy of reading the *Dialogues* as ultimately fiction rather than autobiography. The discursive context set up by Rousseau's speakers clearly includes an essential referential dimension (indicated even by the fact that "Rousseau" is discussing "Jean-Jacques"), and indeed unsettles or disables the very categorical distinction between "fiction" and "autobiography" that O'Dea wants to maintain. As Eakin has recently reminded us in emphasizing "the referential aesthetic of autobiography," it is "the presumption of truth-value" as "experientially essential" that "makes autobiography matter to autobiographers and their readers" (*Touching the World*, 30). Rousseau deploys the fictive device of his interlocutors precisely to establish the elusive and occluded "truth-value" of his life and being.

12. For an analysis of the rhetoric of posterity of *The Reveries*, see my "Autobiography as Revision."

4. GOETHE AND AUTOBIOGRAPHY

Citations of Goethe's *Werke* (Hamburger Ausgabe edition) appear as HA (by volume and page number).

1. According to Müller, "Only with Goethe's *Poetry and Truth* is the transition from a literarized practical prose form [literarisierte Zweckform] to the literary form of autobiography accomplished" (242). Unlike contemporary German autobiography critics, some earlier Goethe scholars have been more chary in their critical assessment. Barker Fairley, for instance, complained of "the curious unreality of *Dichtung und Wahrheit,* by virtue of which it appears rather as a history of literature than as autobiography, more academic than personal." He claims that Goethe "managed seriously to distort the record" of his early life, and that "as he wrote it, [he] was continually touching the fringes of the crucial problem, the problem of his mind and temperament in its first stages, without ever really grappling with it" (52, 57). It seems that Fairley is (unconsciously?) bringing the expectations for the genre established by Rousseau—a more directly introspective and nakedly confessional autobiography—to bear on Goethe's performance. Staiger's perfunctory chapter on *Poetry and Truth* (2:237–60), as opposed to the more than two hundred pages he devotes to *Faust,* part 2, effectively reveals his uncritical valuation of autobiography—even Goethe's—as a subliterary genre, grist for the mill of the biographer.

2. The historicist connection is disputed by Koranyi (94–99), who claims that despite the apparent similarities, Goethe's historical thinking, which takes into account his (the subject's) own viewpoint, differs fundamentally from Ranke's stance of a value-free, scientific, and objective understanding of history.

3. Perloff has argued that although "it is a commonplace that Goethe's lyric poetry was inspired by the pivotal experiences of his own life" (280), the poems "reveal

singularly little about the poet's inner self and about the world he lived in" (281). The reason for this reticence is that "Goethe's innate sense of decorum" as well as his refusal to violate "eighteenth-century rhetorical conventions" (292) "dictated" that "although the poem must originate in personal experience, the experience has poetic value only insofar as it is universalized" (284).

4. Goethe's thesis about the Protestant penchant for autobiography is expressed in a letter of 4 March 1826: "[I]t would be attractive to examine whether Protestants are more inclined to [writing] self-biographies than Catholics" (*Briefe* 4:187).

5. Niggl (102–4) documents several instances of the neologism ("autobiography") in Germany before the turn of the century: "Biographers, and especially autobiographers" (in a work dictated circa 1779 and published in 1791), and "self-biographies or . . . autobiographies" (in a work published in 1795).

6. An *Annals* entry for 1807 makes clear that for Goethe an individual cannot be understood without a corresponding understanding of his century: "I studied Albertus Magnus, but with little success. One would have to picture to oneself the situation of his century, in order to begin to understand more or less what was here intended and done" (HA 10:499).

7. Goethe's experience of the rejection of his new interests was to be repeated a year later with Schlosser, who at the close of *Siege of Mainz* is described as reacting dismissively to Goethe's exposition of his theory of colors and his proposal for collaborative scientific research (Saine, *Poetry and Truth* 775–76).

8. Hammer's conclusion (about the importance of Rousseau to Goethe) is based on a chronological review (offered in his second chapter) of "all references to Rousseau in Goethe's works, letters, diaries, and conversations" (32).

9. Cassirer points out that the only decoration in Kant's Spartan study was "the portrait of Jean-Jacques Rousseau," and that "in other ways also the earliest accounts of Kant's life give varied evidence of his reverence for Rousseau as a person and his admiration for his work" (1).

10. Goethe is praising part 1 of *The Confessions,* which was published in Geneva in 1782; part 2 did not appear until 1789.

11. Goethe's account in book 18 of the disordered behavior of the young Counts von Stolberg acting out the Storm-and-Stress cult of "genius" also suggests a faddish and excessive application of the Rousseau cult of nature and the natural: "Among the crazy notions of the time was one of bathing in the open water under the open sky." Goethe develops this motif in considerable detail and in a manner that both implicates him in and excuses him for these excesses, which are presented with a careful balance of criticism and sympathy. The counts "who could not refrain from this impropriety . . . caused a scandal" in Darmstadt (561), as they do again later on their trip to Switzerland (in book 19), where in fact Goethe becomes temporarily a party to their youthful indiscretions: "I do not deny that I myself joined my comrades for a dip in the clear lake, quite far away from human eyes, or so it seemed. Yet naked bodies gleam afar, and whoever might have seen them took offense" (579).

12. As has been frequently noted, the epistolary style of *The Sufferings of Young Werther* as well as the presentation of Werther's unhappy love for Lotte also seem to owe a good deal to Rousseau's *Julie.*

13. Trunz stresses that Goethe (unlike Rousseau and Jung-Stilling) "offers a life-history, not an analysis of the inner life"; "Goethe described his life not because he

became a psychological problem to himself, but because he became historic to himself" (HA 9:620, 623).

14. Goethe later transposed the terms "truth" and "poetry" in the original title for reasons of euphony.

15. See White's essays on "The Historical Text as Literary Artifact" (81–100) and "The Fictions of Factual Representation" (121–34) in *Tropics of Discourse.*

16. Examples of the conservative view of the role of fiction in *Poetry and Truth* are Alt's assertion a century ago that "Goethe occasionally invented, but invented in such a manner that the Poetry does not contradict the Truth" (80–81), and Bowman's conclusion that "in the last resort his criterion was the poetic eye of memory; 'Erdichtung,' the fabrication of incident, was not allowed" (21).

17. Bowman's characterization of Goethe's "philosophy of life"—"man is to develop and realize at all costs . . . his own manifold potentialities in this world" (138) as constituting a "worldly gospel" (144)—points to Goethe's concept of *Bildung* in *Poetry and Truth* as a secular religion. Stern has speculated about the "compensatory character" of Goethe's biological ("causal-genetic") view of human development as a substitute for the loss of the traditional theological explanations discredited for "the alienated humans" of the Enlightenment and its "condition of autonomy" proclaimed by Kant: "scientific thought appears suddenly no longer as progress, but as the expression of a lack. And in principle that has not changed since Goethe" (278).

18. My discussion of the significance of *Bildung* for Goethe the autobiographer is especially indebted to Bowman, Koranyi, Niggl, Stern, Trunz, and Weintraub.

19. For helpful commentaries on Goethe's "Primal Words," see Trunz (HA 1:674–75) and Weintraub (365–67).

20. It is revealing that the aged Goethe frames this struggle for personal excellence and nobility—"it had become a credo that nobility had to be personally earned, and if any rivalry was shown, it was from above to below"—within the idealized prerevolutionary setting of the bourgeois-patrician city of Frankfurt, "a certain complex . . . that seemed to be knit together of trade, capital, real estate, and delight in knowledge and collections," where "the Lutheran church was in command," and where "no one was excluded from the magistracy" (book 17, 554). His portrait of the social and economic realities of the Frankfurt of his youth, where class harmony supposedly prevailed, was one of the very last passages added to *Poetry and Truth* and is his idyllic and conservative tribute to a world destroyed by the French Revolution.

21. A more nuanced view than Niggl's (of "the daemonic" replacing the organic conception), is Schnur's thesis that after the metamorphosis paradigm for the self that informs parts 1 and 2 became problematic for Goethe in part 3, "the daemonic" represents his attempt at a new formulation of his identity (80–85). In Schnur's psychological interpretation of "the daemonic," the new identity concept that emerges in part 3 and that defines Goethe's outlook in part 4 conflicts with the metamorphic model and poses a problem of autobiographical representation (89) that accounts for Goethe's failure to complete part 4. Particularly suggestive is Schnur's interpretation of Goethe's description in book 10 of the unfinished Cologne cathedral as a poetological parallel to his own autobiography (71–72). Schnur concludes that while Goethe could not reconcile the organic and the daemonic conceptions of his identity, nature is a third term common to both and thus constitutes "the true subject of *Poetry and Truth*" (91).

22. In conversations with Eckermann (March 2 and 8, *Gespräche mit Goethe* 2:443–44), Goethe cited Napoleon as his chief example of the "daemonic" individual ("he was so in the highest degree, so that hardly another can be compared with him"). Goethe also mentioned Byron, Frederick II of Prussia, Peter the Great, and (less credibly?) Paganini and Karl August, Duke of Weimar.

23. I am indebted to Jane K. Brown for pointing out to me the earlier appearance of the renunciation theme in Goethe's writings.

24. Eakin has stressed the identity-enacting and confirming role of autobiography: "The act of composition may be conceived as a mediating term in the autobiographical enterprise, reaching back into the past not merely to recapture but to repeat the psychological rhythms of identity formation, and reaching forward into the future to fix the structure of this identity in a permanent self-made existence as a literary text" (*Fictions* 226).

5. FAMILY RELATIONSHIPS IN POETRY AND TRUTH

1. Modern autobiographical fiction has also explored the family romance in depth, e.g., D. H. Lawrence's depiction of the conflicted Oedipal relationship of Paul Morel with his abusive parents in *Sons and Lovers*.

2. When Madame de Staël visited Frankfurt, the mother of the famous author of *Werther* met her with the proud declaration, "Je suis la mère de Goethe" (Friedenthal 18).

3. Boyle notes that Goethe had eight tutors in all and gives his father credit for his choice of them, "which seems to have had the deliberate purpose of stimulating the children by exposing them to as varied a set of influences as internationally-minded Frankfurt could provide" (54).

4. "My father was particularly obstinate on the subject of completion. Something once undertaken had to be finished, even if in the meantime the inconvenient, tedious, vexatious, nay, useless aspects of the project had clearly revealed themselves" (book 4, 116).

5. Müller has noted that Thoranc becomes "a positive father figure" for young Goethe (293).

6. Goethe's patriarchal outlook is also reflected in the fact that while he paints a detailed portrait in the opening book of his maternal grandfather, his two grandmothers are at best a shadowy presence.

7. Boyle notes that "in all [Goethe] handled only twenty-eight cases in nearly four years, much of the work being taken from his shoulders by the clerk . . . who was paid for by his father" (105).

8. At the beginning of book 18 Goethe offers a vivid account of the visit to Frankfurt of the Stolbergs, including their eccentric and *outré* conduct while dining at his house. At these dinners the presiding figure is Goethe's mother, who in the role of "Dame Aya" (the name of the mother in an old children's story), enters into and enjoys their high-spirited and "youthful fantasies," which also involve a liberal consumption of wine from the father's well-stocked cellar. Now the same father who would not permit the blank verse poetry of Klopstock into his house during Goethe's childhood shows a new forbearance: "my father smiled and shook his head" (559).

9. Friedenthal characterizes Cornelia Goethe as "sensible [gefühlvoll] and frigid, a not unusual but unfortunate combination" (26).

10. In 1772 Cornelia had inscribed on her seal, "La liberté fait mon bonheur" (Michel 60).

11. Witkowski (53–58) offers summary excerpts of this deft sketch by the sixteen-year-old Cornelia that is clearly based on the romantic intrigues of her social circle.

12. For an analysis of such love relationships in European Romanticism, see my article on "The Romantic Idealization of Incest."

13. That Goethe was unable to solve the riddle of his sister's being is the considered conclusion of Witkowski, who rejects Goethe's vision of Cornelia as an abbess as fundamentally misconstrued, given her temperament as a worldly and sociable individual (196).

14. *Sir Charles Grandison* was Cornelia's favorite Richardson novel, and Miss Byron her female and Sir Charles her masculine ideals (Witkowski 48, 63).

15. Two sketches by Goethe of Cornelia in 1770 and 1773 strikingly reproduce the feature of the high and arched forehead and the pulled-back hair (Witkowski 80ff., 96ff.).

16. In an NEH institute on Goethe's *Faust* that I attended at the University of California at Santa Barbara in 1990, the witty consensus of the feminists in our group was that "being Faust means never having to say you're sorry."

6. ROMANTIC LOVE IN POETRY AND TRUTH

1. For an analysis of Goethe's "Trilogy of Suffering" in the context of its biographical setting, see my "Memory, Imagination, and Self-Healing in the Romantic Crisis Lyric."

2. Whereas Jean-Jacques does not feel "the least glimmering of love" for the woman who bore his children ("the sensual needs I satisfied with her were for me purely sexual" [*Confessions*, book 9, 385–86]), "the first and only love in all [his] life" (408), his midlife intoxication with Sophie d'Houdetot, is an unconsummated autoerotic fantasy that fueled the fiction of *The New Héloïse*.

3. The motif of the three apples in "The New Paris" appears to allude to both the Judgment of Paris and the Atalanta myths. The symbolic significance of the colors of the three apples (red, green, and yellow) might be explored by way of Goethe's treatise *On the Theory of Colors*, which has a section on "The Physical and Moral Effect of Colors" ("Sinnlich-Sittliche Wirkung der Farbe"), where he states that "humans generally experience a great pleasure in colors" (HA 13:494). According to Goethe, the colors yellow = plus and blue = minus constitute a basic polarity, the former associated with force, light, warmth, proximity, and rejection, and the latter with shadow, cold, distance, and attraction (478). The polarity seems gendered, but not consistently so; thus the masculine-seeming yellow, "the nearest color to light," is also described in feminine terms as warm, cheerful, comforting, and gently attractive (495–96). Perhaps yellow can be seen as related to the life force. The equal mixture of the polar opposites of yellow and blue yields green (478), a color that produces "a real satisfaction" (501). Yellow heightened or intensified into red gains more energy and splendor (496). Red itself gives a singular impression of seriousness, dignity, and grace that befits the dignity of age as well as the attractiveness of youth (500). Of the three colors of the apples, then, one (green) is the balance of polar opposites and can serve as a symbol of the male-female relationship; the other two have very positive connotations.

4. "Whether there really was a definite attachment to some one person at this time,

whether, if so, her name really was Gretchen, whether any reliance is to be put on the circumstantial detail of Goethe's narrative . . . are all matters subject to varying degrees of doubt" (Boyle 57).

5. Remak has analyzed how in the Gretchen narrative "the autobiographical" and the "novellesque elements enter a complex but happy fusion" ("Autobiography or Fiction?" 54). (See also his "Die novellistische Struktur des Gretchenabenteuers.") Other commentators have noted what Müller calls the "novelistic" shaping of "the Gretchen-episode" (329–30).

6. Goethe's discovery that the young Italian woman is in fact engaged to be married brings about a momentary "Werther-like" *crise de coeur* (*Italian Journey,* HA 11:426–27) that he seeks to master through the aesthetic compensation of landscape painting. For an analysis of Goethe's account of his relationship with Maddalena Riggi, see Remak's "Autobiography or Fiction?"

7. According to some suspicious commentators, "Joseph's behavior during the [coronation] ceremonies was a deliberate and conscientious rejection of old institutions" (Bernard 28).

8. Like that of the Wordsworth deeply depressed by the failure of the French Revolution, the slow recovery of the young Goethe after the Gretchen debacle is a function of the healing impact of nature as well as the ministrations of a loving sister.

9. In a letter to Charlotte von Stein on his surprise visit to Sesenheim in September 1779, Goethe acknowledges, "the second daughter of the house once loved me more than I deserved . . . I had to leave her at a moment when it nearly cost her her life" (*Briefe* 1:272).

10. See Price and Bracht for a detailed overview of the chronological questions involved in Goethe's use of Goldsmith's novel for his Sesenheim narrative. Bracht diverges from the scholarly consensus that Goethe could not have read the novel when he was actually at Sesenheim by leaving the door open to the possibility that he might have heard about it from some other source prior to Herder's reading (Bracht 264–65).

11. For a nuanced discussion of how "the Sesenheim-history is held in suspension between novel and reality," see Müller's section on "Das Sesenheim-Erlebnis" (298–310), which posits that "the Sesenheim-history is admittedly a fictive shaping of experience, but neither novella nor novel" (309).

12. Goethe's "Das Heidenröslein" was based on folk sources and actually taken as a folk ballad by Herder, under whose impetus Goethe had ventured into the Alsatian countryside to collect such traditional popular material.

13. The liminality that allows the figure of Friederike to happily combine normally opposed traits is suggested more than once by Goethe. Her "merits" include "her discreet cheerfulness, her naiveté combined with awareness, her happy disposition combined with foresight—qualities that seemed incompatible but which coincided in her" (book 11, 338).

14. The references to elegant interior decor, including wallpaper, suggest that Friederike will not fit into the house and patrician urban world of Goethe's father.

15. In the last part of book 11 Goethe summarizes in some detail his enthusiastic discovery and championing in his Strasbourg circle of Shakespeare, who "has received more recognition in Germany than in any other nation, perhaps including his own" (365). Goethe makes it clear that he played a leading role in the German cult of the Bard of Avon. Trunz concludes that the "influence that

Shakespeare's spirit and poetic compositions had on Goethe is difficult to overestimate and was acknowledged again and again by the poet throughout his life" (HA 12:668). See also Goethe's essays, "For Shakespeare's Day" and "Shakespeare and No End" (HA 12:224–27, 287–98).

16. Goethe's insistence in a written text (*Poetry and Truth*) on the primacy of voice and speech—a text that today is the only version of Goethe's voice we can have, i.e., an autobiographical voice speaking to us from beyond the grave—can be seen as a special instance of what de Man has identified as "the trope of autobiography," *prosopopeia* ("Autobiography as De-Facement" 75–76).

17. How it is possible for one person to give a reading of *Hamlet* in its entirety—that is, to read *all* the many and very different parts—is a question to be asked.

18. Rousseau states of the Marion episode, "I can affirm that the desire to some extent to rid myself of it [the burden of guilt] has greatly contributed to my resolution of writing these *Confessions*" (book 2, 88).

19. Friederike was still alive when Goethe published his account of their meeting and love in part 2 (book 10) in 1812. She never married, spent her later years in the household of her brother, and died in 1813. In the final period of her life she would not speak of Goethe. After the breakup with Goethe and her illness, she also had to put up with the importunities of Goethe's fellow Strasbourg student and poet, Lenz, who in his envy and incipient madness sought to spy into Goethe's relationship with Friederike and to emulate him by also wooing her (Friedenthal 110–13).

20. Kestner's statement about Goethe's view of Rousseau at the time (the *Werther* period) is quoted in Boyle (131).

21. Friedenthal also views the Lili relationship as deeply passionate, unsettling, and painful for Goethe: "Here, for the first and probably also for the last time, he felt himself caught" (193). Boyle concludes that Lili "was sacrificed" for the same reason as Friederike ("marriage would still have meant . . . the end of desire") (199).

22. As a single example of the later Goethe's gnomic terseness, let me cite one assertion whose irony makes it my favorite. It comes several pages before the close of *Poetry and Truth*: "But that *is* youth, and life in general; we usually perceive the strategy only when the campaign is over" (book 20, 602).

23. According to Goethe, in hindsight the obstacles to a marriage between him and Lili were "at bottom not insurmountable" (Eckermann 2:674, 5 March 1830).

24. Lili's elder brother had doctored the books and later committed suicide. Before the catastrophe, however, Lili made an advantageous marriage (Friedenthal 201).

WORKS CITED

Aichinger, Ingrid. *Künstlerische Selbstdarstellung: Goethes "Dichtung und Wahrheit" und die Autobiographie der Folgezeit.* Bern: Peter Lang Verlag, 1977.

Alt, Carl. *Studien zur Entstehungsgeschichte Goethes Dichtung und Wahrheit.* 1898. Reprint, Hildesheim: Gerstenberg Verlag, 1976.

Augustine, Saint. *Confessions.* Trans. R. S. Pine-Coffin. Harmondsworth: Penguin Books, 1961.

Barner, Wilfried. "Goethes Bild von der deutschen Literatur der Aufklärung: Zum Siebentem Buch von *Dichtung und Wahrheit.*" In *Zwischen Aufklärung und Restauration: Sozialer Wandel in der deutschen Literatur (1700–1848),* ed. Wolfgang Frühwald and Alberto Martino, 283–305. Tübingen: Max Niemeyer Verlag, 1989.

Beaujour, Michel. *Miroirs d'encre: Rhétorique de l'autoportrait.* Paris: Éditions du Seuil, 1980.

Berland, K. J. H. "Didactic, Catecheticall, or Obstetricious?: Socrates and Eighteenth-Century Dialogue." In *Compendious Conversations: The Method of Dialogue in the Early Enlightenment,* ed. Kevin L. Cope, 93–104. Frankfurt: Lang Verlag, 1992.

Bernard, Paul B. *Joseph II.* New York: Twayne, 1968.

Blake, William. *Complete Writings.* Ed. Geoffrey Keynes. Oxford: Oxford University Press, 1966.

Bowman, Derek. *Life into Autobiography: A Study of Goethe's "Dichtung und Wahrheit."* N.p.: Herbert Lang, 1971.

Boyle, Nicholas. *Goethe: The Poet and the Age.* Oxford: Oxford University Press, 1992.

Bracht, Edgar. "Wakefield in Sesenheim: Zur Interpretation des zehnten und elften Buches von Goethes *Aus meinem Leben. Dichtung und Wahrheit.*" *Euphorion* 83 (1989): 261–80.

Brodzki, Bella, and Celeste Schenk. "Introduction." *Life/Lines: Theorizing Women's Autobiography,* 1–15. Ithaca: Cornell University Press, 1988.

Buckley, Jerome Hamilton. *The Turning Key: Autobiography and the Subjective Impulse since 1800.* Cambridge: Harvard University Press, 1984.

Cassirer, Ernst. *Rousseau, Kant, Goethe: Two Essays.* Trans. James Gutmann, Paul Oskar

Kristeller, and John Herman Randall Jr. Princeton: Princeton University Press, 1957.

Coe, Richard C. *When the Grass Was Taller: Autobiography and the Experience of Child-hood*. New Haven: Yale University Press, 1984.

Cranston, Maurice. *Jean-Jacques: The Early Life and Work of Jean-Jacques Rousseau, 1712–1754*. Great Britain: Viking/Penguin, 1982; Chicago: University of Chicago Press, 1991.

———. *The Noble Savage: Jean-Jacques Rousseau, 1754–1762*. Chicago: University of Chicago Press, 1991.

de Man, Paul. *Allegories of Reading: Figural Language in Rousseau, Nietzsche, Rilke, and Proust*. New Haven: Yale University Press, 1979.

———. "Autobiography as De-Facement." In Paul de Man, *The Rhetoric of Romanticism*. New York: Columbia University Press, 1984.

Derrida, Jacques. *Of Grammatology*. Trans. Gayatri Chakravorty Spivack. Baltimore: Johns Hopkins University Press, 1976.

Eakin, Paul John. *Fictions in Autobiography: Studies in the Art of Self-Invention*. Princeton: Princeton University Press, 1985.

———. *Touching the World: Reference in Autobiography*. Princeton: Princeton University Press, 1991.

———. "Relational Selves, Relational Lives: The Story of the Story." In *True Relations: Essays on Autobiography and the Postmodern*, ed. G. Thomas Couser and Joseph Fichtelberg, 63–81. Westport: Greenwood Press, 1998.

Eckermann, Johann Peter. *Gespräche mit Goethe in den letzten Jahren seines Lebens, 1823–32*. 2 vols. Basel: Birkhäuser, 1945.

Egan, Susanna. *Patterns of Experience in Autobiography*. Chapel Hill: University of North Carolina Press, 1984.

Fairley, Barker. *A Study of Goethe*. Oxford: Clarendon Press, 1947.

Ferrara, Alessandro. *Modernity and Authenticity: A Study of the Social and Ethical Thought of Jean-Jacques Rousseau*. Albany: State University of New York Press, 1993.

Fleishman, Avrom. *Figures of Autobiography: The Language of Self-Writing in Victorian and Modern England*. Berkeley: University of California Press, 1983.

Folkenflik, Robert. "Introduction: The Institution of Autobiography." In *The Culture of Autobiography: Constructions of Self-Representation*, ed. Robert Folkenflik, 1–17. Stanford: Stanford University Press, 1993.

Freud, Sigmund. "A Childhood Recollection from *Dichtung und Wahrheit*." In *Collected Papers*, vol. 4, 357–67. Trans. Joan Riviere. New York: Basic Books, 1959.

Friedenthal, Richard. *Goethe: Sein Leben und seine Zeit*. Munich: R. Piper Verlag, 1963.

Gagnebin, Bernard, and Marcel Raymond. "Introductions." In *Les Confessions. Autres Textes autobiographiques*. Vol. 1 of *Oevres complètes*, ed. Bernard Gagnebin and Marcel Raymond, xi–xcv. Paris: Bibliothèque de la Pléiade, Gallimard, 1959–69.

Gibbon, Edward. *Memoirs of My Life*. Ed. Georges A. Bonnard. New York: Funk & Wagnalls, 1969.

Glagau, Hans. "Das romanhafte Element der Modernen Selbstbiographie im Urteil des Historikers." In *Die Autobiographie: Zur Form und Geschichte einer literarischen Gattung*, ed. Günter Niggl, 55–66. Darmstadt: Wissenschaftliche Buchgesellschaft, 1989.

Goethe, Johann Wolfgang von. *Briefe*. 4 vols. Ed. Karl Robert Mandelkow and Bodo Morawe. Hamburg: Christian Wegner Verlag, 1962–67.

———. *Werke*. Hamburger Ausgabe. 14 vols. Ed. Erich Trunz. Hamburg: Christian Wegner Verlag, 1967.

———. *From My Life: Poetry and Truth. Campaign in France/Siege of Mainz*. Ed. Thomas

P. Saine and Jeffrey Sammons. Vols. 4 and 5 of *Goethe: The Collected Works*, ed. Victor Lange, Eric Blackall, and Cyrus Hamlin. Princeton: Princeton University Press, 1994–95.

Gould, Robert. "Obstacles to Artistic Development in Part 4 of *Dichtung und Wahrheit*." *Carleton Germanic Papers* 12 (1984): 67–86.

Grimsley, Ronald. *Jean-Jacques Rousseau*. Brighton: Harvester, 1983.

Guéhenno, Jean. *Jean-Jacques en marge des "Confessions": Roman et verité*. Vol. 1 of *Jean-Jacques: Histoire d'une conscience*. 2 vols. Paris: Gallimard, 1962.

Gusdorf, Georges. "Conditions et limites de l'autobiographie." In *Formen der Selbst-darstellung: Analekten zu einer Geschichte des literarischen Selbstportraits*, ed. Günter Reichenkron and Erich Haase, 105–23. Berlin: Duncker & Humblot, 1956.

———. "De l'autobiographie initiatique à l'autobiographie genre littéraire." *Revue d'histoire littéraire de la France* 75 (1975): 957–94.

Hammer, Carl J. *Goethe and Rousseau: Resonances of the Mind*. Lexington: University of Kentucky Press, 1973.

Hartle, Ann. *The Modern Self in Rousseau's "Confessions": A Reply to Saint Augustine*. Notre Dame: University of Notre Dame Press, 1983.

Hopkins, Brooke. "Pear Stealing and Other Faults: An Essay on Confessional Autobiography." *The South Atlantic Quarterly* 80 (1981): 305–21.

Jackson, Susan K. *Rousseau's Occasional Autobiographies*. Columbus: Ohio State University Press, 1992.

Jay, Paul. *Being in the Text: Self-Representation from Wordsworth to Roland Barthes*. Ithaca: Cornell University Press, 1984.

Jones, James F., Jr. "The *Dialogues* as Autobiographical Truth." *Studies in Eighteenth-Century Culture* 14 (1985): 317–28.

Kamuf, Peggy. "Seeing through Rousseau." *L'esprit créateur* 28, no. 4 (1988): 82–94.

Kavanagh, Thomas M. *Writing the Truth: Authority and Desire in Rousseau*. Berkeley: University of California Press, 1987.

Kelly, Christopher. *Rousseau's Exemplary Life: The "Confessions" as Political Philosophy*. Ithaca: Cornell University Press, 1987.

Kelly, Christopher, and Roger D. Masters. "Rousseau on Reading 'Jean-Jacques': The *Dialogues*." *Interpretation* 17 (1989–90): 239–53.

Koranyi, Stephan. *Autobiographik und Wissenschaft im Denken Goethes*. Bonn: Bouvier Verlag, 1984.

Lejeune, Philippe. *L'autobiographie en France*. Paris: Armand Colin, 1971.

———. "Le 'dangereux supplément': Lecture d'un aveu de Rousseau." *Annales* 4 (1974): 1009–22.

———. *Le pacte autobiographique*. Paris: Éditions du Seuil, 1975.

———. "Le peigne cassé." *Poétique* 7, no. 25 (1976): 1–29.

Lionnet, Françoise. *Autobiographical Voices: Race, Gender, Self-Portraiture*. Ithaca: Cornell University Press, 1989.

Lorgnet, Michèle. *"Rousseau juge de Jean-Jacques—Dialogues:* L'imaginaire de l'argumentation." *Francofonia* 4, no. 6 (1984): 29–41.

McDonald, Christie V. "The Model of Reading in Rousseau's *Dialogues*." *MLN* 93 (1978): 723–32.

Mason, Mary G. "The Other Voice: Autobiographies of Women Writers." In *Autobiography: Essays Theoretical and Critical*, ed. James Olney, 207–35. Princeton: Princeton University Press, 1980.

May, Georges. *L'autobiographie*. Paris: Presses Universitaires de France, 1979.

Mellor, Anne K. *Romanticism and Gender*. New York: Routledge, 1993.

Melzer, Arthur. *The Natural Goodness of Man: On the System of Rousseau's Thought*. Chicago: University of Chicago Press, 1990.

Michel, Christoph. "Cornelia in *Dichtung und Wahrheit*: Kritisches zu einem 'Spiegelbild.'" *Jahrbuch des Freien Deutschen Hochstifts* (1979): 40–70.

Müller, Klaus Detlef. *Autobiographie und Roman: Studien zur literarischen Autobiographie der Goethezeit*. Tübingen: Max Niemeyer Verlag, 1976.

Nabokov, Vladimir. *Speak, Memory: An Autobiography Revisited*. Rev. ed. New York: Paragon Books, 1979.

Nietzsche, Friedrich. *Zur Genealogie der Moral*. Munich: Goldmann Verlag, n.d.

Niggl, Günter. *Geschichte der deutschen Autobiographie im 18. Jahrhundert: Theoretische Grundlegung und literarische Entfaltung*. Stuttgart: J. B. Metzler Verlag, 1977.

O'Dea, Michael. "Fiction and the Ideal in *Rousseau juge de Jean-Jacques*." *French Studies* 40 (1986): 141–50.

Olney, James. "Autobiography and the Cultural Moment: A Thematic, Historical, and Bibliographical Introduction." In *Autobiography: Essays Theoretical and Critical*, ed. James Olney, 3–27. Princeton: Princeton University Press, 1980.

O'Neal, John C. "Rousseau's Narrative Strategies for Readers of His Autobiographical Works." *Bucknell Review* (1985): 106–20.

Pascal, Roy. *Design and Truth in Autobiography*. Cambridge: Harvard University Press, 1960.

Perloff, Marjorie. "The Autobiographical Mode of Goethe: *Dichtung und Wahrheit* and the Lyric Poems." *Comparative Literature Studies* 7 (1970): 265–96.

Pfau, Thomas. "Rhetoric and the Existential: Romantic Studies and the Question of the Subject." *Studies in Romanticism* 26 (1987): 487–512.

Price, Lawrence Marsden. "Goldsmith and Sesenheim." *The Germanic Review* 4 (1929): 237–47.

Remak, Henry H. H. "Die novellistische Struktur des Gretchenabenteuers in *Dichtung un Wahrheit*." In *Stil- und Formenprobleme in der Literatur*, ed. Paul Böckmann, 303–8. Heidelberg: Carl Winter Universitätsverlag, 1959.

———. "Autobiography or Fiction? Johann Wolfgang and Johann Caspar Goethe's 'Schöne Mailänderinnen' and the 'Frankfurter Gretchen' as Novellas." In *Goethe in Italy, 1786–1986: A Bicentennial Symposium*, ed. Gerhart Hoffmeister, 21–54. Amsterdam: Rodopi, 1988.

Rousseau, Jean-Jacques. *The Confessions*. Trans. J. M. Cohen. Harmondsworth: Penguin, 1953.

———. *Oeuvres complètes*. 4 vols. Ed. Bernard Gagnebin and Marcel Raymond. Paris: Bibliothèque de la Pléiade, Gallimard, 1959–69.

———. *Les Confessions. Autres textes autobiographiques*. Vol. 1 of *Oeuvres complètes*, ed. Bernard Gagnebin and Marcel Raymond. Paris: Bibliothèque de la Pléiade, Gallimard, 1959–69.

———. "Pygmalion, scéne lyrique." *La Nouvelle Héloïse Théatre-Poésies Essais littéraires*. Vol. 2 of *Oeuvres complètes*, ed. Bernard Gagnebin and Marcel Raymond. Paris: Bibliothèque de la Pléiade, Gallimard, 1959–69.

———. *Les Rêveries du promeneur solitaire*. In vol. 1 of *Oeuvres complètes*, ed. Bernard Gagnebin and Marcel Raymond. Paris: Bibliothèque de la Pléiade, Gallimard, 1959–69.

———. *Rousseau juge de Jean Jacques: Dialogues*. In vol. 1 of *Oeuvres complètes*, ed. Bernard

Gagnebin and Marcel Raymond. Paris: Bibliothèque de la Pléiade, Gallimard, 1959–69.

——. *Politics and the Arts: Letter to M. d'Alembert on the Theatre.* Trans. Allan Bloom. Glencoe, Ill.: Free Press, 1960.

——. *Emile ou de l'éducation.* Ed. Michel Launay. Paris: Garnier-Flammarion, 1966.

——. *Les Confessions.* Ed. Jacques Voisine. Paris: Garnier, 1980.

——. *Essay on the Origin of Languages. The First and Second Discourses and Essay on the Origin of Languages.* Ed. and trans. Victor Gourevitch. New York: Harper & Row, 1986.

——. *Rousseau's Political Writings.* Ed. Alan Ritter and Julia Conaway Bondanella. New York: Norton, 1988.

Satonski, Dmitri. "Die Entwicklungsidee in Goethes *Dichtung und Wahrheit.*" *Goethe Jahrbuch* 99 (1982): 105–16.

Schlegel, Friedrich. *Dialogue on Poetry and Literary Aphorisms.* Trans. Ernst Behler and Roman Struc. University Park, Pa.: Pennsylvania State University Press, 1969.

Schnur, Harald. "Identität und autobiographische Darstellung in Goethes *Dichtung und Wahrheit.*" *Jahrbuch des freien deutschen Hochstifts* (1990): 28–93.

Schwartz, Joel. *The Sexual Politics of Jean-Jacques Rousseau.* Chicago: University of Chicago Press, 1984.

Sheringham, Michael. *French Autobiography Devices and Desires: Rousseau to Perec.* Oxford: Clarendon Press, 1993.

Smith, Sidonie. "The [Female] Subject in Critical Venues: Poetics, Politics, Autobiographical Practices." *Auto/Biography Studies* 6, no. 1 (1991): 109–30.

Spacks, Patricia Meyer. *Imagining a Self: Autobiography and Novel in Eighteenth-Century England.* Cambridge: Harvard University Press, 1976.

Spengemann, William C. *The Forms of Autobiography: Episodes in the History of a Literary Genre.* New Haven: Yale University Press, 1980.

Staiger, Emil. *Goethe.* 3 vols. Zurich: Atlantis Verlag, 1963.

Starobinski, Jean. "The Style of Autobiography." In *Literary Style: A Symposium,* ed. Seymour Chatham, 285–96. New York: Oxford University Press, 1971.

——. *Jean-Jacques Rousseau: Transparency and Obstruction.* Trans. A. Goldhammer. University of Chicago Press, 1988.

Stauffer, Donald. *The Art of Biography in Eighteenth Century England.* Princeton: Princeton University Press, 1941.

Stelzig, Eugene L. "Romantic Subjectivity: Disease or Fortunate Fall?" In *English and German Romanticism: Cross-Currents and Controversies,* ed. James Pipkin, 153–68. Heidelberg: Carl Winter Universitätsverlag, 1985.

——. "Some Notes on Romantic Subjectivity in the Context of German and English Romanticism." In *Sensus Communis: Contemporary Trends in Comparative Literature Festschrift für Henry Remak,* ed. Janos Riesz et al., 357–67. Tübingen: Günter Narr Verlag, 1986.

——. "Autobiography as Revision: Rousseau's *Reveries.*" *a/b: Autobiography Studies* 4 (1988): 97–106.

——. "Memory, Imagination, and Self-Healing in the Romantic Crisis Lyric: *Trilogie der Leidenschaft* and 'Resolution and Independence.'" *Journal of English and Germanic Philology* 90 (1991): 524–41.

——. "'Though It Were the Deadliest Sin to Love As We Have Loved': The Romantic Idealization of Incest." *European Romantic Review* 5 (1995): 230–51.

Stern, Martin. "'Wie kann man sich selbst kennen lernen?': Gedanken zu Goethes Auto-biographie." *Goethe Jahrbuch* 101 (1984): 269–81.

Stull, Heidi I. *The Evolution of the Autobiography from 1770–1850: A Comparative Study and Analysis.* New York: Peter Lang, 1985.

Taylor, Charles. *Sources of the Self: The Making of Modern Identity.* Cambridge: Harvard University Press, 1989.

Voisine, Jacques. "De la confession religieuse à l'autobiographie et au journal intime: entre 1760 et 1820." *Neohelicon* 2, no. 3–4 (1974): 337–57.

Weinrich, Harald. "Faust's Forgetting." *Modern Language Quarterly* 55 (1994): 281–95.

Weintraub, Karl Joachim. *The Value of the Individual: Self and Circumstance in Autobiography.* Chicago: University of Chicago Press, 1978.

White, Hayden. *Tropics of Discourse: Essays in Cultural Criticism.* Baltimore: Johns Hopkins University Press, 1978.

Williams, Huntington. *Rousseau and Romantic Autobiography.* Oxford: Oxford University Press, 1983.

Witkowski, Georg. *Cornelia die Schwester Goethes.* Frankfurt: Literarische Anstalt Rütten & Loening, 1924.

Wordsworth, William. *The Prelude: 1799, 1805, 1850.* Ed. Jonathan Wordsworth et al. New York: Norton, 1979.

INDEX